INDO-MYANMAR BORDER TRADE

INDO-MYANMAR BORDER TRADE
Status, Problems and Potentials

Edited by

Gurudas Das
N Bijoy Singh
C J Thomas

AKANSHA PUBLISHING HOUSE
NEW DELHI-110 059 (INDIA)

AKANSHA PUBLISHING HOUSE
R-37B, Vani Vihar, Uttam Nagar
New Delhi-110059
Phones: 25640621
Email: ektabooks@yahoo.com

Showroom
4649-B/21, Ansari Road
Daryaganj, New Delhi - 110 002
Phones: 011-23263193, 9811582579

Indo-Myanmar Border Trade: Status, Problems and Potentials

First Published 2005

ISBN 81-8370-007-1

Edn. 2018

PRINTED IN INDIA

Published by M.P. Misra for Akansha Publishing House, New Delhi-110059 and Printed at Tarun Offset Press, Delhi.

Contents

Appendix

Annexure

पी.आर. किन्डिया
P.R. KYNDIAH

मंत्री
जनजातीय कार्य एवं
पूर्वोत्तर क्षेत्र विकास
भारत सरकार
शास्त्री भवन, नई दिल्ली - 110001
MINISTER FOR TRIBAL AFFAIRS &
DEVELOPMENT OF NORTH EASTERN REGION
GOVERNMENT OF INDIA
SHASTRI BHAWAN, NEW DELHI-110001

Foreword

It gives me immense pleasure to write this foreword to the book entitled Indo-Myanmar Border Trade: Status, Problems and Potentials. India shares about 1643 kms. land border with Myanmar, which passes through four North Eastern States. All these States, although bountiful, are landlocked and economically backward and require adequate access to markets. The cross border trade between the North-Eastern Region and neighbouring countries will be mutually beneficial for both the parties.

Government of India's North-East Initiative and Look East Policy are complementary to each other. We need to specialize in lines of our competitive advantage in order to reap the benefits of globalization as well as cross border trade.

I am happy that the contributors in this volume have studied the pros and cons of Indo-Myanmar border trade and I congratulate them for their contribution. Though we need more in-depth studies on mattes of border trade.

I appreciate the efforts made by ICSSR-NERC in this regard. Studies on interfaces between Government and activists do enrich policy making by providing analytical inputs. I wish this volume a wide readership, here and abroad, cutting across academia, policymaking, business and research.

(P.R. Kyndiah)
Minister for Tribal Affairs &
Development of North Eastern Region
Government of India
Shastri Bhawan, New Delhi - 110 001

Dated: 11th February, 2005

Preface

There has been a metamorphosis in India's Myanmar policy–from idealist to realist–from disengagement to engagement. This is most evident in economic field rather than in political arena. Since early 1990s, with the adoption of India's Look East Policy, India-Myanmar engagement has been growing on substantive ground and increasingly getting structured.

India has become the largest export market for Myanmar accounting for nearly one fourth of Myanmar's export. The construction of Moreh-Kalemo-Kaleya road that leads to Mandalay connecting the two countries across the international boundary is an indication that shows India's constructive engagement with Myanmar. Besides Western and South-East Asian firms, Indian oil companies also have taken keen interest in exploration and marketing of Myanmar's rich oil and gas reserves. Both, India and Myanmar, being the members of Bay of Bengal initiative for Multisectoral Techno-Economic Cooperation (BIMSTEC), originally started as Bangladesh-India-Sri Lanka-Thailand Economic Cooperation (BIMST-EC), are committed to use the synergies in their capabilities and resource endowments for their mutual interest and development.

Because of neighbourhood, the North Eastern Region of India is supposed to be directly benefited out of this growing Indo-Myanmar economic cooperation. This book, the outcome of a national seminar on ***Promotion of Border Trade Between India's North-East and Myanmar: Problems and Prospects,*** held on November 8-9, 2004, organized by the Indian Council of Social Science Research, North-Eastern Regional Centre (ICSSR-

NERC), Shillong, examines this hypothesis in relation to cross-border trade that flows between India's North-East and Myanmar.

We are grateful to the Ministry of Development of North-Eastern Region (DoNER), Government of India, New Delhi, and North-Eastern Council (NEC), Shillong, for their financial support towards this Seminar. We put on record our appreciation for the encouragement we received from Professor Mrinal Miri, Vice-Chancellor, North-Eastern Hill University (NEHU) and Chairman, ICSSR-NERC, Shillong; Dr. Surjit Mitra and Dr. T. Kumar, Joint Secretaries of DoNER, New Delhi; and Dr. Kamal Taori, Secretary, NEC.

We are thankful for the helps which we received during the seminar from the officials of Manipur University and the staff of NERC-ICSSR. Ms. Christine Blah and Ms. Narisha Kharbuli, deserves special appreciation for all their meticulous and ungrudging secretarial assistance. Lastly we appreciate Mr. M.P. Misra of the M/S Akansha Publishing House for the keen interest to bring out this volume on time.

—Editors

सत्यमेव जयते
GOVERNOR OF MANIPUR

RAJ BHAVAN
IMPHAL-795001

Inaugural Speech

—S S Sidhu

It gives me great pleasure to be with you all for the inauguration of the National Seminar on "Promotion of Border Trade Between India's North East and Myanmar—Problems and Prospects". Institutionalized interactions among business leaders, academicians and policy makers are a crucial part of our strategy to speedily bring about peace, prosperity and all-round progress in the North-Eastern States.

As you know, the First India-ASEAN Motor Car Rally is going to be organized by the Ministry of External Affairs and the Confederation of Indian Industry (CII) from 22nd November to 6th December 2004 to demonstrate the proximity of India with the ASEAN countries. This is an outcome of the signing of India-ASEAN Agreement on 8th October 2003 at Bali of Indonesia.

We are particularly determined to attend to the developmental needs of our States in the north-eastern region. This region is blessed with tremendous diversity and richness, both in its natural resources and human capital. However, it is a matter of deep concern to us that slower economic growth has implied lesser opportunities of employment and progress for its people. The resultant discontent is exploited by certain extremist organizations to foment violence and divisiveness.

With the opening up of Indo-Myanmar border trade in 1995, Manipur has entered into the global market. The volume of trade, as per record of Land Customs Station, Moreh (border town of Manipur) upto the end of March 2004 was Rs. 204.26 crore in cumulative. The main items of exports were wheat-flour, fenugreek seed, ani seed, cumin seed, soyabari, dry chilly, suman rose powder, agarbatti, pea, garlic, dried buffalo offals, etc., and that of imports were betel nut, turmeric, red kidney bean (Rajma), kuth root, gram, resin, reed-broom, dry ginger, etc. These items were falling with the 22 items listed in the agreement.

In the meantime, Mizoram has also started the border trade with Myanmar in January this year.

Considering the large volume of unofficial trading activities, the State Government has been consistently pressing to increase the potential exchangeable items within the parameters of EXIM Policy, now Foreign Trade Policy, announced on 31st August 2004.

The State Government has initiated various steps to improve the infrastructure at the border town of Moreh by providing trade centre, warehouse, convention hall and stay facility centre, upgradation of Land Customs Station, interconnectivity roads and street lighting.

In order to sort out the various problems of the exporters and importers of Myanmar and India through border trade, operationalization of I/C documents is one of the prime needs. The hindrances faced by the traders along the route between Pallel and Moreh are to be looked into by the respective organizations in the larger interest of the border trade as have been practiced at Mizoram sector.

Above all, the proposed Trans-Asian Highway will certainly boost the export to Myanmar, in particular and other South-East Asian countries in general. Till now, Myanmar is the transit route of exporting to other neighbouring countries like Thailand, Laos, Korea, Singapore, Malaysia, Indonesia and even China.

Friends, when we look at the North-East, we also naturally look at India's extended neighbourhood in South-East Asia. This is a region where truly historic socio-economic transformation is taking place. Because of its proximity to South-East Asian markets, India's North-Eastern region enjoys a locational advantage of great importance. Our North-Eastern States can become the economic bridgehead to South-East Asia. Equally, vibrant exchanges with South-East Asia can galvanize growth and development in the North-East. I would urge all the eight States in the region together to prepare the ground to participate vigorously in the emerging opportunities with our South-East Asian neighbourhood. This also includes tourism, where we see a major synergy between the North-East and ASEAN countries.

I hope, the organizing of such Seminar with the experts in the field will help in resolving the problems for promotion of export and import through border trade in the State. I trust that this Seminar will be a good foundation for the development of border trade, investment, tourism and people-to-people links between North-East of India and ASEAN countries. The deliberation of the Seminar will hopefully provide the framework and identify the issues for discussion in the forthcoming Seminar on Indo-Myanmar Trade & Economic Co-operation being scheduled on 25th November 2004 at Mandalay.

Thank you.

(S.S. Sidhu)
Governor of Manipur
Raj Bhavan, Imphal-795 001

Presidential Speech

N Bijoy Singh

The northeastern region of our country shares ninety-eight per cent of its border with the neighbouring countries of Bangladesh, Bhutan, China and Myanmar, and only two per cent with the mainland India. Though the main stream administrative and political structures were introduced in the region, the development of the region has been far from satisfactory. This has led to the perpetuation of backwardness and weak structural links in the regional economy.

The region is rich with bio-diversity, hydro-potential, oil and gas, coal, limestone and forest wealth. The forest resources are bountiful, offering valuable wood, medicinal plants and roots, orchids, cut flowers, etc. The region is also well known for its traditional art and crafts, especially in the field of handloom textiles and handicraft products. These products are currently exported outside the region through the custom check posts located on the international borders in the region. The commodities are exported to Bangladesh, Myanmar, Bhutan and China either through formal or informal trade.

The geographical location and proximity to the neighbouring countries is an added trade advantage to the region. In fact, these countries had been the traditional markets for a variety of goods and services produced by the people of this region before its traditional links were disrupted following the partition of the country.

The Government of India, to renew the long tradition of trade between Manipur and Myanmar, signed Indo-Myanmar Border Trade Agreement in January 1994. The cross-border trade, through Moreh of Manipur, became operational in April 1995.

The volume of official trade between 1995 and 2000 is reported to be one hundred and thirty-five crores of rupees. However, the estimates for unofficial trade range between one thousand and six hundred and two thousand five hundred crores of rupees annually. The local business people claim that the clandestine trade, including drugs and precious stones, would amount to not less than rupees two thousand and five hundred crores per annum. As the clandestine trade exceeds the official ones, the government loses much of its revenue.

We need to focus on border trade in view of the need to forge closer commercial and economic links with the larger markets in the fast developing South-East Asian economies. The northeastern States have already established a large volume of informal trade with Myanmar and also with Bangladesh. With appropriate policies and programmes, the region can become an important gateway to affluent Asian markets. We have to identify the potentials, taking into account the historically developed patterns of exchanges across the border and the present volume of cross-border informal trade.

The border trade between India and Myanmar has been operational for nearly a decade now. It is high time now to assess the benefits accrued from the trade and also to study the lacunae that might hinder the trade. I am glad that this seminar would focus on the assessment of trade relations, trade flow, regional development, etc., and suggest a framework to facilitate and strengthen the cross border economic integration between the northeastern region and Myanmar.

I wish the seminar all success.

Contributors

Bhattacharyya, Rahul. Chief Officer, United Bank of India, International Banking Division, Kolkata.

Das, Gurudas. Department of Economics, North-Eastern Hill University, Shillong.

Das, H. N. Former Chief Secretary, Government of Assam, Guwahati

De, Prabir. Advisor (Hony.), South Asia Research Society, Kolkata & Research Associate, Research and Information Systems for the Non-Aligned and other Developing Countries, New Delhi.

Haokip, Lunminthang. Additional Deputy Commissioner, Kampopi, Senapati District, Manipur.

Khathing, J. S. R. Chief Commissioner of Central Excise & Customs, North-Eastern Region, Shillong.

Kumar, Sunil. General Secretary, North-East Federation of International Trade, Shillong.

Mero, M. K. Joint Director General of Foreign Trade, Ministry of Commerce, Office of the Joint Director General of Foreign Trade, Guwahati.

Phanjoubam, Pradip. Editor, Imphal Free Press, Imphal, Manipur.

Prasain, G. P. Associate Professor, Department of Commerce, Manipur University, Manipur.

Raychaudhuri, Ajitava, Professor, Department of Economics, Jadavpur University, Kolkata.

Sailo, Lallura. Director, Trade and Commerce, Government of Mizoram, Mizoram.

Sharma, Amiya K. Economist, North-Eastern Development Finance Corporation Ltd., Guwahati.

Sharma, D K. Secretary General, North-East India Chamber of Commerce, Guwahati.

Sidhu, S. S. Governor, Manipur.

Singh, Konsam Ibo. Associate Professor, Department of Political Science, Manipur University, Imphal, Manipur.

Singh, N. Bijoy. Vice Chancellor, Manipur University.

Thomas, C Joshua. Acting Director, Indian Council of Social Science Research, North-Eastern Regional Centre, Shillong, Meghalaya.

Yumnam, Amar. Professor, Department of Economics, Manipur University, Imphal, Manipur.

List of Tables

List of Figures & Maps

1

Economy of Myanmar: Trends, Structure and Implications for Border Trade with India's North-East

—Gurudas Das and C J Thomas

India shares about 1643 km border with her north-eastern neighbour Myanmar (formerly Burma). This border touches four out of seven north-eastern states of India, viz., Arunachal Pradesh (520 km), Manipur (398 km), Mizoram (510 km) and Nagaland (215 km)(Egreteau:2003-49). Although cross-border contact and movement of people are known throughout, but they have not led to any strong economic interdependence between the two regions, viz., north-eastern region (NER) of India and Myanmar. In pre-colonial era, cross-border contacts used to take place mainly through distance trade (Das:1995-42/3), war and invasion, and common racial affinities.

However, the land-based agriculture oriented feudal and tribal economies provided little scope for intensive trading and cross-border economic cooperation. During the colonial era, the British security perception, her policy of frontier management, and above all her imperial interest did not allow local economic potential to grow across the border. The state-centric security perception of the post-colonial states including India and Myanmar treated the borders as peripheries and considered them vulnerable. As a result, the idea of "shared border" and border area development through mobilizing the synergies across the borders did not receive due attention from the national power centres. The geo-economic potentials of the border regions were overlooked for geo-political considerations. The situation has, however, changed following the end of the cold-war paradigm, rise of East Asian tigers, and release of forces of globalisation. While the demise of the bi-polar world has freed the nations, who seek to forge new strategic partnership, the globalising forces have brought economic interest in the forefront of nation's foreign policy. With the growth of regional trading arrangements, border areas are now visualized as economic corridors. It is in this perspective, which has dawned in both India and Myanmar in the early 1990s that this chapter seeks to analyse the economy of Myanmar to find whether there exists any complementarity across the border for mobilizing the synergies for the development of the north-eastern region (NER) of India. Needless to mention that for Arunachal Pradesh, Manipur, Mizoram and Nagaland, cross-border markets in Myanmar are nearer than the far away main market centres in the country. Thus, cross-border markets may act as "vent" for the surplus produced in NER as well as source of cheaper imports.

I

Economy of Myanmar: The Trajectory of Development

Myanmar, having 678,500 sq km area for about 50 million people, is rich in natural resources. Fertile cultivable land, valuable forest (343,767 sq km), large water bodies (20,760 sq km), huge deposits of strategic and critical minerals like coal (15 million tonnes), oil (7 million tonnes), natural gas (283 billion cubic metre), hydro potential (108,000 MW) (RIS:2004-51), limestone, copper, lead, zinc, iron, granite, tin, nickel, marble, tungsten, antimony, gold and precious stones — all these have made Myanmar a great economic power house. But all these potentials have not been realised. In fact, it is a country of huge potential with very weak resource-industry linkages.

Post-independent (Myanmar attained her independence on January 4, 1948) economic development in Myanmar may be analysed into three distinct phases, viz., the phase of integration and consolidation (1948-62), seclusion and socialism (1962-87), and liberalisation (1988 onwards).

The Phase of Integration and Consolidation (1948-62)

During this phase Myanmar was ruled by civilian governments under the leadership of U Nu, the first Prime Minister, except a brief spell of General Ne Win's care taker government (September 1958-March 1960). The national government sought to change the colonial economic and resource-ownership structures. Independent Burma inherited an economy where strengths were rooted in agriculture, forestry, and extraction of minerals. Except rice milling, timber processing, industrial activities were conspicuously absent all along the colonial era. British economic policy was focussed on production and export of rice and extraction of minerals like oil, tungsten, tin, nickel, zinc, copper and lead. By 1939-40, Myanmar's average annual output of rice reached 4.94 million metric tons (Ghosh:1989-4). From 1870 to 1940, rice export increased from 3,99,000 tons to 3,141,000 tons from Lower Burma alone (Ghosh:1989-4). By 1940-41, about two-thirds of Burma's total acreage was planted with rice, i.e., 12,518,000 acres out of a country wide total of 18,814,798 acres (Ghosh:1989-5). In fact, it was the colonial government who realised the rice producing potential, projected Burma as a granary, encouraged immigration and the process led to large scale land alienation. The number of landless labourers increased from 27 per cent to 40 per cent of the total peasant population between 1921 and 1931(Ghosh:1989-5). By 1930, Chettyars (a distinct group of Indian money lenders from Chettinad in Madras) owned about 25 per cent of the holdings (Ghosh:1989-5).

At the end of British rule, two-thirds of all the rice lands were held by non-resident landlords (Ghosh:1989-8). Apart from land alienation, non-Burmese actors were dominating the trade, mining and service sectors — particularly British nationals in trade, both Indians and Chinese in trade, retail business, mining and other services. Thus, on independence, Burmese occupied the political space but the economic space was held by the non-Burmese (Donnison:1970-197). Moreover, Japanese occupation during the World War II had severely affected the economy of Burma. The acreage of rice came down to nearly 7,200,000 acres in 1943-44 from a pre-war level of 12,400,000 acres (Ghosh: 1989-7).

On Independence, the national government, therefore, adopted a policy of "nationalisation", "Burmanisation" and "industrialisation". In order to translate these goals, a Two-Year plan was devised in April, 1948, but could not be implemented due to political instability. Later on, a Five-Year plan for Agricultural and Rural Development and another Eight Year Programme for Industrialisation had been adopted in 1952. All these plans and programmes aimed (i) to increase agricultural output to the pre-war level by the end of 5 years, (ii) to restore pre-war export surplus of rice, (iii) to supply agricultural inputs through state enterprises, (iv) to modernise rice-milling, (v) to nationalise land, and (vi) to industrialise using the surplus earned from rice-export. For the 8 years, from 1952-53 to 1959-60, the average public capital expenditure made in agriculture was 9.2 per cent, in industry 8.4 per cent, in transport 18.6 per cent, in power 10.3 per cent, in construction 9 per cent and in defence 19.8 per cent (Ghosh:1989-36).

The national government prepared a road map for speedy industrialisation. While the basic industries were reserved for the public sector, small mining and consumer goods industries were kept open for the private sector. A joint sector had been conceived with the large operators in the mining and processing sector. Nationalisation of basic industries was one of the prime goals.

The strategy of industrialisation focussed on the establishment of resource-based industries like pulp and paper, demand based industries like chemical fertiliser for the use of agricultural sector, processing units like rice bran oil and forest-based industry. The state manufacturing programme included a pharmaceutical plant, a steel mill, a jute mill, two sugar mills, a brick and a tile factory, a cotton spinning and weaving mill, a central factory and a tea packing plant (Ghosh:1989-33).

Resources for industrialisation were supposed to come from rice export. Foreign aid was not favoured due to strings usually tied to them. But because of fall in the price of rice in the international market, in spite of increase in the production much could not be gained from rice export. Moreover, many countries attained self-sufficiency in food and hence it was not possible even to gain by increasing the volume of export. As the demand for rice is income inelastic, it neither helped Burma to export more to high-income countries. In fact, Burma's rice economy was in crisis as other countries ensured their food security.

The alternative source of revenue like forestry and mining could not be realised due to ethnic insurgency. Forests and mines were located in the fringe areas where minority tribal groups like Karens, Shans, Mons, Kachins, Arakanese and Chins had strong holds who were contesting against Burmanization of national identities and advocating for their accommodation preferably within a federal framework which would ensure their local autonomy. Besides ethnic insurgency, political insurgent groups like Burmese Communist Party and Kuomintangs were also having their strong holds. The operation and sabotage activities of these insurgent groups had severe adverse impact on the efforts towards economic development.

Not only sabotage activities of the insurgent groups raised the maintenance cost of the oil pipelines, they also led to sub-optimal resource extraction as well as high defence expenditure. Levy imposed by the insurgent groups on productive and profitable activities worked as disincentives.

Besides the menace of insurgency, lack of indigenous technical and managerial manpower had led to a high degree of dependence on foreign technicians and thereby high remittance abroad.

Moreover, over emphasis on industrialisation at the cost of agriculture had led to stunted growth of both the sectors. As financing the industrialisation programme was modelled on the return from rice export, the fall in export price of rice coupled with slow growth of the agricultural sector had dried the pipeline. Due to scarcity of resources, many industrial projects had to be completed in a truncated way while some other could not be operationalised. All these had led to the failure of the early efforts towards industrialisation.

In fact, the failure of the U Nu government in both economic as well as political fronts and the rising insurgent activities had created the ground for army take over in 1962.

The Phase of Seclusion and Socialism (1962-1988)

On March 2, 1962 General Ne Win overthrew U Nu government through a lightening *coup d'etat* and assumed power in Burma. He ruled the country for twenty-six-and-a-half years (till he resigned on July 23, 1988) by instituting an autocratic military regime. He floated Burma Socialist Program Party (BSPP) to carry his programmes to the people. Except BSPP, all types of political activities were banned. He renamed the country as the Socialist Republic of the Union of Burma on January 4, 1974, with a new constitution.

The "Burmese Way to Socialism", the politico-economic agenda, drawn up by Ne Win and BSPP also adopted the policy of nationalisation and Burmanisation as strategies for the economic development and national integration. The space for public sector had largely been widened at the cost of private sector. State controlled enterprises and cooperatives were formed to undertake production, trade and distribution. The programme of nationalisation was pursued vehemently. Most of the businesses run by the non-Burmese were nationalised immediately leading to large-scale outmigration of non-Burmese entrepreneurs, traders, businessmen, professionals, technicians and managerial personnel.

Non-Burmese labour, entrepreneurs, traders and bankers,

particularly Indian, used to play a prominent role in the colonial and post-colonial economy of Burma. In fact, Indians were the largest non-Burmese group in Burma. Throughout the 100 years (1852-1948) of colonial rule, Indian labour, professionals, entrepreneurs and bankers kept on penetrating Burma under British patronage. As per 1931 census, Indians constituted 53 per cent of Rangoon's population. Only 30.46 per cent were Burmese, and 7.65 per cent were Chinese (Mahajani:1960-4). In 1941 the Burmese labour force in industries numbered 28,033 while the Indians were 74,516 or about 69 per cent of the total. While 36 per cent of skilled labour came from the indigenous population, 55 per cent came from the Indians. Similarly, while 23 per cent of unskilled labour was indigenous, 73 per cent were Indians (Mahajani:1960-8). While the majority of the immigrant Bengalis, Tamils and Oriyas were working in government establishments, conducting retail trade and acting as professionals; Telagus were chiefly employed in mills, factories, shipping companies and also working as rickshaw pullers and handcart men. People from Bihar and Uttar Pradesh, Nepalese and Bhutias were manning the fourth grade jobs and also running petty businesses. Marwaris, Gujratis and Parsis were in business. Chettiars were working as financiers and bankers. In 1930, 1655 Chettiar firms were reported functioning in Burma (Mahajani:1960-17), with a working capital of Rs.750 million, (Mahajani:1960-19) and advanced about Rs.400 millions loans (Mahajani:1960-19) to non-Chettiars, largely to the Burmese agriculturists. In fact, it was the Chettiar capital that led to the phenomenal development of Burman agriculture. This large presence of Indian labour force and the firm grip of the Indian business and banking communities in the economy had led Burmese nationalism to become anti-Indian.

Ne Win's government confiscated all private banks, domestic as well as foreign. It nationalised private press, banned private imports and exports, confiscated all trading companies and cooperatives, oil companies, mining companies, consumer goods factories like soap, cigarette, private schools, mission hospitals, cinemas, shipping companies. The confiscations led to the departure of around 3 lakh Indians and Pakistanis, who abandoned some 11,000 shops (Tucker:2001-190). The shops were handed over to military personnel, who rented or sold them. Between 1962 and 1965, more than 2 lakh Indians escaped Burma (Egreteau:2003-49). The private manufacturing and commercial sector of the economy diminished from 493 firms employing 17,947 people in 1963 to 267 firms employing 6887 people in 1972 while the state sector rose from 31.6 per cent in 1962-63 to 46.4 per cent in 1977-78. Twenty-four state stores distributed merchandise formerly handled by 12,212 private stores. The number of government employees almost doubled from 3,68,301 in 1962 to 6,23,529 in 1973, while less than 1 per cent of Burma's workforce was employed in the state sector in 1931, it had gone up to 10 per cent in 1985 (Tucker:2001-191).

Having established state monopoly over the resources, productive capacity, and trade, government aimed at diversifying the export trade. It followed an industrial policy of import substitution. It controlled the private sector through its monopoly on raw materials and foreign exchange. Unlike U Nu government, Ne Win realised that Burma's industrialisation would not meet with success without foreign aid. Many believe that Ne Win's adoption of a new constitution in 1974 was a cosmetic gesture to attract foreign aid (Tucker:2001-192). In fact, the average amount of annual foreign donor loans and grants to Burma had significantly increased from $65.5 million for the period 1974-77 to $348.5 million for the period 1978-86. But state control of productive resources, trade and distribution had led to the growth of large-scale corruption and black market in the economy. Goods were smuggled into Burma from Thailand and smuggled goods constituted as much as four-fifths of domestic consumption and had a turnover equal to, or even higher than official trade (Graves: 1999-63). Besides cross-border smuggling, the restrictions on economic activity in the private sector gave rise to a flourishing black economy, in which individual soldiers took bribes from the traders for grants of licences and permits and sold goods from government stocks to which they enjoyed privileged access (Tucker:2001-192). This rent seeking practices had jerked up the cost of production and made the home production costlier than foreign goods. The economy nosedived, the flourishing black market and increasing injections of foreign aid enabled Burma to avoid starvation. In order to alleviate interest on foreign loans, Ne Win regime applied to the United Nations to accord it least developed country status which had been formalised at UN in December 1987. Ne Win also lifted restrictions on private trading. But the black market economy had thrived to such an extent, no option left to the regime other than to demonetise large bank notes of 75 and 25 Kyat on September 5, 1987. As most Burmese accumulated vast cash savings in black money, it wiped out most of the people's savings. On the face of stiff public protest, General Ne Win suddenly resigned on July 23, 1988, bringing and end to his twenty six and half years autocratic rule.

The Phase of Liberalisation (1988 onwards)

With Ne Win's resignation, Burma slipped into unprecedented political turmoil. Sein Lwin, Anti-Riot Police Chief, who replaced Ne Win tried to quell the mass agitation in iron hand but failed and resigned. General Saw Maung, Minister of Defence in Ne Win's last government and his associates, assumed power on September 18, 1988 by a new *coup d'etat*. They abrogated the 1974 Constitution and constituted a new military government under the banner of State Law and Order Restoration Council (SLORC). In the parliamentary election held on May 27, 1990, people overwhelmingly voted for Suu Kyi's National League for Democracy (NLD) which won 80 per cent of the Assembly, and rejected SLORC rule as National Unity Party, which was formed by SLORC, won only 10 seats. However, SLORC refused to step down and came down heavily on the pro-democracy movement. It banned all political parties, arrested NLD leaders and strengthened its hold.

During these years of political turmoil, Burma suffered negative growth while most of the South East Asian countries were experiencing lightning economic growth. In order to combat imminent economic disaster, SLORC has come out of the Ne Winian policy prescription and put an end to policy of isolation and state control. It has taken steps to liberalise the economy through privatisation and industrialisation. It has opened up Myanmar for foreign direct investment. Both export and import have been largely decontrolled. It has tried and is being trying to strike deals with ethnic insurgencies through accommodating some of their concerns. In agricultural front it has focussed on diversification in order to shed the dependence on rice cultivation alone. It has been entering into joint ventures with multinationals of various origins in order to bring new technology and foreign investments. Instead of only sending the army to quell the rebellion in the border regions, SLORC has successfully utilized the economic synergies across the border through opening them for trade and cross-border development projects.

All these measures have started bearing fruits as the economy has shown the signs of improvement since 1995-96.

Since 1995, Myanmar economy started growing at an accelerated rate. From 2.9 per cent in 1985, growth rate more than doubled in 1995 and it is doing extremely well since 1999 (Table 1.1).

Table 1.1
Myanmar: Growth Rate of GDP (% per year)

Year	*GDP Growth Rate*
1985	2.9
1990	2.8
1995	6.9
1996	6.4
1997	5.7
1998	5.8
1999	10.9
2000	13.7
2001	11.3
2002	10.0
2003	10.6

Source: Compiled from Asian Development Bank (2004) and Okamoto et al. (2003)

Primary sector activities have mostly been privatized. Although government controls a large part of forestry and logging; agriculture, livestock and fishery, and mining activities are mainly in the hands of private operators (Table 1.2). In case of the secondary sector activities, production and distribution of energy and power are strictly under government control. Private operators have not been allowed to play any role in these areas. Even in case of construction, about 62 per cent output comes from the state sector. However, in manufacturing and processing private initiative are fast growing (about 72 per cent) (Table 1.2).

Table 1.2
Gross Domestic Product by Form of Ownership, 1999-2000 (Provisional)

(in percent of sectoral output)

Sectors	*State*	*Cooperatives*	*Private*
Productive Sectors	**12.3**	**1.5**	**86.2**
Agriculture	0.2	1.9	97.9
Livestock and Fishery	0.2	1.0	98.8
Forestry	47.9	0.7	51.4
Energy	99.9	0.1	0.0
Mining	5.6	1.6	92.8
Manufacturing & Processing	26.5	1.1	72.4
Power	99.9	0.1	0.0
Construction	61.9	0.2	37.7
Services	**53.8**	**3.0**	**43.2**
Transportation	27.3	1.0	71.7
Communication	100.0	0.0	0.0
Financial Institutions	57.0	15.9	27.1
Social & Administrative Services	88.0	0.8	11.2
Rental and Other Services	3.5	3.3	93.2
Trade	**20.04**	**2.4**	**77.2**
Gross Domestic Product	**21.8**	**2.0**	**76.2**

Source: IMF (2001)

In case of tertiary sector activities, communication has remained exclusively under state control, while private operators are doing well in transport (72 per cent). Even finance and banking have been opened up. Although state has considerable control (57 per cent) in this strategic area, private operators (27 per cent) also play a significant role. Most importantly, following the withdrawal of restrictions on internal distribution as well as export and import, private operators are playing the dominant role (77 per cent) in trade. As a whole, in 1999-2000, 76 per cent of GDP has come from the private sector and only 22 per cent from the state sector (Table 1.2). Thus, under SLORC, a considerable degree of decontrol and privatisation has taken place.

Economy of Myanmar: Structure and Trends in Sectoral Change

Agriculture

Agriculture has been and is the most important sector in Myanmar economy. In 2003, cultivable land constitutes 16 per cent of the total land area of Myanmar. Of the rest, forest covers 50 per cent, wasteland constitutes 10 per cent and land under non-agricultural use constitutes another 25 per cent[1]. Fifty-five per cent of agricultural land is under paddy cultivation. Dry land constitutes 31 per cent, garden covers 7 per cent, alluvial land forms 5 per cent and shifting cultivation covers another 2 per cent[2].

Out of 11.75 million hectares under major crops in 1999-2000, about 53 per cent has gone for paddy cultivation, 22 per cent for pulses, 9 per cent for sesame, 5 per cent for groundnuts, 4 per cent for sunflower, and 3 per cent for cotton (IMF:2001). Between 1995-98 and 1999-2000, there has been marginal increase in acreage under paddy, wheat, maize, groundnuts and sesame. Increase in acreage under pulses, sunflower and sugarcane has been substantial. Acreage under crops like jute, cotton and rubber has been marginally declined (Table 1.14A). This shows that agriculture in Myanmar is diversifying in favour of pulses, sunflower and sugarcane.

For the same reference period, i.e., between 1995-96 and 1999-2000, except sesame, jute and rubber, there has been an increase in the level of output in case of paddy, wheat, maize, pulses, groundnuts, sunflower, cotton, sugarcane and tobacco. But except, paddy, wheat, pulses, cotton and tobacco, the yield has decreased for others (Table 1.15A).

The figures suggest that except cotton, increase in production in case of other crops is due to the increase in acreage. As the land-man ratio is favourable in Myanmar compared to other South East Asian countries, extensive cultivation is more in practice rather than intensive cultivation. Lack of irrigation, limited availability and high price of fertilizers, low consumption of energy appear to be the causes of slow growth of agriculture. Because of the ban on private sector export of rice, the price of rice at domestic market is about half the international price. As the price of privately imported fertiliser has been fully liberalised, this has resulted into higher input price but lower price for output. As a result, imported fertilizers are almost beyond the means of most farmers (IMF:1999-10). Lack of adequate irrigational facilities has kept agricultural activities depended on the vagaries of monsoon. In spite of being rich in water resources, having 828 cubic km[3] potential for surface water and 495 cubic km[4] for ground water, only 0.36 per cent of total paddy land were under irrigation in 2003. Thus, irrigation potential is yet to be realised. As far as consumption of energy inputs is concerned, agriculture absorbed about 11 per cent of total petroleum products in 1999-2000 (IMF:2001-15). However, consumption of electricity in this sector has been negligible.

Compared to 1980s, agriculture has grown at a higher rate in the 1990s. Apart from the fact that agriculture is subject to diminishing returns, the fluctuation in the growth rate is also partly explained by the variations in natural factors like rainfall, drought, etc. Severe flood in 1997 and drought in 1998 had contributed to slow growth in corresponding years (Table 1.3).

The contribution of agriculture to GDP is declining over the years (Table 1.3). So also the share of agriculture in total export (Table 1.3). There has been a perceptible change in the cropping pattern as well as export of agricultural crops. Once Myanmar was the largest exporter of rice in the world, now pulses have become the largest foreign exchange earning crop, accounting for about 15 per cent of total export. The annual growth rate of production of pulses averaged 11 per cent during 1994/95–1998/99. Besides pulses, sunflower and sugarcane production also recorded strong growth in 1998-99 (IMF: 1999-10).

Table 1.3
Myanmar: Economy and Agriculture

Year	*Growth Rate of Agricultural Sector*	*Agricultural Sector's Share in GDP*	*Agricultural Sector's Share in Export*
1985-86	2.2	39.7	42.4
1990-91	2.0	38.7	31.8
1995-96	5.5	37.1	46.0
1996-97	3.8	36.2	36.1
1997-98	3.0	35.2	30.3
1998-99	3.5	34.5	28.0
1999-2000	10.5	34.4	17.9
2000-2001	9.5	33.1	18.9

Source: Okamoto *et al*., 2003

However, in spite of declining importance of agriculture in relation to its contribution to GDP as well as export, it is still the main source of livelihood in Myanmar. About 64 per cent of the total labour force was engaged in agriculture in 1995-98. By 1997-98, this figure was reduced only by 1 per cent. Taking the primary sector[5] together, 68 per cent of the labour force was employed in it in 1995-96 which came down to 67 per cent in 1997-98.

Industrialization

It has already been pointed out that efforts towards industrialisation made during the integration and consolidation phase (1948-62) by the U Nu government had failed. Till 1974, Ne Win also made futile efforts to industrialise Myanmar. As the source of finance for industrialisation was modelled on rice export, its success was contingent upon the success of rice export and international price of rice. This model faced twin challenges. Firstly, falling international price of rice with most countries attaining self-sufficiency in food, and second, aggravating food insecurity within with the growth of domestic population. Ne Win tried to maximise export earning as well as ensure food security in the country by nationalizing export trade. As rice is the staple food in Myanmar, it was important for the stability of his government to keep the domestic price of rice lower than the international market price. As a result, government procurement price was kept very low. This acted as a disincentive to the farmers who, in turn, preferred to supply low quality rice by way of levy to the government. This, in turn, led to the fall in export earning from rice.

By early 1970s, Ne Win realized that industrialisation of Myanmar is not possible without external aid which he avoided so far. On assuming power in 1962, Ne Win led Myanmar to isolation. Even he denied joining ASEAN when it was established in 1967, although joining this group would have been of much benefit. However, since 1970s, there had been a policy shift in favour of foreign aids. Myanmar turned to World Bank in 1972 and joined the Asian Development Bank in 1973. It started borrowing from international financial institutions and began to accept loans and grants from the foreign governments (Chaudhary:2000-430). On assuming power, SLORC enacted the Foreign Investment Law in 1988. It has identified areas for foreign direct investment. It has encouraged FDI in joint ventures.

For six years, 1994/95–1999/2000, a sum total of about 6 billion dollar FDI proposals have been approved for investment.

However, about a little less than 50 per cent of the approved amount has actually been received (Table 1.4). The annual average actual inflow during this period has been little less than half a billion which is, in a sense, negligible compared to the very high inflow of FDI in the South-East Asian neighbours like Thailand, Malaysia, Hong Kong, Republic of Korea and Singapore. But compared to her past, this is also no less significant for a country like Myanmar where volatile political and social environment has kept business confidence perpetually low.

Table 1.4
Myanmar: Foreign Direct Investment 1994/95-1999/2000

(in Millions of US dollar)

Year	*Approved*	*Actual*	*Growth Rate of Actual FDI (in per cent)*
1994-95	1351.9	135.0	-
1995-96	668.3	317.5	135.18
1996-97	2814.2	580.7	82.90
1997-98	1012.9	878.8	51.33
1998-99	54.4	683.6	(-) 22.21
1999-2000	58.1	304.2	(-) 55.50
Total	5959.8	2899.8	

Source: Calculated from Table-39, IMF (1999,2001)

A sector-wise analysis of actual FDI inflow for the same period shows that the lion's share has gone to country's rich oil and gas sector (54.45 per cent), followed by hotels and tourism (19.03 per cent), manufacturing (9.54 per cent), mining (7.75 per cent), transport (4.14 per cent) and real estate (3.22 per cent) (Table 1.5).

Table 1.5
Myanmar: FDI Inflow by Industry, 1994-2000

(in Millions of US dollar)

Industry	*Approved*	*Actual*	*Percentage Realisation*
Agriculture	11.7	0.5	4.27
Manufacturing	1401.7	276.7	19.74
Oil and Gas	1927.2	1578.9	81.93
Mining	358.8	224.8	62.65
Fishery	192.7	28.0	14.53
Hotels and Tourism	572.0	551.9	96.49
Transport	274.4	120.0	43.73
Real Estate	997.2	93.5	9.38
Industrial Estate	193.1	18.6	9.63
Others	31	6.9	22.26
Total	5959.8	2899.8	48.66

Source: Calculated from Table-39, IMF (1999 , 2001)

However, privatisation appears to have made hotels and tourism sector as a favourite destination for FDI. The percentage realisation (actual as percentage of approved FDI) is the highest in this sector (98.49) followed by oil and gas (81.93) and mining (62.65). The percentage realisation in each of these three sectors is much higher than the national average (48.66 per cent). This indicates extractive activities are more lucrative than manufacturing in Myanmar.

Inflow of FDI in Myanmar originates mainly from two regions, viz., developed countries of the West and South-East Asian countries. Firms of United Kingdom, France and United States together have contributed about 61 per cent of actual inflow (Table 1.6) during the six years (1994/95–1999/2000). Lion's share of the FDI from the developed world has gone into the oil and gas sector. Western oil barons like Texas, Royal Dutch, Amoco, Unocal, Kirkland, Premier, Clyde, and Total — all have developed a significant stake in Myanmar's rich oil and gas resource. Singapore, Thailand, Japan, Hong Kong, Malaysia and Republic of Korea based firms together have contributed around 45 per cent of total actual inflow of FDI in Myanmar (Table 1.6). These firms are investing mainly in areas like fishery, logging, mineral extraction, and manufacturing through joint ventures with the Myanmar state enterprises and departments.

Table 1.6
Myanmar: FDI by Country, 1994/95–1999/2000

(in Millions of US dollar)

Country	*Approved*	*Actual*	*Percentage to total Actual FDI*
United Kingdom	1339.3	997.9	34.41
Singapore	1243.3	645.1	22.25
France	460.4	508.4	17.53
USA	365.1	250.6	8.66
Thailand	1053.4	192.6	6.64
Japan	132.4	87.7	3.02
Hong Kong	76.7	54.6	1.88
Malaysia	533.4	50.1	1.73
Republic of Korea	43.4	36.1	1.24
Others	712.4	76.7	2.64
Total	5959.8	2899.8	100.00

Source: Calculated from Table-40, IMF (1999, 2001)

In fact, SLORC, later renamed as State Peace and Development Council (SPDC) in 1997, considers joint ventures as preferred route for the inflow of FDI than any other forms. In spite of encouraging private initiative in manufacturing, resource extraction and trade, state control over critical and strategic sectors like power, communication, banking and construction, has not been loosened (Table 1.3). Moreover, state enterprises also play a significant role in forestry, mining, manufacturing and processing, transportation and trade (Table 1.3).

It may be pointed out that SPDC exercises a considerable indirect influence over a significant part of private enterprises run or control by the army personnel. As the programme of privatization in Myanmar is more of regime engineered rather than market structured, permits and licenses have been given to the cronies who dance in tune with the interest of the regime. As a result, the degree of privatization and its quality in terms of market competitiveness are not as large as data presented in Table 1.3 suggest us to believe.

Be that as it may, of the total actual inflow during 1994/95–1999/2000, about 35 per cent have been routed through joint ventures with the state enterprises (Table 1.7).

Table 1.7
Myanmar: FDI Inflow by Types of Venture, 1994/95–1999/2000

(in percentage)

Types	*Approved*	*Actual*
Solely Foreign Owned Venture	44.63	33.55
Joint Venture	27.17	35.06
Others	28.20	31.39
Total	100.00	100.00

Source: Calculated from Table-38, IMF (1999, 2001)

Joint Ventures

State enterprises like Myanmar Automobile and Diesel Engine Industries (MADI), Myanma Agricultural Machinery Industries (MAMI), Myanma Machine Tools and Electrical Industries (MTEI) and Myanma Tyre and Rubber Industries (MTRI), under the Ministry of Industry, play important role in joint ventures. It is these enterprises who participate in joint ventures with the foreign firms. These enterprises, created in the 1960s and 1970s, have been restructured under SLORC/SPDC so that they can play more effective role in transforming the agrarian economy into an industrial one. Besides these state enterprises, SLORC created Union of Myanmar Economic Holdings Company Limited (UMEHC), where majority of the shares are held by government and military personnel, and a number of its subsidiaries like Myanmar Oil and Gas Enterprise (MOGE), in order to control joint ventures particularly in mining and extractive activities.

Myanmar Fritz Werner Industries, established in 1985, has been a joint venture between MAMI and Fritz Werner Industries of Germany. MAMI holds 60 per cent of equity while Werner holds the rest 40 per cent. It produces industrial goods. Myanmar Daewoo Electronics Company Limited is another joint venture between MTEI and Daewoo Electronics of South Korea established in 1990. MTEI is holding 45 per cent of equity and the rest 55 per cent is held by Daewoo Corporation. It produces television, cassettes, refrigerator, washing machine and other home appliances. Myanmar Suzuki Motor Company Limited established in 1998 is a joint venture enterprise between MADI and Suzuki Motor Corporation of Japan. MADI holds 30 per cent of equity while the Suzuki Motors holds the rest 70 per cent. Myanmar Matsushita Electric Works Limited is another joint venture enterprise between MTEI and Matsushita Electric Works of Japan established in 1999. While MTEI holds 30 per cent of equity, the rest 70 per cent is held by the Japanese company. It produces wiring devices and other electrical materials. Myanmar Ekarat Transformer Company Limited is another joint venture between MTEI and Ekarat Engineering of Thailand established in 1999 to produce distribution transformers.

In most joint ventures in extractive activities, UMEHC acts as controlling partner. UMEHC's subsidiary MOGE entered into joint ventures with Unocal and Total in oil and gas sector.

As Myanmar has neither the technology nor the resources, it is to her advantage to enter into joint ventures so that the technology and expertise can be internalised in the long run which will empower her to efficiently use her rich natural resources for future development.

Besides state enterprises and joint ventures, SLORC/SPDC has also emphasized the growth of small-scale units under private sector. Industrial zone approach has been adopted for the development of small-scale sector. Myanmar Industrial Development Committee (MIDC) has been constituted in 1995 in order to frame policy direction for the growth of the small-scale sector. MIDC works through a Working Committee (MIDWC) which implements the guidelines framed by it. The MIDC has established 18 industrial zones all over the country. In every zone industrial estates have been constructed. So far, 26 estates have been constructed in 18 zones. A total of 7112 industrial units are housed in these estates[6].

Low rate of domestic saving in Myanmar has led to low rate of capital formation. This low rate of capital formation, in turn, slows down the pace of industrialisation. However, in recent years, private fixed investment has surpassed its public counterparts (Table 1.16A).

Manufacturing and processing activities absorb around one fifth of the banking system loans (Table 1.17A), employ about 9 per cent of the total employed workforce (1997-98) (IMF:2001-18) and contributes about 9 per cent to GDP (1998-99)[7]. The share of manufactured goods in total export is also rising albeit slowly from 6 per cent in 1980-81 to 8 per cent in 1990-91 and to 16 per cent in 1997-98, the average annual increase in the percentage share of manufactured goods being

0.5 per cent. This is indeed abysmal performance compared to the achievements made by other South-East Asian countries.

Trade

The geo-economic location of Myanmar provides her ample scope for both sea trade with 2832 km long coastline, and overland trade with neighbouring China, Thailand, Laos, Bangladesh and India with whom she shares 2,185 km, 1800 km, 235 km, 193 km and 1,463 km borders respectively. In pre-colonial era, royal dynasties benefited from long distance intra-Indian Ocean trade (Myint-U:2001-46). However, from the 17th century onwards, following the move of the capital from Pegu to Ava, the importance of maritime trade had declined. The pre-colonial trade was characterized by export of agro-forest and mineral based products and import of manufactured goods. Export basket predominantly consisted of rice (with occasional Royal ban), ivory, pepper, cutch, teak, other timber, lac, cotton, tea, gold and silver whereas import basket usually included firearms, silk, paper, textiles and various manufactures (Myint-U:2001-47).

Although there had been an enormous change in the scale of production and export during the colonial era essentially due to inflow of large British capital, the essential structure of trade had remained the same. Myanmar remained producer and exporter of primary goods, *a la*, other British colonies, and importer of British manufactures. With British capital flowing into rice trade, logging and oil exploration–rice, teak and oil became three important building blocks of Myanmar's export (Myint-U:2001-227).

This structure of trade continued in post-colonial Myanmar till late 1990s. About 90 per cent of her exports composed of primary goods, i.e., agro-forest-mineral based products in 1980-81 (Table 1.8). By mid 1980s, i.e., just before liberalisation, primary goods contributed about 92 per cent of Myanmar's total domestic export (Table 1.8). By early 1990s, things started changing and by late 1990s, the share of the primary goods came down below 50 per cent of the total domestic exports (Table 1.8). Moreover, there is a clear trend which shows that Myanmar has come a long way in transforming its rice-based agriculture into a multi-crop one.

Table 1.8
Myanmar: Domestic Export of Principal Commodities

(in million Kyat)

Commodity/Group	*1980-81*	*1985-86*	*1990-91*	*1995-96*	*1999-98*
1. Agricultural Products	1761	1126	942	2321	1952
	(55.45)	(43.88)	(31.90)	(46.12)	(31.03)
of which:					
Rice and Rice Products	1355	763	172	440	38
Pulses	152	238	515	1358	1403
2. Timber	793	1046	999	1048	853
	(24.97)	(40.76)	(33.83)	(20.82)	(13.56)
3. Base Metals and Ores	190	114	72	70	30
	(5.98)	(4.45)	(2.44)	(1.39)	(0.48)
4. Precious Stones and Minerals	105	74	86	137	207
	(3.31)	(2.88)	(2.91)	(2.72)	(3.29)
5. Other Commodities	327	206	854	1457	3248
	(10.29)	(8.03)	(28.92)	(28.95)	(51.64)
Total Domestic Export	3176	2566	2953	5033	6290
	(100.00)	(100.00)	(100.00)	(100.00)	(100.00)

Source: http:www.myanmar.com/Ministry/commerce/data_chart/domestic_export_principal.htm

Note: Figures from different sources are cross-verified and then adjusted against "other commodities" in order to arrive at the given annual total export. Figures in brackets are percentages.

Export of rice constituted 77 per cent of total agro exports in 1980-81, it came down to 68 per cent in 1985-86, and then to 18 per cent in 1990-91 (Table 1.8). The fall in export of rice over the years has been compensated by the rise in export of pulses. The share of pulses in total agro export was 7 per cent in

1980-81 and it has gone up to 55 per cent in 1990-91. Because of the severe flood in 1997-98, the share of rice in total agro export had touched its bottom at 2 per cent, while that of pulses had reached to 72 per cent (Table 1.8). Besides pulses, diversification has also taken place in favour of sugarcane, sesame, sunflower and cotton, the contributions of all those crops to total agro exports are also increasing over time.

Table 1.9
Myanmar: Composition of Imports

(in million Kyat)

Commodity/Group	*1980-81*	*1985-86*	*1990-91*	*1995-96*	*1999-98*
1. Capital goods	2496.3 (53.85)	2741.3 (57.09)	1905.6 (34.50)	3644.5 (35.38)	6172.1 (43.29)
2. Intermediate goods	1863.1 (40.20)	1484.7 (30.92)	1661.6 (30.09)	2376.8 (23.07)	3350.1 (23.50)
3. Consumer goods	275.6 (5.95)	576 (11.99)	1955.6 (35.41)	4280.3 (41.55)	4735.2 (33.21)
Total	4635 (100.00)	4802 (100.00)	5522.8 (100.00)	10301.6 (100.00)	14257.4 (100.00)

Source: http:www.myanmar.com/Ministry/commerce/data_chart/composition_of_imports.htm

Note: Figures in brackets are percentages

While the composition of exports reflects the resource base and productive capacity of an economy, the composition of imports represents the demand structure. Being primary goods producing economy, Myanmar has to import capital goods in a big way. The share of capital goods in total imports was 54 per cent in 1980-81 (Table 1.9). It has further gone up to 57 per cent in 1985-86, just before Myanmar liberalised her economy since 1988. In post-liberalised 1990s, although the percentage share of capital goods in total import bill has come down, it has remained as the principal component of Myanmar's import (Table 1.9). The share of consumer goods in total import was

5.95 per cent in 1980-81 and 12 per cent in 1985-86 (Table 1.9). With trade liberalisation in 1988, the value of import of consumer goods has gone up 3 times in the 1990s. While machinery and transport equipments constitutes the single largest item in capital goods, manufactured goods constitutes the bulk of consumer goods. The manufactured goods basket is dominated by chemicals, medicines, textiles, edible vegetable oils; dyeing, tanning and colouring materials, fertilizers, cotton yarn, paper and paper board, cement, rubber manufacturer, electrical goods, etc.

Thus, the composition of export and import shows that Myanmar is basically a producer and exporter of primary goods and importer of capital as well as manufactured goods. Although there is a change in the composition of export basket in late 1990s, it cannot be inferred at the moment as to whether this change is a temporary phenomenon or it is because of the change in the fundamentals of the economy of Myanmar.

Myanmar economy is more integrated with the economies of neighbouring South-East Asian countries. Singapore, Japan, Hong Kong, Korea, Thailand and Malaysia have been the major trading partners all along. While 39 per cent of Myanmar's total export in 1980-81 went to these countries, it went up to 60 per cent in 1990-91 (Table 1.18A). Since the 1980s, Myanmar products have been increasingly received in both India and China.

While China absorbed 1.33 per cent of Myanmar's export in 1980-81, and 13.55 per cent in 1990-91, India absorbed 1.80 per cent and 17.92 per cent respectively. In 1997-98, about 12 per cent of Myanmar's total export has gone to China while India absorbed 23 per cent (Table 1.18A). Thus, by late 1990s, India emerged as the largest export market for Myanmar.

As far as the sources of Myanmar's imports are concerned, Japan played the dominant role in the 1980s. About 45 per cent of Myanmar's total import originated from Japan in 1980-81 as well as in 1985-86. About 63 per cent of Myanmar's total import originated from South-East Asian countries and China in

1980-81 which gone up to 70 per cent in 1990-91 and further to 82 per cent in 1997-98 (Table 1.18A). By late 1990s, Singapore has emerged as the major source of imports for Myanmar.

It may be noted that although India has become the major destination of Myanmar's exports during the 1990s, she remained as a poor source for Myanmar's imports. Indian imports constituted only 0.54 per cent of Myanmar's total imports in 1980-81, it went up marginally to 0.68 per cent in 1990-91, and then to 4.65 per cent in 1997-98 (Table 1.18A). Thus, Myanmar enjoys a huge positive trade balance from her trade with India, although she has been experiencing overall negative trade balances with the rest of the world (Table 1.19A).

Table 1.10
Myanmar: Share of Export and Import in GDP, 1995/96–1999/2000

(in Million Kyat)

	1995-96	*1996-97*	*1997-98*	*1998-99*	*1999-00*
GDP at Market Prices	604,729	791,980	1,119,509	1,609,776	2,190,301
Exports	5033	5488	6290	7700	9394
Imports	10,302	11,779	14,258	16,941	15,248
Percentage share of Export in GDP	0.8	0.7	0.6	0.5	0.4
Percentage share of Import in GDP	1.7	1.5	1.3	1.1	0.7

Source: IMF (2001)

However, in spite of trade liberalisation, the external sector of the Myanmar economy is not performing well. The ban on Myanmar imposed by USA and EU because of the failure of installation of popular government following the 1990 election has hit hard on the external sector of the economy. The percentage share of exports in GDP has been continuously falling. It was 0.8 per cent in 1995-96 and has slided down to

0.4 per cent in 1999-2000 (Table 1.10). As GDP is rising at a faster rate, there is a need to accelerate exports as well. Otherwise, it will be difficult to sustain the growth rate.

Myanmar's Border Trade

In order to expand trade, since early 1990s Myanmar has started promoting border trade with the neighbouring countries of China, Thailand, Bangladesh and India. Along Myanmar-China border, it has opened three border trade posts at Muse, Lwejel and Lizer; four posts along Myanmar-Thailand border at Tachilek, Myawaddy, Kawthaung and Myeik; two posts along Myanmar-Bangladesh border at Sittwe and Maungdaw and one post along Myanmar-India border at Tamu.

Table 1.11
Myanmar: Volume of Border Trade

(in Millions US dollar)

Year	*Export*	*Import*	*Volume of Trade*
1995-96	43.15	292.80	335.95
1996-97	58.40	298.72	357.12
1997-98	154.97	102.09	257.06
1998-99	146.30	153.97	300.27
1999-2000	196.40	147.99	344.39
Total	599.22	995.57	1594.79

Source: http:www.myanmar.com/Ministry/commerce/Border trade/FSbodertrade.htm

The average annual volume of trade for 1995/96–1999/00 flowed through all these border trade posts is accounted for about US $319 million (Table 1.11). The total volume of export has gone up from US $ 43.15 million in 1995-96 to US $ 196.40 million in 1999-2000 (Table 1.11). The import has declined from US $292.80 million in 1995-96 to US $147.99 million in 1999-2000. The trade balance, within these five years, has improved from a deficit of US $249.65 million in 1995-96 to a surplus of

US $48.41 million in 1999-2000 (Table 1.11)[8]. By adopting a policy of export first and import later, Myanmar has succeeded to have a positive trade balance in her border trade.

Much of Myanmar's cross-border trade flows across China. Next to China, the second highest volume of trade flows across Thailand. The volume of trade along Myanmar-Bangladesh border is also increasing gradually. However, compared to other neighbouring countries, the volume of trade along Indo-Myanmar border is small.

Border Trade of NER

This is also evident when one looks at it from India's point of view. Indo-Myanmar border trade flows through Moreh (Manipur)-Tamu (Myanmar) sector. While the north eastern region (NER) has 32 land custom stations (LCS) along Bangladesh border and 3 LCS along Bhutan border, it has only 1 LCS along Myanmar border (Das:2000-28/30). For the last five years (1998/99–2002/03), the average annual export of NER to neighbouring countries amounts to US $87.32 million. The average annual import stands at US $4.38 million and average volume of trade stands at US $ 91.7 million (Table 12).

Table 1.12
NER's Border Trade with Neighbouring Countries, 1998/99–2002/03

(in Millions US dollar)

Year	*Export*	*Import*	*Volume of Trade*
1998-1999	92.55	5.67	98.22
1999-2000	91.37	4.29	95.66
2000-2001	88.46	4.28	92.74
2001-2002	79.50	3.34	82.84
2002-2003	84.74	4.30	89.04
Total	436.62	21.88	458.50

Source: Office of the Commissioner of Customs, Shillong.

However, for the same period, NER's annual average export to Myanmar stands at US $0.89 million which is only 1 per cent of NER's annual average export to the neighbouring countries (Table 1.13). As far as NER's imports for this period is concerned, the annual average imports from Myanmar amounts to US $1.66 million which is 38 per cent of NER's annual average import from all the neighbouring countries (Table 1.12 and 1.13). Thus while NER enjoys favourable balance of trade in her cross border trade, she suffers from negative trade balance with Myanmar.

Table 1.13
NER's Border Trade with Myanmar Through Moreh

(in Millions US dollar)

Year	*Export*	*Import*	*Volume of Trade*
1998-1999	1.20	1.47	2.67
1999-2000	0.77	1.55	2.32
2000-2001	1.2	2.70	3.90
2001-2002	0.26	0.16	0.42
2002-2003	1.03	2.44	3.47
Total	4.46	8.32	12.78

Source: Office of the Commissioner of Customs, Shillong.

NER Vs Myanmar: Is there any basis for trade?

The reason for the slow volume of cross-border trade between India and Myanmar appears to lay in the similarity of resource base and production structure across the border. North-Eastern Region of India (NER) which shares border with Myanmar also rich in natural resources. Like Myanmar, NER also exports primary products. Agro-horticultural goods, minerals like coal, limestone, boulder stone, crushed stone, etc. constitute her export basket. For the period 1998/99–2002/03, the average annual share of agro-horticultural and mineral products to total exports of NER has been 98.58 per cent[9].

About 95 per cent of NER's export goes to Bangladesh. While the complementarity between the resource base of NER[10] and demand structure of Bangladesh provides a firm basis for cross border trade between them (Das:2000), the competitive resource base of both NER and Myanmar hardly provides any strong basis for trade.

Apart from similar resource base, both NER and Myanmar are industrially weak and require huge investments in order to strengthen resource industry linkages. Both import manufactured goods. The similarities in resource base, production structure and demand structure between NER and Myanmar seem largely to explain the reasons for small volume of trade between them across the border.

However, besides formal trade, for which data have been presented, and on the basis of which structure of trade has been analysed so far, there exists large-scale informal trade across Myanmar borders. Since pre-colonial era, Myanmar had strong informal trade across the border with China and Thailand. Myanmar observers feel that the volume of informal Sino-Myanmar trade is about three fold more than its formal counterparts (Egreteau:2003-80). In fact, it is difficult to estimate the volume of informal trade as it is carried out clandestinely. It is believed that the volume of the informal Indo-Myanmar trade is at least 10 times more than its formal counterparts[11]. Manufactured goods of third country origin like clothes and blankets from China, Japan and other South-East Asian countries are imported into NER informally and medicines, bicycle parts, chemicals and other pharmaceutical products, fertilizers procured from other regions of India, are exported to Myanmar informally (Rao, et al:2004-10). Although there is not much of scope for NER-Myanmar commodity trade, the volume of informal trade indicates a large scope for transit trade.

As it has already been pointed out that the economy of Myanmar is more integrated with the economies of South-East Asian countries rather than developed western economies, the prospect of reaching the markets of these newly industrialised countries through Myanmar has further brightened with her entry into ASEAN in 1997. India's Look East Policy precisely wants to achieve this goal for her industry and business.

Concluding Remarks

Although the instrumental value of NER-Myanmar trade in terms of generation of economic growth is negligible at present, the intrinsic value of cross border trade is, no doubt, immense as it eases out life of the people living in the border areas. For border trade to promote the economic development of the border areas, it has to be integrated with the overall development strategy of the border states. Unless the border states mould their development strategy focussing on border trade and adjust their sectoral strategies accordingly, the cross border trade is unlikely to pay any dividend. The production structure of the border states needs to be reorganised in line with the demand structure of the neighbouring country. As the import basket of Myanmar mainly consists of manufactured goods, NER could benefit from trade with Myanmar only if she could industrialise herself. It is, thus, important to have a market survey in Myanmar and identify the products which NER can produce at competitive costs preferably using her own resources. In doing this, states in NER may follow export processing zone approach to negotiate with her internal forces of rigidities like rigidities associated with land transfer and labour mobility. Besides this, anciliarisation approach towards industrialization seems to be the best way to produce quality products at competitive price rather than state-led industrial development approach.

Given the weak manufacturing base, trans-border trade in services like education, health and tourism may be of immediate benefit for NER. Both education and health services are far better in NER compared to the bordering regions of Myanmar. Appropriate policy response needs to be evolved in these areas.

Although Indo-Myanmar border trade is essentially transit in nature and is not organically linked with the local economy at present, promotion of this trade may, in the long run, lead to the development of transport sector as well as assembly line industrialisation. These may, in turn, lead to the strengthening of resource-industry linkages in the regional economy. While Indian industry and business seeks to use both NER and Myanmar as corridors to reach South-East Asian markets, this may build a partnership between local and national capital which, in turn, will facelift the local economy. State policies need to be woven in building this partnership.

Finally, Indian state needs to consider "border trade" as a strategy for the development of the border areas. A "shared border" approach will lead to better border management which is a *sine qua non* for the promotion of cross border trade. India needs to engage Myanmar more intensely and play more substantive role in the development of Myanmar *a la* China. Border states in India need to adopt corporate approach as far as their development activities are concerned. Federal government may think of empowering the border states so that they can strike business deals with entities across the border.

NOTES

1. http://www.fao.org/ag/agl/sw/wpnr/reports/y_ta/z_mm/mmtb28p.htm
2. http://www.fao.org/ag/agl/sw/wpnr/reports/y_ta/z_mm/mmtb282.htm
3. http://www.fao.org/ag/agl/sw/wpnr/reports/y_ta/z_mm/mmtb311.htm
4. *ibid*
5. Agriculture, livestock and fishery, forestry and mining constitute the primary sector here.

6. www.myanmar/directorate of myanma industrial planning-5.htm

7. At constant 1985-86 prices.

8. Border trade statistics of Myanmar available in IMF (2001, table 35) do not tally with the same available at the website of the Department of Border Trade, Government of Myanmar. Here we have used the latter source as it is consistent with the data available with the Office of the Commissioner of Customs, Shillong, on the Indo-Myanmar border trade.

9. Calculated from data collected from the Office of the Commissioner of Customs, Shillong.

10. For details on resource base of NER , see (Das: 2005_a, Das: 2005_b)

11. Rao, *et al* (1997) estimated the volume of informal trade through Moreh-Tamu sector at Rs 1300 million annually.

REFERENCES

Asian Development Bank, 2004, Asian Development Outlook, Oxford University Press, Hong Kong.

Choudhary, Nilufar, 2000, "Burma's Foreign Policy: Continuity and Change", in Verinder Grover, (ed), *Myanmar: Government and Politics*, Deep and Deep Publications, New Delhi.

Das, Gurudas, 1995, *Tribes of Arunachal Pradesh in Transition*, Vikas, New Delhi.

Das, Gurudas, 2000, "Trade Between the North-Eastern Region and Neighbouring Countries: Structures and Implications for Development", in Das, Gurudas and R K Purkayastha, (eds), *Border Trade: North-East India and Neighbouring Countries*, Akansha Publishing House, New Delhi.

Das, Gurudas, (ed), 2005_a, *Structural Change and Strategy of Development: Resource-Industry Linkages in North East India*, Akansha Publishing House, New Delhi.

Das, Gurudas, 2005_b, "Sino-Indian Border Trade for Frontier Development: The Case of India's North East and China's South West", in Ray, Jayanta Kumar and Prabir De, (eds), *India and China in an Era of Globalisation: Essays on Economic Cooperation*, Bookwell, New Delhi.

Donnison, F S V, 1970, *Burma*, Praeger Publishers, New York.

Egreteau, Renaud, 2003, *Wooing the Generals: India's New Burma Policy*, Authors Press and Centre De Sciences Humaines, Delhi.

Ghosh, Anjali, 1989, *Burma: A Case of Aborted Development*, Papyrus, Calcutta.

International Monetary Fund (IMF), 1999, Myanmar: Recent Economic Development, IMF Staff Country Report No 99/134, IMF, Washington, D C.

International Monetary Fund (IMF), 2001, Myanmar: Statistical Appendix, IMF Country Report No 01/18, IMF, Washington, D C.

Graves, Mikael, 1999, (2nd ed), *Nationalism as Political Paranoia in Burma: An Essay on the Historical Practice of Power*, Curzon, Richmond.

Mahajani, Usha, 1960, *The Role of Indian Minorities in Burma and Malay*, Vora & Co, Bombay.

Myint-U, Thant, 2001, *The Making of Modern Burma*, Cambridge University Press, Cambridge, UK.

Okamoto, Ikuko, Kurita, Kyosuke, Kurosaki, Takashi and Koichi Fujita, 2003, "Rich Periphery, Poor Centre: Myanmar's Rural Economy under Partial Transition to Market Economy", in Online Burma/MyanmarLibrary, http://www.ibiblio.org/obl/show.php?cat=895

Rao, V L, Baruah, Srinath and Ram Upendra Das, 1997, *India's Border Trade with Select Neighbouring Countries*, Research and Information System for the Non-Aligned and other Developing Countries (RIS), New Delhi.

RIS, 2004, *Future Directions of BIMSTEC: Towards a Bay of Bengal Economic Community*, RIS, New Delhi.

Tucker, Shelby, 2001, *Burma: The Curse of Independence*, Pluto Press, London.

APPENDIX

Table 1.14A
Myanmar: Harvested Acreage Under Major Crops, 1994/95-1998/99

(in thousands of hectares)

	1994-95	*1995-96*	*1996-97*	*1997-98*	*1998-99*
Paddy	5,743	6,033	5,768	5,408	5,751
Wheat	107	91	90	88	102
Maize	167	161	165	161	168
Pulses	1,693	2,006	1,932	2,046	2,391
Groundnuts	497	515	478	446	464
Sesame	1,132	904	1,015	774	673
Sunflower	179	216	122	115	287
Cotton	178	324	298	246	313
Jute	37	47	43	34	37
Sugarcane	53	66	84	106	127
Myanma tobacco	28	25	29	33	28
Virginia tobacco	3	4	4	4	5
Rubber	52	49	46	48	50
Total	9,869	10,441	10,074	9,509	10,396

Source: IMF (1999)

Table 1.15A
Myanmar: Output and Yield of Major Crops, 1994/95-1998/99

	1994-95	1995-96	1996-97	1997-98	1998-99
	(In thousands of metric tons)				
Output					
Paddy	18,195	17,953	17,673	16,651	17,848
Wheat	89	78	87	92	92
Maize	284	275	286	308	303
Pulses	1,109	1,337	1,370	1,597	1,678
Groundnuts	500	593	559	540	502
Sesame	304	304	344	296	186
Sunflower	117	164	92	90	184
Cotton	86	165	168	164	189
Jute	35	43	39	33	33
Sugarcane	2,375	3,342	4,042	5,136	5,927
Myanma tobacco	35	41	47	57	46
Virginia tobacco	18	22	23	25	29
Rubber	27	26	26	27	26
	(In kilograms per hectare of harvested area)				
Yield					
Paddy	3,168	2,976	3,064	3,079	3,103
Wheat	832	857	967	1,045	902
Maize	1,701	1,708	1,733	1,913	1,804
Pulses	655	667	709	781	702
Groundnuts	1,006	1,151	1,169	1,211	1,082
Sesame	269	336	339	382	276
Sunflower	654	759	754	783	641
Cotton	483	509	564	667	604
Jute	946	915	907	971	892
Sugarcane (mt per ha)	45	51	48	48	47
Myanma tobacco	1,250	1,640	1,621	1,727	1,643
Virginia tobacco	6,000	5,500	5,750	6,250	5,800
Rubbers	519	531	565	563	520

Source: IMF (1999)

Table 1.16A
Myanmar: Investment and Savings, 1995/98–1999/2000

	1995-96	1996-97	1997-98	1998-99	1999-00 Provisional
(In millions of kyats at current prices)					
Gross capital formation	86,122	97,051	139,964	199,308	290,019
Fixed investment	82,582	118,313	150,240	206,912	241,694
Public	41,035	57,275	68,402	79,598	81,806
Private	41,547	61,038	81,838	127,314	159,888
Change in Stocks	3,540	-21,262	-10,276	-7,604	48,325
National saving	83,383	94,317	135,882	195,911	288,190
Domestic saving	81,484	91,732	133,059	192,815	285,381
Net factor income plus net unrequited transfers from abroad	1,899	2,585	2,823	3,096	2,809
Foreign saving	2,739	2,733	4,082	3,397	1,829
(Percentage share in GDP)					
Gross capital formation	14.2	12.3	12.5	12.4	13.2
Fixed investment	13.7	14.9	13.4	12.9	11.0
Public	6.8	7.2	6.1	4.9	3.7
Private	6.9	7.7	7.3	7.9	7.3
National saving	13.8	11.9	12.1	12.2	13.1
Domestic saving	13.5	11.6	11.9	12.0	13.0
Foreign saving	0.5	0.3	0.4	0.2	0.1

Source: IMF (2001).

Table 1.17A

Myanmar: Banking System Loans by Sector, 1996-2000

(In percentage)

	1996	1997	1998	1999	2000
Primary sector	**12**	**7**	**6**	**6**	**6**
Agriculture	11	5	3	3	3
Others	1	2	3	3	3
Secondary sector	**29**	**22**	**25**	**27**	**29**
Manufacturing and Processing	22	17	18	20	23
Others	7	5	7	7	6
Tertiary sector	**59**	**71**	**69**	**67**	**65**
Trade	25	51	49	46	45
Others	34	20	20	21	20
Total	100	100	100	100	100
Total loans (in million of Kyats)	31,627	77,198	116,913	142,393	188,658

Source: IMF (2001)

Table 1.18A
Myanmar: Direction of Foreign Trade

(in percentage of total)

Country/	1980-81		1985-86		1990-91		1995-96		1997-98	
Region	Export	Import	Export	Import	Export	Import	Export	Import	Export	Import
Singapore	13.02	8.47	13.38	9.57	28.91	9.78	19.77	17.97	13.30	31.84
Japan	8.53	45.36	7.53	45.52	7.62	16.58	5.14	24.75	3.85	15.64
Hong Kong	7.89	0.46	12.47	1.33	8.48	0.59	7.20	1.67	5.84	2.68
Korea	4.49	1.35	0.66	1.84	0.54	3.66	1.44	3.98	0.88	5.65
India	1.8	0.54	7.15	0.11	17.92	0.68	20.77	3.41	22.81	4.65
China	1.33	4.75	6.26	3.84	13.55	22.14	3.91	14.16	10.72	9.6
Thailand	1.75	0.33	5.10	0.5	13.26	10.19	10.72	13.03	12.02	10.02
Malaysia	2.88	2.58	3.52	1.15	1.40	7.04	2.96	6.08	2.65	7.14
Sri Lanka	5.07	-	2.67	-	2.3	-	0.29	-	0.36	-
North-West Europe	13.42	20.81	11.28	24.22	2.86	10.29	2.62	6.33	5.08	3.25
Africa	9.71	0.04	10.47	1.66	1.84	0.33	0.65	0.08	0.07	0.54
Others	30.11	15.31	19.51	10.26	1.32	18.72	24.53	8.54	22.42	8.99
Total	100.00	100.00	100.00	100.00	100.00	100.00	100.00	100.00	100.00	100.00

Source: http://www.myanmar.com/Ministry/commerce/data_chart/all_export.htm
http://www.myanmar.com/Ministry/commerce/data_chart/import_by_country.htm

Table 1.19A
Myanmar: Value of Foreign Trade

(in Million Kyat)

Year	*Export*	*Import*	*Balance of Trade*
1980-81	3176.4	4635.0	(-) 1458.6
1985-86	2566.1	4802	(-) 2235.9
1990-91	2952.6	5522.8	(-) 2570.2
1995-96	5032.7	10301.6	(-) 5268.9
2000-2001(p)	3982.5	6979	(-)2996.5

Source: http://www.myanmar.com/Ministry/commerce/data_chart/value_ft.htm
Note: 1990-91 onward data include border trade
P = Provisional

2

Indo-Myanmar Border Trade

—J.S.R. Khathing

Introduction

Trade is an engine of economic growth. It is widely acknowledged that low income countries are characterized by smaller sized markets that fail to absorb sufficient volume of output which in turn leads to low incentive for investment. International trade can expand the size of markets leading to an increase in the incentive for investment and promotion of growth of income and savings through more efficient allocation of resources. It also helps to transform the subsistence sector into a monetized sector by providing a market for farm produce and raises the income level and standard of living of people. Higher levels of output and income achieved through international trade can help to break the vicious circle of poverty and promote economic development.

In this context border trade will have a special significance to the economies of the Northeastern States due to their seemingly disadvantageous geographical location *vis-à-vis* the rest of the country. These States share 99.56 per cent of their borders with neighbouring countries and a negligible 0.44 per cent with mainland India. With the exception of the tiny *"chicken's neck" (22 km wide)* connecting Assam with West Bengal, the rest of the border *(5000 km)* is shared with Bangladesh, China, Bhutan, and Myanmar. This, coupled with poor infrastructural facilities within the region, has led to a situation where each of the States tends to look more to neighbouring countries than to mainland India for economic sustenance and subsequently, economic growth.

Myanmar

Myanmar, the largest country of mainland Southeast Asia, has an international border of 5,858 km with India and Bangladesh on the northwest; and Laos and Thailand on the southeast. Myanmar and India share a common border of 1,643 km covering four Indian States in the Northeast *viz.* Arunachal Pradesh, Manipur, Mizoram, and Nagaland. Myanmar's coastline, which is about 2822 km, with a continental shelf of about 228,781 sq km, defines the eastern shore of the Bay of Bengal, running from the Bangladesh border in the northwest down to the Malay Peninsula and Thai territory in the southeast.

Myanmar is essentially an agricultural economy, where almost three-quarters of Myanmar's population either grows or processes crops, with roughly ten per cent working in the industrial sector. Forests reportedly cover 51 per cent of the total area and the potential in trade of Myanmar teak and hardwood is huge. Similarly, the long coastline and the large perennial rivers endow the country with a variety of marine resources. The country also has deposits of mineral resources, which include a variety of precious and semi-precious stones that have good demand in the international markets.

North-East India

The North-Eastern Region, though a landlocked region in the relatively remote northeast of India, has several advantages that if properly channelised will boost foreign trade with its neighbouring countries. To name a few:

- The region has about 5000 km of international borders with the countries of Bangladesh, Bhutan, China and Myanmar that can be made into India's gateway to the entire South-East Asian region.

- It has one of the most fertile stretches of land along the Brahmaputra valley, whose potential for the cultivation of a wide variety of cash and food crops on a commercial basis is yet to be fully realised. Agro-economic potential is high.
- Rich mineral resources, many of which have not yet been fully exploited.
- Abundant forest resources with many ethnic products, which are unique to the region.
- One of the largest perennial water system in India (Brahmaputra and its tributaries) with immense potential in the areas of energy, irrigation and transportation.
- Oil, tea and hydrocarbon processing industry.

Overview of trade between North-East India and Myanmar

A Memorandum of Understanding (MOU) between the Government of India and Myanmar on cooperation between Civilian Border Authorities of the two countries was signed on 21st January 1994. Thereafter, on 10th June 1994 certain decisions were arrived at, at the Delegation-Level talks Co-chaired by the Commerce Secretary of India and the Director General, Directorate of Trade, Ministry of Trade, Myanmar and the Agreed Upon Minutes signed. The items discussed and minuted included Banking and Trading arrangements, Immigration and Customs Inspection Arrangements and timing for Border Trade.

Formal Trade between the two countries through the Moreh Land Customs Station in Manipur was opened on 12th April 1995 by the Hon'ble Minister of State for Commerce, Government of India, Shri P Chidambaram along with his Myanmar Counterpart Lt. Gen. Tun Kyi, the Minister of Trade, Myanmar. Presently, Moreh is the only Land Customs Station through which trade across land route from India to Myanmar takes place.

Interestingly, despite the enormous potential that both Myanmar and the North-East region of India possess in terms of contiguity of border, proximity of markets and natural resources, the value of export/import trade between India and Myanmar through North-East represents a small fraction of the total export/import trade of the entire North-East as can be seen from the figures for the last five years appended below:

Table 2.1
Total Value of Export and Import (EXIM) Trade

	Entire North East Region (Rs. Crore)	*Across Indo-Myanmar border (Rs. Crore)*	*% share of Indo-Myanmar trade vis-à-vis total EXIM trade of the NE Region*
1999-00	414.46	9.99	2.41
2000-01	423.64	17.88	4.22
2001-02	395.09	8.82	2.23
2002-03	430.91	16.03	3.90
2003-04	468.29	18.25	3.90

Source: Office of the Commissioner of Customs, Shillong

As can be seen from Table 2.1, the average value of EXIM trade in the entire North East during the last five years was Rs. 426.48 crore, while that across the Indo-Myanmar border it was Rs. 14.19 crore, constituting just 3.33 per cent of the total trade. This chapter will attempt to analyze the reasons for the huge disparity in performance of cross border trade across the Indo-Myanmar border.

Cross-border trade/movement prior to the introduction of the 'Indo-Myanmar Trade Agreement'

The hill people inhabiting the border areas along India and Myanmar have traditionally been allowed free movement up to 40 km on either side of the entire length of the 1643 km International Border between India and Myanmar. Owing to absence of defined markets, medical facilities, etc., in most of the bordering areas, tribals of these remote areas frequently cross over to the other side for availing of such facilities.

Though there was no bilateral agreement between India and Myanmar on the regulation of movement of local tribals, there was, however, a tacit understanding that there would be no restriction on such movements, which have continued since time immemorial owing to close economic and cultural ties among the tribals of the area. This tacit understanding between the two governments is reflected in the reciprocal notifications issued during 1948-50 amending their respective *Passport Rules* so as to provide for and accommodate the continuance of the traditional practice regarding travel across the border of indigenous tribals in either country up to 25 miles (40 km) in the other country.

The Myanmar Passport Rules, 1948 contained a provision to the effect that "indigenous nationals of those countries whose land borders are co-terminus with the border of Myanmar are exempt from Passport requirements, provided they were members of Hill Tribals inhabiting areas adjacent to the land border and did not proceed beyond 25 miles across the Land Border." Subsequently, in December 1948, this provision was modified and it was stipulated that the continuous stay of tribals crossing over would not exceed 30 days.

Through a Notification dated 26th September, 1950, the Government of India exempted the indigenous tribals inhabiting areas within 25 miles of the Indo-Myanmar frontier, from passport and visa requirements provided any such national of the Union of Myanmar did not proceed beyond 25 miles (40 km) from the land border. Tribals from both sides enjoyed this exemption until June 1968 when the Government of India through a Notification unilaterally introduced a permit system to regulate their movement with a view to prevent entry of undesirable elements and checking insurgent activity. The system of permits *(which is still in vogue)* stipulated that Indian and Myanmar tribals would have to carry permits for travelling across the border and that these would be granted liberally to persons who are required to travel frequently in pursuit of their normal vocation and for other bonafide purposes. Instructions were also issued to the concerned State authorities to refuse permits to undesirable elements.

In reality, however, the local ethnic tribals take very little effort to obtain such permits to visit places on either side of the border on account of inconvenience with the absence of check posts on the international border to regulate such movement.

Cross-border trade/movement after the introduction of the 'Indo-Myanmar Trade Agreement'

Types of Movements permitted under the Trade Agreement

The *'Indo-Myanmar Trade Agreement'* provides for two types of movement across the border. These are:

Free Movement *not related to trade,* regulated under a simple Border Pass/Permit issued by the immigration authorities of either country. This is restricted to 12 hours per day and takes place between Tamu/Namphalong (Myanmar) and Moreh (India). This form of movement is restricted to ethnic locals living on both sides of the border, up to a distance of 40 km on either side of international border and is in keeping with the customary practice existing prior to the introduction of formal trade. Traditional free movement/exchange in the form of visits, not related to trade does not entail exchange or barter of local produces for commercial purpose. Consequently, free movement/exchange taking place all along the international border are not regulated by Customs or DGFT. However, this sort of movement as indicated in *Article-II* of the *'Indo-Myanmar Trade Agreement'* restricts goods to local produce only and its consumption within the 40 km zone.

Movement in connection with **'Regulated Trade'** is

permitted through a *'Special Identity Document'* called *Travel Pass,* which is equivalent to and similar to a Passport. Visits of such pass holders are restricted to a period of 7 days with an option for Indian traders to travel up to Kalemyo - Mandalay in Myanmar; and for Myanmarese traders up to Imphal in India.

Free movement, related to trade, regulated under a simple Border Pass/Permit issued by the immigration authorities of either country. This is restricted to 12 hours per day between Tamu/Namphalong (Myanmar) and Moreh (India). This sort of movement restricts trade to the exchange of locally produced commodities (as contained in the *Annexure-I* of the *Indo-Myanmar Trade Agreement*) in headloads and on payment of customs duty. The value of the goods so traded are not to exceed US $ 1000/- per transaction and are exempt from declaration on the prescribed *Guurunteed Receipt (GR) Form,* in terms of the Reserve Bank of India Notification No. FEMA.23/2000-RB Dated 03.05.2000. However, such exchange under simplified documentation without Import Export Code (IEC) are to be balanced within a day or two.

Problems associated with free movement

The movement of people (not related to trade) takes place through all the gates along the Moreh Township and other parts of the border, which is totally porous. It should be kept in mind that the *'Indo-Myanmar Trade Agreement'* does not appear to confine such free movement/exchange only through the areas along Moreh Township. It envisages that as per the prevailing customary practice, free movement including exchange of locally produced commodities shall continue. This implies that such movement may take place all along the border; and so it does.

Unlike other international borders, the position of Indo-Myanmar border along Moreh is different. Here there are four entry/exit points namely Gate No. 1 and 2 in addition to two other unofficial entry/exit points locally known as Gate No. 3

and 4. This is complemented by numerous foot tracks within a very short stretch in between Border Pillars No. 77 and 80. The movements in connection with trade and traded goods requiring Customs clearance are exclusively channelised through Gate No.1 at Moreh Land Customs Station. This gate straddles the Burma Road, the only road connecting India with Myanmar. It is a notified authorized route and all legal export/ import trade is carried out through this Gate.

Traditional free movement between India and Myanmar takes place through Gate No. 2 as also the entire length of the 1623 km Indo-Myanmar border. No formal trade takes place through this gate. Movement of people with head loads is very heavy across this gate as it straddles the foot-track connecting the two main markets of *Namphalong* (Myanmar) and *Moreh* (India). If this gate is closed all traditional free movement can take place through gate No 1.

Prior to the *'Indo-Myanmar Trade Agreement'* and channelisation of trade through Moreh Land Customs Station situated at Gate No.1, all four gates were manned round the clock by BSF personnel. However after the implementation of *'Indo-Myanmar Trade Agreement'* the Customs and Immigration personnel man Gate No. 1 and 2 from 5 AM to 5 PM beyond which the gates are manned presently by the Assam Rifles. The other two entry/exit points are however, under the exclusive control of the Assam Rifles authorities.

All movement to and from Moreh (India)/Namphalong-Tamu (Myanmar) are not strictly subjected to restrictions under immigration law. Here people are allowed to visit either side on the basis of simple passes/travel documents issued by the immigration authorities. However, this simple minimum formality is not uniformly implemented across the Indo-Myanmar border.

The entire stretch of border including the areas adjoining Moreh is totally porous and virtually unmanned barring a small distance between Border Pillars 77 and 80.

The problems associated with unregulated free movement across the border is further aggravated by a permanent shopping complex constructed at Namphalong (Myanmar) in early 1997 in close vicinity of Gate No. 2 at Moreh. Goods, consisting of primarily cheap consumer items of Chinese origin from this shopping complex easily find their way into India unhindered owing to the unrestricted movement of the people.

With this backdrop, the only control that can reasonably be exercised by the Customs is anti-smuggling measures, which are enforced quite satisfactorily. For fencing of borders and permanent closure of Gate Nos. 3 and 4 the State Government's active participation and sincere intention would be essential, though this measure is not likely to solve the problem. Instead the expense on fencing should be diverted to the building of good roads, perhaps of world-class quality and 4-laned. Such an advance mode of surface transport will bring down the cost of carriage for legal trade and will enable legally imported goods compete and become preferable to crossings via free movement.

Types of trade allowed under the Trade Agreement

Unlike trade through other land borders, as per the Indo-Myanmar Trade Agreement a *three-tier system of trade* was introduced. These are:

(i) **Traditional exchange** of locally produced items up to US $ 1000 between indigenous people residing up to 40 km on either side of the border under simplified documentation without GR formalities, on payment of customs duty.

(ii) **Barter Trade** of 22 agreed upon exchangeable items up to US $ 20,000 with GR formalities as per DGFT PN No. 289(PN) 92-97 and on payment of customs duty. Under this system traders should possess IEC allotted by Director General of Foreign Trade (DGFT). The items that can be traded under this system are locally produced commodities, mainly agricultural produce and minor forest products as appended below:

Mustard/Rape seed, Pulses & Beans, Fresh Vegetables, Fruits, Garlic, Onion, Chillies, Spice (excluding nutmeg, cloves, mace, cassia & cinnamon), Bamboo, Minor forest products (excluding teak), Betel Nuts & leaves, Food items for local consumption, Tobacco, Tomato, Reed broom, Sesame, Resin, Coriander seeds, *Katha*, Ginger, Soyabean, Roasted sunflower seeds.

(iii) ***Normal or Regular Trade*** under the Letter of Credit System *as per EXIM Policy guidelines.*

To complement the trade agreement and to facilitate and encourage trade, the Central Board of Excise and Customs (CBEC) vide Notification No. 9/95 dated 06.03.1995 notified the items mentioned in (ii) above, attracting a concessional rate of duty @ 5% ad valorem under barter and normal trade through the Moreh Land Customs Station.

The Reserve Bank of India also formulated their policy in line with *Article-II* of the *Indo-Myanmar Trade Agreement*, which, *inter alia*, laid a condition that imports from Myanmar to India,

(i) Shall precede exports from India to Myanmar and such exchange should be balanced within six months from the date of import, in case of barter trade up to US $ 20,000, and

(ii) Preferably within a day or two, in case of traditional exchange of locally produced items up to US $ 1000.

Trade through Moreh Land Customs Station

Cross-border trade with Myanmar through Moreh Land Customs Station, which initially gained momentum and reached its *peak in 1998* started declining due to a number of reasons as can be seen from the table below:

Table 2.2
Export-Import through Moreh

Year	*Import (Rs. Crore)*	*Export (Rs. Crore)*
1995-1996	5.39	00.46
1996-1997	16.17	29.80
1997-1998 *	37.19	25.17
1998-1999	3.75	4.88
1999-2000	6.68	3.31
2000-2001	12.35	5.53
2001-2002	7.59	1.23
2002-2003	11.83	5.00
2003-2004	8.85	9.41

Source: Office of the Commissioner of Customs, Shillong

* due to high demand of wheat flour from Myanmar during the period.

Reasons for the decline in trade through Moreh Land Customs Station

Border trade through Moreh Land Customs Station could not sustain the initial thrust due to the following reasons:

Limitation / Similarity in the list of barter and exchangeable items

Trade in the barter/exchange mechanism is restricted to only 22 items as mentioned above. Obviously, therefore, there is a dearth of commodities that can be exchanged/bartered. Moreover, the 22 listed items are grown and available on both sides of the border, although Myanmar has a surplus.

What actually can be profitably bartered/exchanged, for forest/agricultural/mineral produce from Myanmar is our very own manufactured Indian goods, which enjoy a strong demand in Myanmar. All such consumer goods fall under the OGL so there is no problem from the licensing angle either. Export smuggling of goods like motor cycles/parts, textiles and ready-made clothing, leather goods and footwear, medicines, motor-vehicle/bi-cycle and their parts, health beverages like Maltova/Horlicks/etc., bear testimony to this. Here it should be kept in mind that Myanmar is not an industrialized nation and the demand for manufactured products in the country are by and large met by imports. Traders have been persistently requesting for the inclusion of more items, especially manufactured goods in the list of exchangeable items. It is imperative, therefore, that the list of goods that can be traded under the barter mechanism be expanded.

MOU yet to be signed between designated banks

To understand why no MOU has been signed between the two designated banks of India/Myanmar one has to first understand the existing exchange rate mechanism in actual operation along the border:

The existing rate of exchange is approximately:

Official	*Unofficial (approx value)*
US $ 1 = 6 Kyats	US $1 = 1000 Kyats
US $ 1 = Rs.48	
Kyat 1 = Rs. 7	*Re.1 = 15-20 Kyats*

The unofficial exchange rate of currency appears to benefit our traders, being closer to reality instead of the artificially propped *Kyat* of the Myanmar Government. As a consequence, therefore, traders are reluctant to transact business under Regular Trade under the Letter of Credit system. In the circumstances, barter/exchange being the only viable solution, trade practice along the border is also along these lines.

From the above it should be apparent as to why no MOU can be possible between the two banks.

Restrictions on export of plant and plant materials

The little that's left of export trade from India to Myanmar has been adversely affected because of the restrictions on export of plant and plant materials by the Ministry of Agriculture, which allows export of such items only through the ports of Mumbai, Kolkata, Cochin, Delhi, Chennai, Tutticorin and Amritsar.

Collection of sales tax etc by the State Government

Collection of Sales tax, forest royalty and other taxes on import/export goods, including imported agricultural/horticultural and forest produce of Myanmar origin by the State Government of Manipur has added to the tax burden of the Indian importers, thereby reducing their competitive edge. It must be noted here that the main market for import goods as well as the source of export goods are mainly outside North East. Transportation costs are very high on account of the remoteness and treacherous terrain cutting the competitive edge of the importers at the national level.

Import of Timber

The Supreme Court vide its judgment dated 15.01.1998 banned the felling and movement of domestic timber. The Apex Court's order does not appear to have banned movement of timber imported through licit channels, subject to the EXIM Policy in force and payment of Customs Duty. As per the EXIM Policy in force wood/timber are freely importable under normal trade, subject to the payment of Customs Duty. The DGFT Public Notice No. 289 (PN) 92-97 dated 10.04.1995 also provides for the import of minor forest products *(excluding teak)* under the barter mechanism. This is complemented by the CBEC Notifications 9/95 dated 06.03.1995 and 24/02 dated 01.03.2002 that allows wood in several forms to be imported at a concessional rate of duty of 5% ad valorem under both barter and normal trade.

However, till recently, import of timbers could not take place through Moreh Land Customs Station as the High Powered Committee (HPC) for North Eastern Region *(constituted by Supreme Court's order dated 04.03.1997in WP (Civil) No. 202/95)* did not accord approval to allow movement of timber imported from Myanmar, either by road or otherwise, and in case such timber was imported, the same was to be detained under intimation to the HPC.

Thus there was a situation where timber from Myanmar was allowed through every port in the country except through Moreh Land Customs Station.

However, upon constant persistence from the State Governments of the North East, the HPC has recently decided to allow import of timber from Myanmar through Moreh Land Customs Station, subject to the following conditions:

(a) Import of timber by the HPC cleared wood based units located inside approved industrial estates for their own use will be permitted through Moreh gate. No import will be allowed for trading purpose.

(b) To begin with import of teak and *dipterocarpus indica (garjen)* with a minimum girth of 150 cm will be permitted for manufacture of face veneer for plywood except for Manipur, where import of timber for core veneer will also be permitted. For the time being, import of timber for preparation of sawn timber of veneer as the end product will not be permitted. Such permission will be considered after reviewing the effect of allowing import of timber by the plywood units.

(c) The wood based industries who intend importing timber for preparation of face veneer for plywood manufacturing (and for core in Manipur) may seek permission from the HPC through respective State Government giving species wise details of total quantity of timber to be imported and period of import alongwith source of timber for core veneer together with an undertaking that the unit will send monthly account of receipt and utilisation of such timber to the Principal Chief Conservator of Forest (PCCF) with a copy to the Regional Chief Conservator of Forest, Shillong and that the imported timber will be used by the units for its own production.

(d) No import disproportionate to the capacity of the wood based units will be permitted.

(e) After import of the timber, the details of the imported timber along with purchase documents, customs clearance together with related documents and a Xerox copy of the measurements recorded at the weigh bridge at Moreh gate shall be sent by the unit to the PCCF with a copy to the Regional Chief Conservator of Forest, Shillong.

(f) For Manipur, for the time being import of timber for core will also be permitted. However, in case the working plans are not prepared and approved within a period of one year, no further import will be permitted.

(g) For Nagaland, the permission for import will be considered after the State of Nagaland provides details about availability of timber under the sanctioned working plans, timber available for preparation of core veneer by the plywood units after deducting sawn timber being sent outside Nagaland and being used locally by the veneer units and for other purposes.

It may be mentioned here that there is a tremendous potential for timber imports from Myanmar as the location of Moreh is in the vicinity of vast timber producing areas of

Myanmar and the scarcity of timber in our own country holds a natural advantage for trading in Myanmarese timber. Nevertheless, despite allowing import of timber, subject to conditions as mentioned above, and concurrence given by the HPC for import of timber by six wood based industries of Assam, timber import has not taken off through Moreh Land Customs Station.

Recently, the HPC has also allowed the State of Mizoram to import 500 cu.m of teak from Myanmar. However, the State of Mizoram has to import this through Moreh Land Customs Station in Manipur *(thus resulting in higher costs)* as Zokhawthar, the Land Customs Station on Indo-Myanmar border in Mizoram is not an authorized entry point for import of plant and plant products as per Ministry of Agriculture. Further, it has been experienced that *conditional permission* given to six wood based industrial units of Assam has not resulted in any import yet. Therefore it is to be seen whether such permission granted to State of Mizoram by the HPC will ultimately lead to any import or not.

Multiple check-posts on NH-39

Multiple check posts and obstruction on movement of import/export goods on the National Highways-39 and 53 running through the State of Manipur/Nagaland have been a major stumbling block. Representations received from the trade indicates that there are 53 check posts of various departments/ organisations of the Governments of Manipur and Nagaland from Moreh to Dimapur on National Highway 39 and as many as 12 check posts of the Government of Manipur on National Highway 53.

Present status of infrastructure at Moreh Land Customs Station

The Land Customs Station is housed in Departmental building and the space available is presently sufficient for office purpose and parking. A warehouse has been constructed by the State Government but is yet to be made functional. Further, there are no cold storage facility available for the storage of perishable export/import items.

Similarly, though a weigh bridge has been constructed, it is yet to be made operational. The electricity available in the Land Customs Station is also erratic and drinking water facility is lacking.

The Land Customs Station is not rail linked. The nearest railhead is at Dimapur (Nagaland), which is about 329 km. from Moreh (Manipur). The average value of export/import trade through this station during the last five years was Rs.14.19 crore only. A railway connection with other parts of the region in particular and the country in general will surely boost this figure.

Other Land Customs Stations along Indo-Myanmar Border

Zokhawthar (Champhai) Land Customs Station in Mizoram

Though Champhai town in the Champhai District of Mizoram was declared a Land Customs Station, trade across Indo-Myanmar border through this trade point could not take off mainly because Champhai is situated about 25 km from the international border, as a result of which it was not a suitable location for cross border trade.

However, owing to the persistent demand of the State Government, and also in view of the concurrence of the Union Ministry of Commerce, the Commissioner of Customs NER, Shillong vide Notification No.1/2004(NT) dated 28.01.2004 relocated the Champhai Land Customs Station to Zokhawthar, which is in close proximity to the 'zero-point' under intimation to the Central Board of Excise and Customs (CBEC), New Delhi. The matter relating to de-notification of Champhai Land Customs Station and notification of Zokhawthar as a Land Customs Station is pending with CBEC. The Commissioner of

Customs, Shillong has also reallocated the staff of Champhai Land Customs Station to Zokhawthar to facilitate trade.

Despite such relocation, till date there has been no export/ import through this trading point. The main reason for this is the following:

(a) The Indo-Myanmar Trade Agreement limits barter trade between the two nations to agricultural and minor forest produces only and Zokhawthar is not a declared entry point for import of Plants and Plant products as per Schedule-I, II and III of the Plant Quarantine (Regulation of Import into India) Order, 2003, of the Ministry of Agriculture, Government of India effective from 1st January, 2004. Hence, in the absence of Zokhawthar being a notified as an entry point for plant materials, trade through this sector cannot take off.

(b) At the zero point and across the bridge over the River Tiau is Rih on the Myanmar side, where a small office housing Myanmarese Customs and Immigration personnel has recently been set up. The nearest regular Myanmarese Customs Station is at *Kalemyo*, about 80 miles from Rih. It is connected to Rih by only a fair weather road. Thus necessary infrastructure has to be built if international trade is to take off and flourish through this route.

It is interesting to note that as far as infrastructure in our side is concerned, only an Assam type temporary building (40' X 12') has been built by the Government of Mizoram to house Customs Office and Immigration Office. Other necessary infrastructural facilities like electrification, water supply, staff quarters, bank, office space for Plant Quarantine officers etc. are yet to be completed.

Nampong Land Customs Station in Arunachal Pradesh

The only Land Customs Station across Indo-Myanmar border at Arunachal Pradesh is Nampong. The Land Customs

Station is situated at a distance of 12 km from the Pangsau Pass on Indo-Myanmar border and 80 km from Digboi (Assam), and is in the Changlang District of Arunachal Pradesh. It is strategically located on the famous "Stilwell Road" linking India with Myanmar and China. It is said the road, which was built to meet military requirements, was in use till about 1963 after which it fell into disuse.

Today, 61 km of the Stilwell road is in India, 1033 km in Myanmar and 632 km in China. Nampong (Changlang District, Arunachal Pradesh) situated around 50 km from the railhead at Ledo, is the last township in India on this gigantic serpentine road before it plunges into Myanmar through the Pangsau Pass (Pangsau means a thing, which cannot be seen due to mist) situated barely 12 km from the town and forming a natural corridor between India and Myanmar in the Patkai Range. The place during the Second World War was known as the *"Hell Gate"* or *"Hell Pass"*, as crossing this town/pass to Burma was considered dangerous and hazardous as *"Hell"* considering the active war theatre, not to speak of hostile terrain that lay beyond.

Nampong is presently the last outpost of the Indian Customs in the North-East Region. The Land Customs Station building standing on a land that belonged to the erstwhile North Eastern Frontier Agency, has been under occupation of the Department since 1954, essentially to regulate trade/passenger movement between the two newly independent nations. The last movement of goods across this LCS was during 1962. With no Customs Station in the immediate vicinity on the Myanmarese side (the nearest Land Customs Station is reported to be at Tamai, a small Myanmarese village at a distance of 66 km from Pangsau Pass) dilapidated road condition and insurgency, it is unlikely that commercial Border Trade will resume in the near future through this Station. There is another Land Customs Station at Myitkyina, at a distance of 342 km from Pangsau Pass. It takes not less than 7(seven) days to reach Myitkyina, on foot, as there is no other means of transport. The portion of Stilwell Road between Pangsau Pass and Myitkyina, is reported to be in a crumbling state due to non-maintenance.

Today, Nampong is probably fated to be a forgotten milestone on a historical road whose glorious days have been short lived. However, a point to ponder is that the distance between Nampong and New Delhi by road/rail is approximately 2600 km whereas it is only 1726 km from Kunming, a bustling commercial centre in China well connected with major port cities like Shanghai. While the North-Eastern Region will always be a remote corner of India due to its distance from New Delhi and Mumbai, places such as Nampong can be utilized to leverage their location to turn the region into a bridge that connects the fastest growing commercial hubs of the South-East Asian countries by reconstructing historical linkages such as the Stilwell Road. Presently, it is reported that the road stands barricaded near *Singbwiyan* in Myanmar. The present state of the road is not conducive for heavy traffic and the task of redeveloping the Stilwell Road is a gigantic one. It will involve three countries — China, Myanmar and India. Hundreds of kilometres have to be rebuilt, almost from scratch, an arduous task considering that no complete survey of the route appears to have been done in recent times.

A few measures suggested for boosting Indo-Myanmar trade

Expansion of list of exchangeable items

Myanmar is not an industrialized nation and its demand for manufactured products is met through imports. In order to arrest the declining trend of export/import trade across the Indo-Myanmar border it is suggested that manufactured goods of Indian origin be included and the list of exchangeable items expanded accordingly. Studies undertaken indicate that there is a strong demand in Myanmar for the following Indian made items:

Bi-cycles and its parts, Life saving drugs, Fertilizers, Insecticides, Cotton fabrics including *lungies*, Stainless steel utensils, Menthol, *Agarbati* and Perfumery compounds, Spices, Chemicals, Cosmetic, Cotton yarn, Textile and dress materials,

Pan *masala* and *zarda*, Animal skin/hides, Soya nuggets, Other food items and Motor cycles.

Similarly items like *Agarwood*, raw cotton, teak furniture and herbs and roots for medicinal purpose appear to have good demand on the Indian side.

Inclusion of third country goods within the purview of barter trade

It may perhaps be a good idea to include third country products falling under OGL on payment of duty at normal rates (not concessional) within the purview of barter trade. This will also help the Myanmarese traders to balance their barter trade. Critics may suggest that inclusion of third country goods will make our markets susceptible to the onslaught of cheap Chinese imports. However, large quantities of Chinese manufactured products are already finding their way into the Indian market by way of legal imports through the major ports of the country. Thus, under such circumstances some import of unrestricted third country goods through Moreh Land Customs Station will not affect the economy adversely, rather it will boost revenue generation. Further, since imports by way of barter have to be balanced, with an increase in import from Myanmar, more Indian products will be exported. However, inclusion of Indian manufactured products in the list of exchangeable items should precede trade in third country goods.

Permit import of timber with fewer restrictions

As has been mentioned above, the import of timber through Moreh Land Customs Station is yet to take off. Allowing import of timber by simplified procedures will help boost trade in the item. Inclusion of teak for trade under barter mechanism, at least till the MOU between the Designated Banks in India and Myanmar is signed to facilitate normal trade system, will definitely help to enhance the trade through Moreh Land Customs Station.

Review India-Myanmar Border Trade Agreement

MOU yet to be signed between designated Banks Expansion of list of exchange items and Remit import at timber with fewer restrictions ought to be taken up for review in the next round of talks between India and Myanmar under *Article IV* of the Agreement between the two countries on border trade.

Declare Zowkhathar in Mizoram as an entry point for import of plant and plant materials

Develop border areas and improve/augment available infrastructure

Today, the pulse is one of global aspirations and one that seeks to break down narrow domestic walls. As a long-term measure, therefore, it is essential to look beyond our immediate neighbours and envisage trade with South-East Asian and Far Eastern Countries, which have the reputation of having the best potential among emerging markets. The North East has the potential to emerge as a strategic base for foreign and domestic investors to tap the vast potential of contiguous markets of Myanmar, China, Malaysia, Thailand, Philippines, Cambodia, Indonesia and other East and South-East Asian countries.

Concluding Remarks

In order to give shape to this regions dream of making the 21st Century into an Asian Century, it is imperative that the North-East Region is brought out of its isolation by making it India's main trade route for trade with South-East Asia. However there are major question marks here: Firstly, what kind of infrastructure do we have in North-East that will enable large scale movement of goods and passengers to take place? Secondly, what kind of infrastructure do we need to build to enable huge volumes of goods to pass through?

To be honest, we have pathetic roads, no river transport worth the name, our river ports and Land Customs Stations are nowhere near International standards. For example, the Land Customs Station at *Bukit Kayu Hitam* (near Malaysia-Thailand border) has full office automation and duty free shops comparable with some international airports in India. How can we think of garnering the benefits of foreign trade if we do not improve our trade routes and border areas? This is serious business and needs serious consideration and answer. Just thinking and wishing that foreign trade is going to grow by leaps and bounds by opening Land Customs Stations along the international borders is certainly wishful thinking. Many of the Land Customs Stations in the North-East do not even have basic amenities like safe drinking water, electrification, proper office accommodation and staff quarters. The border areas of the North-East are mostly underdeveloped, remote and often difficult to access. Similarly, the levels of infrastructure available in the countries with which we have contiguous borders are also not upto the mark. For instance, there is no Customs station across Nampong and Zowkhathar in Myanmar. This brings into focus the willingness of our neighbours for enhanced trade with India. Thus it may be pertinent to mention that before rushing into opening our borders for cross border trade in a hasty manner, the viewpoints of the neighbouring countries need to be taken into consideration too with realism and honesty. Obviously, they will look at what will benefit them and not necessarily what will help us. That is how, even in the age of regional cooperation, all nations and sensible businessmen think. A lot of homework and improvement of infrastructure is called for with determination, if the North East is to march on the road to prosperity.

3

Indo-Myanmar Border Trade in the Light of India's Look East Policy

—M.K. Mero

Following the signing of Indo-Myanmar Border Trade on January 21, 1994 Indo-Myanmar Border Trade came into operation on April 12, 1995 through Moreh Border. Under the Agreement, import and export has been classified into 3 categories.

(i) **Traditional Exchange** under barter mechanism of locally produced items upto US Dollar 1000 between local people residing upto 40 km. on either side of the border under simplified documentation without Importer Exporter Certificate from DGFT, GR formalities and by way of head load or non motorised transport system.

(ii) **Barter Trade** of 22 agreed upon exchangeable items upto $ 20,000 with Guarantee Repayment (GR) formalities as per DGFT PN No.289(PN)/92-97. Under this system traders should possess IEC allotted by Director General of Foreign Trade (DGFT). The items that can be traded under this system are locally produced commodities, mainly agricultural produce and minor forest products.

Complementary to the trade agreement and to facilitate and encourage the trade, the Central Board of Excise and

Customs (CBEC) vide Notification No.9/95 dt.6.3.1995 notified a concessional rate of import duty @ 5% ad valorem for 21 items under barter trade and normal trade through the Moreh Land Customs Station.

The Reserve Bank of India also formulated their policy in line with Article-II of the Indo-Myanmar Trade Agreement, which, *inter alia*, laid a condition that imports from Myanmar to India.

(a) Shall precede exports from India to Myanmar and such exchange should be balanced within six months from the date of export or, on the due date of import whichever is earlier in case of barter trade upto US $ 20,000, and

(b) Preferably within a day or two, in case of traditional exchange of locally produced items upto US $ 1000.

(iii) **Normal Trade** where transactions will be through banking channels for all freely permissible items of export and imports and with licenses for restricted items as per Foreign Trade Policy guidelines.

Problems Associated with Barter Trade

(i) The 22 items identified under barter trade are mostly importable items and not exportable items. As a result the traders are finding difficult to balance/adjust their export/import within 6 months as per the RBI guidelines.

(ii) Collection of sales tax, royalty and other taxes on import/export goods, including imported agricultural/horticultural and forest produce of Myanmar origin, by the State Government of Manipur has added to the tax burden of the Indian importers, thereby reducing their cost-effectiveness. It must be noted here that the main market for import goods as well as the source of export goods are mainly outside North East.

(iii) Transportation costs are very high because of the remoteness and treacherous terrain cutting the competitive edge of the importers at the national level.

(iv) Multiple check posts and obstruction on movement of import/export goods on the National Highway 39 and 53 running through the State of Manipur/ Nagaland have been a major stumbling block. Representations received from the trade indicate that there are 53 check posts of various departments of the Governments of Manipur and Nagaland from Moreh to Dimapur on National Highway 39 and as many as 12 check posts of the Government of Manipur on National Highway 53.

Problem Associated with Normal Trade

Both India and Myanmar are Asian Clearing Union (ACU) countries and as such the transaction through Letter of Credit for normal trade has to be in ACU dollar. However, due to imposition of USA banning on the use of dollar for trade transaction with Myanmar, operationalisation of LC is not possible for the moment. In addition, the exchange rate poses problem as shown below:

Exchange Rate of Currencies

The existing rate of exchange is approximately:

Official	*Unofficial (approximate value)*
US $1 = 6 Kyats	US $1 = 1000 Kyats
US $1 = Rs. 48	
Kyat 1 = Rs. 7	Re.1 = 15-20 Kyats.

Since the unofficial exchange rate of currency appears to benefit the Myanmarese traders, they are not willing to transact business under the Normal Trade system under a Letter of Credit. Under such circumstances, barter/exchange appears to be the only viable solution. At the same time, it is to be noted that unless normal trade is operationalised, the exporters/importers will not be able to avail the various incentives such as Duty Entitlement Pass Book Scheme (DEPB), Export Promotion of Capital Goods (EPCG) Licence, Duty Free Advance Licence and Duty Credit Scrip. In addition, the State Government will not get Assistance to State for Development of Export Infrastructure (ASIDE) fund as deserved.

It is also a matter of concern that the 22 specified items for exchange under barter mechanism are levied custom duty @ 5% ad valorem, whereas all the third country products and non specified barter trade items are entering in unspecified quantity from Gate No.2 without levying any duty.

Security of Moreh LCS

Lack of security at LCS Moreh is a prime concern. As Moreh LCS is at the extreme border, it is very vulnerable to the activities of the anti-social elements. The valuable equipment of weigh-bridge is still at the Police Station of Moreh and the costly equipment of Plant Quarantine Unit, Moreh in LCS Building has not been installed due to lack of security.

Problems of Infrastructure

Under the Critical Infrastructure Balance (Scheme) (CIB)/ASIDE Scheme of the Department of Commerce, GOI, various projects such as construction of trade centre at Moreh, warehouse, custom house, weigh bridge, boundary fencing, road improvement and installation of street lights in Moreh town are being done. However, a lot need to be done such as:

(i) Overall improvement and widening of road from Imphal to Moreh,

(ii) Truck parking bay for loading and unloading.

(iii) Improvement in power and water supply at Moreh town.

(iv) Setting up of export processing zone or special economic zone in Moreh town.

(v) Improvement of telecommunication system and other services such as hotels, tourist lodge for visitors.

(vi) Construction of sentry post and security barrack inside LCS.

Suggestions

(1) There is a need for regularization of import/export from Moreh border. All the freely importable and exportable items may be included in the list of exchangeable items under barter mechanism by levying custom duty at the entry point for import of items exceeding specified value.

Benefits

(a) This will increase exports of goods from the country and help the growth of industry in the domestic market.

(b) Revenue collection can increase substantially for development purpose.

(c) It will help the exporters and importers to balance/ adjust their exports and imports.

(d) It will legalise the import and export and reduce the harassments at the check gates and the fear of seizure from the custom authorities.

(e) The export and import business will become more viable and profit from exporting and importing will increase.

(2) Under normal trade, instead of ACU dollar, Euro may be permitted for opening Letter of Credit for trade transaction with Myanmar.

India's Look East Policy and Prospects of Indo-Myanmar Border Trade

India has got a new dimension to its Look-East vision, developing its north-eastern States by linking them to South-East Asia through road and rail links via Myanmar. It is part of a larger project to build Eurasian land and rail corridors that could connect Singapore to Istanbul and Europe via both India and China. The trans-continental highway and railway could lead to the ultimate link up of China, Russia and Central Asia, bringing immense benefits to all the countries. China has already agreed in principle to build a highway connecting Bangkok with Kunming in the thriving Yunan province of China, through Laos.

There is also a possibility of building a railway line between the Chinese cities of Kunming and Mytikyina on the Myanmar border, where both the roads – Ledo to Patkai Range and Ledo to South Myanmar–meet. The Asian Development Bank has given a loan to the Myanmar Government to construct the railway through northern Myanmar linking India with China. India thus wants to develop its North-East by using Myanmar as a bridge to economically leverage with China and the other ASEAN nations.

The essence of this triangular road and rail diplomacy among India, China, Myanmar and Thailand is also about ultimately linking the Indian Ocean to the South China Sea. In economic and strategic terms, India wants to develop the North-East by increasing its connectivity with the rest of the world through commercial linkages with Asean. By taking advantage of Myanmar's links with other Asean countries, India hopes to transform the North-East from a security burden into a land of economic opportunity.

In pursuance of India's "Look East" Policy, it has moved

purposefully in developing a broad economic and strategic partnership with the dynamic countries of South-East Asia.

At the second Indo-ASEAN Summit in 2003, India acceded to the Treaty of Amity and Co-operation (TAC) in South-East Asia, signed a declaration to combat international terrorism, and agreed on comprehensive economic co-operation to step up their current trade turnover of $ 12 billion. A Free Trade Agreement (FTA) between India and ASEAN would come into being in 10 years, and India is committed to aligning its peak tariff to East ASEAN levels by 2005.

The highlights of the framework agreement lays down that negotiations on FTA in goods would begin in 2004 and conclude by 2005. Talks on FTA in services and investments would start in 2005 and conclude by 2007. Areas of economic co-operation would include trade facilitation measures, sectors of co-operation and trade and investment promotion measures. The framework agreement provides for exchange of tariff concessions on the "Early Harvest Programme" (EHP). Concessions and differential treatment have been given to Cambodia, Laos, Myanmar and Vietnam, the lesser-developed members of ASEAN. India also signed a landmark FTA with Thailand and four other accords for enhancing co-operation in agriculture, tourism and science. This will provide a free trade area in goods, to begin with, by 2010 and, in services and investments from 2006. The two countries have also slashed tariffs by 50 per cent on 84 products under an early harvest scheme with effect from September 1, 2004.

Further, India has offered a unilateral "Open Skies" Policy and announced India's unilateral decision to connect all 10 ASEAN capitals with four metropolises in India through daily flights without further bilateral discussions. Indo-ASEAN cooperation has progressed substantially in many spheres—science and technology, information technology and electronics, human resource development, transport and infrastructure, space technology, tourism and trade and investment. These initiatives are, however, not adequately reflected in trade figures.

The Indo-ASEAN two-way trade grew 30 per cent from $ 7.6 billion in 1999 to $ 10 billion in 2002. ASEAN's trade to India is still at a very low level, accounting for only 0.9 per cent of ASEAN's global trade in 2002, while India's trade to ASEAN countries still hovers around 7 per cent of its global trade. The volume of trade is still small, considering the vast potential for trade that exists amount countries of over 1.5 billion people, and it is hoped the target of $ 30 billion will be reached by 2010. The list of goods for which duties are brought down to zero by 2006 include petrochemicals and polyesters, apart from marine foods, white goods, electrical machinery, precious stones, office equipments, printed circuits and key auto components such as gear box and petrol engines. The pact with Thailand is to be followed by a similar agreement with Singapore and, ultimately, the entire ASEAN region.

The terms of Indo-ASEAN engagement needs to be taken much more seriously. The possibilities for functional cooperation are limitless, and enthusiasm should translate into tangible gains. India also needs to deepen its links with the Mekong Ganga Cooperative forum (MGC)—a new co-operative forum floated by India with five of its eastern neighbours, Myanmar, Thailand, Cambodia, Vietnam and Laos. Tourism, culture and education are given precedence and priority in the cooperative framework. Transport, communications and infrastructure will be prioritised in the next phase. The MGC also provides immense opportunities for India's private sector to create a niche in the region. Indo-ASEAN cooperation in tourism, culture and education can also be strengthened in Indonesia and Malaysia. It must be remembered that India's cultural footprints in South-East Asia have been left because of trade and religion.

India's relations with ASEAN also assume significance in the light of the various cultural similarities it shares with the region. Buddhism is the natural link to South-East Asia, particularly the Mekong basin. The cultural ties with South-East Asia also need mention. ASEAN can also source its manpower requirements–technical and managerial--from

India, as it both competitive and culturally compatible. Indian professionals teaching English and computer skills can raise the standards of education and knowledge base. The ASEAN-India human resource development programme needs to be strengthened further.

It is assumed that bilateral trade between India and Myanmar can double within the next two years to 1 billion dollar. Several proposals and measures such as transport subsidy package are under the consideration of the Ministry of Commerce in order to make North-East a natural base for trade from Myanmar. Special emphasis has been given in building infrastructure facilities in the North-East including roads and Airports to develop the region as a bridgehead of the country for entering into the South-East Asian markets.

In order to promote export from the region, emphasis must be given on product development for marketing purpose based on resources available in the region. Unless we create good quality products for market, we will not be able to survive the intense global competition.

(i) The region's climatic and soil condition is suitable for growing variety of fruits and vegetables. Hence, stress must be given to develop agricultural and horticultural products on a commercial scale in a contiguous area.

(ii) Since the region do not have much scope for development of heavy industries, emphasis must be given on home based processing units as well as cottage and small scale industries.

(iii) Resource based and export oriented industries must be identified and promote the setting up of such units for export marketing.

(iv) Opening up of more border trading points with adequate infrastructure facilities.

(v) To facilitate the easy flow of foreign tourist in the region, creation of air travel circuit between

Singapore–Bangkok, Yangoon–Dhaka, Guwahati–Kathmandu is required. Early resumption of international flight from LGB Airport, Guwahati is a must.

(vi) Inland container transport facility need to be introduced for smooth transportation of export and import consignments.

(vii) A composite check gate at Moreh or Pallel in Manipur should be set up by removing existing multiple check gates.

Conclusion

The North-East Region must be developed at par with other parts of the country to enable its people to take advantage of the changing international scenario characterised by increasingly free of trade restrictions. Execution of various development projects must be properly synchronized, well coordinated and in a time bound manner. The perception regarding the North-East as being an isolated and difficult area with little prospect for self-sustaining growth must go. The mindsets of both people at the policy making level in Delhi as well as of those in this region must change to make this region a vibrant, dynamic and prosperous one.

4

Indo-Myanmar Trade through Moreh: Status and Assessment

—Amar Yumnam

Introduction

Traditionally the importance of trade is appreciated within the framework of comparative advantage of the countries concerned. But this understanding has undergone a large transformation due fundamentally to theoretical and empirical developments in recent years. It has been found that there are no immutable comparative advantages of countries. Further there is the increasing global reality of trade taking place within regional arrangements. These have stimulated the examination of Regional Trading Arrangements (RTA)/ Regional Integration Arrangements (RIA)/ Preferential Trading Arrangements (PTA) as mechanisms creating cumulative causation of trade and growth, and as instruments for trans-border diplomacy. Further the significance of trade and regional cooperation in the development of a country is a fairly well researched area. But the role of trans-border cooperation and trade in the development of the border regions is a relatively recent field. Further if the border region happens to be one where the state is contested and conflict situation prevails, the role of trade and cooperation is altogether different from the conventional ones. Here the issues to be addressed by cooperation and trade are much wider and the conflicting interests are also broad. This chapter is an attempt to assess the existing border trade between Myanmar and India through Moreh in Manipur. It shall attempt to situate the existing border trade within the possible classifications of border trade while appreciating it in the context of the agreement and the theoretical and empirical issues. It shall also try to highlight the distinguishing characteristics of it so that the differences between the traditional understanding and the current practice come out glaringly for an assessment of the real and potential impacts.

This chapter is an attempt at providing an analytic narrative of the Indo-Myanmar trade through Moreh in Manipur.

The Moreh Trade[1]

The Indo-Myanmar trade through Moreh in Manipur and Tamu in Myanmar under the new dispensation is about a decade old since it was formally launched under an agreement on 12 April 1995. Before we proceed, I must hasten to add that the agreement was just an official stamp of recognition to an already existing exchange. Historically there have been forces for integration in the goods market between the two sides of the border with the presence of strong agglomeration economies. The RTA under the new agreement was, on the face of it, an attempt to exploit these economies for development of border areas. But the arrangement is much more restrictive than a traditional RTA and restricted to border exchange of limited number of items.

Here it would be in place to dwell a little on the background and nature of the RTA in place. Until recently the East Asian countries were not very active in forming RTAs. In fact, the ASEAN Free Trade Area (AFTA) established in 1992 was the only major RTA before the Japan-Singapore Economic Partnership Agreement enacted in November 2002. Vietnam, Myanmar, Cambodia and Laos joined the AFTA only in the second half of the 1990s. It was during this period only that the Border Trade Agreement was signed between India and Myanmar on 21 January 1994 to provide for "establishment of trade on the basis of equality and mutual benefit". It provided for establishment of border trade through (a) Moreh in India and Tamu in Myanmar; (b) Champai in India and Hri in Myanmar; and (c) other places that may be notified[2]. It provides for border trade under barter mechanism, limited exchange of goods by traders and regular trade under the existing government policies.

We may think of FTA in terms of three possible types:

(i) Between countries of the North;

(ii) Between a country of the North and another of the South; and

(iii) Between countries of the South.

The FTA between India and Myanmar is of the third type with the rider that

(a) the exchange passes through politically and spatially difficult terrain in both the countries; and

(b) it has objectives other than that of trade as well.

The Trade-Off

While discussing the Indo-Myanmar trade we generally forget the fact that the trade agreement was only one of the two agreements signed between the two countries on the same day. The other agreement was on *Memorandum of Understanding on Cooperation between the Civilian Border Authorities* of the two countries to prevent illegal and insurgent activities. This common background of the trade and the security agreements has led to the imperfect alignment of interests

1. leading to the divergence between the flesh and spirit of trade; and
2. between inter-country approaches and within country objectives.

To begin with Manipur saw the legalized Indo-Myanmar trade as an opportunity for enhancing the general standard of living of the population whereas the government of India saw it more as a "signalling device to monitor the movement of commodities and people" and an insurance against the perceived threat of Chinese dominance of the region. The enthusiasm of the people in the beginning was definitely palpable but has not been sustained thanks to the excessively controlled nature of the trade and accompanying "unofficial payments". This is evident from the volume of trade figures given in the Appendix. Despite the rise in the overall volume of trade between India and Myanmar, that through the Moreh-Tamu route has been declining over the years.

The Myanmar side also seems to have an objective similar to the one of the people of Manipur. Given the economic and political intractability of the border regions of the country, Myanmar saw in the agreements with Thailand and India an opportunity to develop its border regions.

Besides the various disturbances caused to the traders by the security forces within the Indian borders raising trading costs by insisting on unofficial monetary and physical payments, the Indian side has been doggedly insisting on the rule of origin (ROO) in her trade with Myanmar. This is despite the insistence from the Myanmar side to drop the ROO clause as hers is a less diversified economy and hence needing to balance her trade through third country exports.

Despite the internationally increasing significance of RTA, the Indian side has all along shown resistance to treat the Indo-Myanmar Agreement as one but has seen it as a limited arrangement for exchange at the border. In other words, the border trade agreement between India and Myanmar through the Moreh route was not accompanied by domestic economic reforms on the Indian side as expected in a normal RTA, and consequently the trade has not shown the potential buoyancy. We shall have more to say on this later in this chapter.

Until the recent move for *Looking towards the East* Myanmar has never been economically significant to India. First, scientifically and technologically, Myanmar has very little, if anything, to offer India. Secondly, the size of the Myanmar market is very small to be of attractiveness to the Indian business. Thirdly, Indian policy makers thought the Chinese economic influence could be countered by isolation.

However, with the collapse of Doha round of WTO negotiations implying the increasing importance of bilateralism rather than multilateralism and importance of Myanmar as a bridge to the economies of South-East Asia, the significance of Myanmar has dawned on the Indian policy makers. Further, in the process of countering the rising economic and consequent political influence of China, India necessarily has to take Myanmar along the path to growth and transformation. In other words, India has to use trade as a diplomatic tool to keep Myanmar on our side and balance Chinese influence[3]. Still further, Myanmar is also important to address the security concerns in the region as well.

Rule of Origin (ROO)

We said earlier that India's strict insistence on ROO has not served the cause of Moreh-Tamu trade. In normal circumstances and other things remaining the same, the ROO has its own logic and validity. But the empirics in the present case are such that the other things do not remain the same. In these circumstances, insistence on strict application of ROO would fail to serve the cause of trade and growth.

First, the problem to be addressed by the RTA in Manipur, unlike in other cases, is not one of reallocation of employment but one of creating employment and earning opportunities. Like the classic example of benefits from exchange in the prison, the RTA in this case should be rather to benefit the regional population from the trading exchanges. There is the need for introducing the regional population on either side of the borders to the dynamics of technology and investment emerging out of active trading relationships.

Secondly, the RTA, with an unhindered application, would enable the regional population to go for a re-fusion of cultural civilizations given the long and common historical roots—a kind of brush with futurism with a foundation in history. This is significant in the light of the distance and accompanying high transaction costs involved in trading with the main markets in either country.

Thirdly, the local as well as the traditional exchange market between the two countries is not large enough as to sustain an RTA for regional growth. International evidence establishes that being restrictive helps the big markets but small markets can prosper better in a liberalised environment.

Fourth, given the fact that Myanmar is already a member of ASEAN, insistence on ROO is illogical for entering into an agreement with any member of the group should imply access into and from any market of the trading partners.

The Fallout

The fallout of the concatenation of security perspective and ROO has been that the Indo-Myanmar trade through Moreh has been marked more by overregulation seeing trade only as exchange of commodities instead of seeing it as a means for flow of ideas and opportunity for raising per capita income as well. The usual benefit of trade expansion is that it drives bad firms and bad traders out of business and fosters good firms and good traders. Normal trade enhances the opportunity for firms and traders engaged in normal goods whereas restrictions create an incentive for engaging in contraband and harmful goods commanding super-normal profits despite the higher risks; instead of spending energy to get normal goods through the restrictions, it is better to get the non-normal but higher-profit-yielding goods through.

But the overregulation in the present case has had the impact of decreasing the volume of trade in right goods though enhancing that in wrong goods as evident from the decline in the volume of normal trade but not so in the volume of smuggling. Further instead of fostering trade for general growth and welfare, the present pattern of trade has generated a vested interest among the security forces. In the absence of hard data, but on the basis of operational dynamics during the last decade we can estimate in a conservative way that the security forces alone have amassed property ranging from at least Rs. 24 crore to about Rs. 75 crore during the last decade from the Indo-Myanmar trade[4]. This sum has a much higher negative multiplier impact on trade. First, since the amount was generated mainly from small 'collections', the dampening impact on trade and growth is immense. Secondly, it generates more of trade in wrong goods on sharing basis rather than the normal trade in right goods – a classic case of bad trade driving out good trade out of business under overregulation by the security forces. The contraband trade is estimated to be about ten to fifteen times of the normal trade of non-listed items.

Capturing Rent

Another very unfortunate fallout has been the disappearance of the Prem Nagar Market on the Indian side and the replacement of it by the Namphalong Market on the Myanmar side, which is within one kilometre of the Prem Nagar Market, since November 1998. This had to happen given the demand pattern for commodities, the differing approaches of the two governments and the scope for exploiting rent through limit pricing provided by these. In fact, the replacement by the Namphalong Market is such a case of capturing the rent through pricing.

Despite

Despite the overregulation and restrictiveness, the Moreh trade has had some positive effects. First, it has generated a financial capital base of about, at a very conservative estimate, Rs. 1000 crore in the State. Secondly, the recent limited phenomenon of people exiting from this trade and entering other trade proves the potential for this trade in the sense that it enabled certain people to competitively join other business with the capital base built out of it.

The Way Forward

It is in this context that the ongoing *Look East Policy* becomes significant. There now arises the necessity of separating the security and trade perspectives. In other words, the time has now come for a genuine RTA, genuine from the angle of economics and not security, for a real trans-border trading relationship with South East Asia. Such a genuine RTA would have the capability of simultaneously addressing many issues.

First, there is the problem of insurgency to be tackled on the sides of both countries. An economically genuine RTA shall have the potential to eventually sideline and control these. This is because the scope for cumulative causation in the potential trade is immense. An economically genuine RTA would throw open routes for growth through normal ways. This aspect is particularly significant in the context of conflict situation. In conflict management, the state should be able to kill two birds with one stone. On the one hand, the state should be able to retain the non-insurgent population on her side while at the same time providing economic opportunities for growth. On the other hand, the economic opportunities being opened up by genuinely economic RTA should slowly entice and seduce the members of the insurgent groups towards joining the market.

Secondly, there is the potential for a strong RTA to serve the purpose of diplomacy and enhance the level of trust between India and South-East Asia, including Myanmar. It would help in removing the Chinese psychosis of India.

Thirdly, an economically genuine RTA has the inherent feature of locking-in reforms. This is very important to restore the credibility of the government in a conflict situation as it would do away with time inconsistency in policy issues.

Fourth, there are many instances of people transforming from an originally contraband smuggler to legal traders with the profit earned from the first trade. Such transformations would become more frequent and new entrants would rather go for legal trade in the context of an economically genuine RTA.

Conclusion

The Indo-Myanmar trade through Moreh has failed to generate the expected growth bonus for it has been subject to overregulation, and thereby leading to trade more in the wrong goods. There is now an imperative to separate the security and trade perspectives in this RTA so that the growth bonus from trade can be generated and cumulative causation put to work.

NOTES AND REFERENCES

1. I avoid discussion of some of the features as it would be repetitive of my earlier paper. See my paper, "Indo-Myanmar trade through Moreh: time to sow, time to reap", presented at the *Seminar on Transborder Trade in North East India,* 28 July 1999, Guwahati, Sponsored by Society for Conflict Analysis and Resolution and organised by the OKD Institute of Social Change and Development.
2. There is of course the fact that Myanmar had established legalised border trade with Thailand effective from 1989.
3. Trading relationships are now emerging as the most powerful tool in international diplomacy as they enhance credibility between the partner countries "by locking in domestic economic policy reforms."
4. This amount does not include the amount and volume of trade and purchases done by the security forces themselves.

APPENDIX

Table 4.1A
Volume of Moreh Trade

(Rs. Million)

Period	*Export*	*Import*	*Total*
1995-96	104.5	53.8	158.4
1996-97	317.0	151.[illegible]	468.8
1997-98	224.5	350.8	557.3
1998-99	50.6	37.4	88.0
1999-00	32.6	36.8	69.4
2000-01	52.9	1.9	54.8
2001-02	12.5	82.9	95.4

Note: The trade is subject to a list of items revised from time to time.

Table 4.2A
Volume of Indo-Myanmar Trade

(Million US $)

Year	*Export*	*Import*
2000-01	52.71	181.69
2001-02	60.89	374.43
2002-03	75.07	336.04

Source: Ministry of Commerce and Industry

5

Indo-Myanmar Border Trade: Imperatives and Present Status

—Konsam Ibo Singh

Informal border trade between Myanmar on the one hand and its neighbouring countries China, Thailand, Bangladesh, India on the other have been going on since a long time. However, these activities continued to prosper with the participation and under the protection of trans-border ethnic minorities who inhabit on both sides of the international borders. The Kachins in Myanmar-China border, the Karens in Myanmar-Thailand border, the Rohingyas in Myanmar-Bangladesh and the Tamil Chettiars and Nagas and the Kuki, Chin and Mizo in India-Myanmar border have been carrying on border trade. It was mainly because of this fact that the hill tribals inhabiting the border areas along the Indo-Myanmar border enjoyed the facility of free movement up to 40 kilometres on either side on the entire length of 1643 kms. The reason being that they had close affinity and cultural and economic ties. They enjoyed this facility until June 1968. Then the Government of India introduced a permit system unilaterally to check entry of undesirable elements and insurgents. Even though the permit system was introduced, the tribals were not much bothered about the new restrictions placed and continued to enjoy the free movement as before[1].

The above centres of border trade were not under effective control of Yangon. They were mostly inaccessible and were under the control of ethnic armies who rose against Yangon.

The survival of ethnic armies mostly depended on the taxes, revenues and protection fees they collected mainly from smugglers and black marketers for passing through the territory under their control[2]. The business included jade, gems, antiques, minerals, teak and returned with items for their consumption which included electronic goods, bicycles, motorcycles, house-wares, medicines etc. In course of time they included narcotics and small arms. Their trade was informal and illegal.

In 1966 the Government of Myanmar brought 426 consumer items under its control. These items were to be sold at government shops only[3]. However, these consumer items were not available at the government shops. They became scarce. Almost all the controlled items were sold at 400-500 per cent higher than the government-controlled price[4]. Shortages, to some extent, were, no doubt, met with supplies coming from across the border. The result was that black marketeering became a thriving business.

Yangon's inability to control the border areas, inaccessibility, neglect caused to prosper border trade in its own way. At the same time Myanmar's economy deteriorated mainly due to nationalisation of key sectors of industries and control of 426 consumer items. Probably 30 per cent of the country's domestic commerce was transacted in the shadow market. Annual per capita income shrank from $ 670 in 1960 to $ 190 in 1987. Official consumer price inflation was around 25 per cent[5]. In 1987 foreign debt stood at $ 5.3 billion. 1986/87 reports say that border trade was opened in several sectors with the connivance of the Myanmar's authorities as the popular discontentment increased. In November 1988, the informal border trade, which amounted to an estimated 50 to 100 per cent of the foreign trade, was regularised firstly with China and later with Thailand and Bangladesh[6]. It was in the same year that, acting on the application of the Myanmar Government; the United Nations declared the country as the Least Developed country in the world.

Deterioration in its economy prompted the military government to adopt drastic policy reforms even before the coup of September 1988. No doubt, it was in 1989 that the State Law and Order Restoration Council (SLORC) officially revoked the Law of Establishment of Socialist Economic System of 1965; and there inaugurated a transition from 'socialist command economy' to one driven by market forces and private enterprises. A look at the economic policy reform measures adopted by the Government of Myanmar from 1987 to 1994 clearly indicate a transition from socialist economy to market economy[7].

Reforms undertaken by the SLORC had three main objectives: (i) to transform the rigid and inefficient socialist economy into one suited to a market oriented economy; (ii) to encourage private investment and entrepreneurial activity at home; and (iii) to open the economy to direct foreign investment and also to promote exports. In 1989 border trade was regularised by the SLORC as an important aspect to improve its economy and also an item of liberalisation[8].

While border trade was formalised with China, Bangladesh and Thailand as already mentioned earlier, India remained strongly committed to the restoration of democracy in Myanmar. It was during this time (1989-1991) that a number of officials from the foreign office, defence and intelligence establishment opposed the Government of India's support extended to the pro-democracy movement and the "limited support" extended to the Myanmar's rebels. These officials strongly felt that transition from military rule to democracy in Myanmar was a distant dream; and it was necessary "to emulate the ASEAN's policy of "Constructive Engagement" with the junta. This group included senior military officials like General Shankar Roychoudhuri, and the military intelligence chief Lt. General Ravi Sawhney, some navy and Research and Analysis Wing (RAW) officials and a few in the Foreign Ministry. They argued that if India did not improve relations with the junta and since democratic transition was a far-cry Myanmar would become a Chinese satellite"[9]. In line with the assertion made by them Government of India extended an invitation to U Ba Swe, Vice Foreign Minister, Government of Myanmar to visit

India. U Ba Swe visited India in August 1992. During his stay he conferred with Indian officials and identified concrete areas for bilateral cooperation including border trade, prevention of narcotics trafficking and contacts between the civilian and military authorities in the border regions of the two countries to prevent illegal activities.[10] His visit was reciprocated by two visits of India's Foreign Secretary J.N. Dixit in March and August 1993. In his memoirs Dixit writes, (i) Attempts should be made to normalize relations whatever the government is in control of Myanmar; (ii) Myanmar is geo-strategically important to India as it borders with China and Bangladesh. Its closeness to the Indian territories of Andaman and Nicobar islands is relevant to India's security, (iii) Indo-Myanmar cooperation is necessary to counter smuggling, drug crimes, and insurgency causing security threats to India's Northeast.[11] After ten months an agreement was signed between India and Myanmar to formalize border trade at two centres: (i) Moreh-Tamu sector and Champai-Rhi sector identifying 22 items for barter trade under the agreement.

The above developments clearly indicate three things. First, from the Indian side Chinese economic and strategic penetration into Myanmar is a serious concern to India. Secondly, at the same time it was more concerned with insurgency causing security threats to India's Northeast. Thirdly, of course, measures for checking drug smuggling, drug crimes were not less important. For these three aspects India strongly felt that co-operation with Myanmar was absolutely necessary. In later years, economic co-operation, trade, cross border projects and activities like international terrorism, drug trafficking etc. became aspects of mutual interest. The above security considerations is supplemented by recommendations of Shukla Commission, Indian Institute of Foreign Trade reports which underlined the prospects and benefits of opening border trade with Northeast India's neighbours. One of the main considerations to promote border trade is the availability of commodities from a convenient commercial centre from a short distant and less time taken place. Of course, fraternal ties of the transborder tribes requirement for cheaper and affordable items are other considerations. No doubt, in the age of globalisation and liberalisation national boundaries have little meaning in terms of trade. In connection with Indo-Myanmar border trade Arvind Dave, Governor of Arunachal Pradesh, while inaugurating the National Seminar on Cross-Border Trade of Arunachal Pradesh: "Retrospect and Prospect" said that the Indo-Myanmar border trade would bring about "greater economic security and prosperity to the population of North-East India as well as Burma". He believed that engagement of youths in trade would minimise the degree of unemployment as well as militancy in the region. He further expected that the opening of the 144 km long Tamu–Kalewa road would bring India and Myanmar closer and would help both the countries in preventing cross-border terrorism and provide the North-Eastern region an "Eastward Outlet" for improving its economic links[12]. Dave's assessment emphasizes two aspects i.e. prevention of cross border terrorism and economic benefits from trade. However, considering the timing and the circumstances leading to the understanding for improving bilateral relationship between India and Myanmar security considerations far outweigh economic considerations.

What would be the impact on Manipur? We all know that Dimapur–Imphal national highway is regarded as the lifeline of Manipur through which all the important items are brought from mainland India. The number of trucks passing through this route comes to around 250 to 300 per day. Many of these trucks bring in essential commodities. This highway has become the haven of both underground and over ground elements for extortion and levying of illegal taxes. A report filed with the ***Imphal Free Press***[13] says that around Rs. 3000 per truck is to be spent as tips at police stations, excise, traffic narcotic and drugs, motor vehicle counters, and as taxes levied by several organizations. In addition to this, every truck loaded at Dimapur has to pay annual taxes ranging from Rs. 1500 to Rs. 3000. These tips and taxes have caused to have an inflated price for essential commodities. For instance the retail price of potato at Dimapur is Rs. 5 while in Imphal it is Rs. 8 to 10 while the retail price of onion at Dimapur is only Rs. 6 while at Imphal it is Rs. 15, the newspaper points out. It is applicable in all the items brought through Nagaland. During the time of economic blockade, bandhs along this highway, which is not rare, the traders have mostly depended on the imported items from Myanmar through Moreh-Tamu border trade sector to meet the demand. Fully aware of this aspect some of the political parties have proposed even for establishing highway protection force and emphasised the importance for a more vigorous and unrestricted trade with Myanmar and Southeast Asia through Manipur[14].

Border trade is important and significant to Myanmar for it served as the lifebelt of Myanmar's sinking economy. While the West and Japan imposed different forms of sanctions and bans, China first and followed by member countries of the ASEAN and India, now, has taken the initiative to take advantage of the developments. To be to the point, border trade with Myanmar's neighbouring countries constitute from 50 to 100 per cent of her total trade.[15] If we rely on a slightly old data, from 1992-93 to 1998-1999 Myanmar's border trade with China accounted for 62 per cent while with India it was only 4 per cent of its total trade[16]. Thailand and Bangladesh shared the rest.

Myanmar is predominantly an agricultural economy. With agriculture (including forestry and fishing) contributed 58.6 per cent of GDP in 1997-98 and 43.5 per cent of GDP in 1998/99. Exports from these sectors accounted for more than 75 per cent of total exports in 1995/96. Therefore agriculture is still considered to be the most important sector in its economy. At the same time slightly less than half of its land is available for its cultivation. Land for cultivation of pulses and beans, important items for border trade with India occupied 14 per cent; sesame another 10 per cent and sugar for 0.7. Though teak production is on the decline, it still earns 25 per cent of the foreign exchange despite continuing large scale illegal felling and smuggled into Thailand[17] and also to India.

In view of this, 22 items were identified for exchange under the barter system as per the Indo-Myanmar Border Trade

Agreement. However, shortage/non-availability of some of the items is reported thereby causing obligation problems[18], one scholar points out. An official of the Customs Preventive, Shillong, Gaigongdin Panmei has suggested to include Indian products like bicycles, medicines especially life-saving drugs, fertilizers, insecticides, cotton fabrics including lungie, stainless steel utensils, menthol, *agarbati,* and perfumery compounds, spices, chemicals, cosmetic, cotton yarn textile and dress materials, *pan masala* and *zarda*, animal hides and skin, soya nuggets, other food items and motor cycles from India which are in great demand in Myanmar. Similarly items like *agarwood,* raw cotton, teak furniture and herbs and roots having medicinal value have a demand on the Indian side[19]. His suggestion is made on the basis of a study carried out, he says. Clearly border trade has attracted customers from both the sides. At the same time the following table shows the present status in terms monetary value.

Table 5.1
Value of Cross Border Trade through Moreh (India, Manipur)

Year	*Import (Rs. Crore)*	*Export (Rs Crore)*
1995-96	5.39	00.46
1996-97	16.17	29.80
1997-98*	37.19	25.17
1998-99	3.75	4.88
1999-00	6.53	3.11
2000-01	3.40	5.53
2001-02	7.59	1.23
2002-03	11.83	4.96
2003-04	8.86	9.46

Source: Gaigongdin Panmei, "Indo-Myanmar Border Trade" ***Souvenir : Seminar on Indo-Myanmar Border Trade,*** held at Imphal on 18-10- 2004 on the Occasion of Ist India-ASEAN Motor Car Rally (22 Nov.-11 Dec. 2004), organised by Department of Commerce and Industries, Government of Manipur, sponsored by Department of Commerce, Ministry of Commerce and Industry, Govt. of India.

* Due to high demand of wheat flour from Myanmar during the period.

An Assessment

The opening of Southeast Asia to India through Manipur is integral to India's Look East Policy formulated by India's former Prime Minister P.V. Narasimha Rao during his tenure as Prime Minister. India's trade links with ASEAN, no doubt, is enhanced. India is an active participant in the ASEAN+4 (China, Japan, Korea, and India) and BIMST-EC. In view of this border trade between India and Myanmar assumes importance.

An important observation is that border trade is so important to Myanmar with its neighbouring countries considering its volume it contributes to its trade and economy. This is the reason why pro-democracy activists of Myanmar in India strongly objected to the formalisation of border trade. Their main objection was that border trade would help to save the military government when the West and Japan orphaned it. China, ASEAN and later India seized the opportunity for their own political and economic objectives i.e. China for expanding its economic activities and influence while ASEAN under "Constructive Engagement (means a policy of non-interference in the internal affairs of Myanmar while actively participating in the economic activities of the country). For India it was for security reasons; and specially to counter insurgency in Northeast India. At the same time, closely associated with the issue of checking of drug smuggling and small arms trade is insurgency for which Myanmar has been a classic example. Along with the legalised and formalised trade there is another trade, which is done in the shadow market. Transaction is reportedly huge in low volume but highly lucrative items like precious stones, gold bars, drugs and small arms. Lastly, as the standard of living of the Myanmarese is poor and the amount of salaries and wages of their workers get are low[20], roughly only one tenth of the amount their counterparts of their neighbouring countries of Thailand or India get, anyone including the government functionaries are likely to be tempted to resort to lucrative illegal business. This is one issue, which cannot be solved so easily which means smuggling of lucrative items, which are compact and easily transportable, will definitely continue. At the same time economic benefits from

Indo-Myanmar border trade would be minimal at the present rate. Security considerations far outweigh economic considerations. However, agreement on border trade may be regarded as a beginning for opening more avenues for India in the coming years.

NOTES AND REFERENCES

1. Gaigongdin Panmei, "Indo-Myanmar Border Trade" *Souvenir : Seminar on Indo- Myanmar Border Trade,* pp.9-17 held at Imphal on 18-10- 2004 on the Occasion of Ist India-ASEAN Motor Car Rally (22 Nov.-11 Dec. 2004), organised by Department of Commerce and Industries, Government of Manipur, sponsored by Department of Commerce, Ministry of Commerce and Industry, Government of India.

2. Frederica M. Bunge, *Burma : A Country Study* (Washington, 1983), pp. 228-29.

3. F.S.V. Donnison, *Burma* (New York: Praeger, 1970), p. 199.

4. Kalyani Bandhyopadhaya, *Burma and Indonesia: Comparative Political Economy and Foreign Policy* (New Delhi: South Asian Publishers, 1983), p. 86.

5. The author heavily depended on a chapter entitled "Myanmar's Economic Policy before 1988: Initiatives and Fallouts" in Langpoklakpam Suraj Singh, *Movement for Democracy in Myanmar: 1988-1997,* unpublished Ph.D. thesis submitted to Manipur University.

6. Myat Thein and Mya Than, "Transitional Economy of Myanmar : Performance, Issues, **and** Problems" in Seiji Finch Naya and Joseph L.H. Tan, ***Asian Transitional Economies : Challenges and Prospects for Reform and Transformation*** **(Singapore,** Institute of Southeast Asian Studies, 1995), pp.210-261.

7. 1987: Participation of private and co-operative sectors in foreign trade

   Relaxation of government's monopoly in the domestic marketing of rice and some important crops

1988: Removal of restrictions of private sector participation in domestic and foreign trade

Introduction of liberal Foreign Investment Law

Restitution of small and medium-sized establishments

1989 : Decontrol of prices

Official revocation of the 1985 Law of Establishment of Socialist Economic System

Regularisation of border Trade

Introduction of state economic enterprise law allowing private sector participation in economic activities

Relaxation of restrictions on private investment

Introduction of the Central Bank of Myanmar Law

Introduction of Myanmar Tourism Law

Introduction of 100 per cent retention of export earnings law

Introduction of Financial Institutions of Myanmar Law

Introduction of Myanmar Agricultural and Rural Development Law

Promulgation of Commercial Tax Law

Announcement of the Central Bank of Myanmar Rules and Regulations

Reestablishment of Myanmar Chamber of Commerce and Industry

Announcement of lease inefficient state-owned factories

Announcement of denationalization of nationalized saw mills

Announcement of sale of government palm oil firms

Announcement of establishment of four more private banks

Introduction of domestic investment law

Announcement of establishment of three or more private banks

Announcement of licensing of representative offices of eleven foreign banks.

8. Ibid.

9. Subir Bhaumik, " Burma Policy and Its Impact on Its (India's) Northeastern Region", paper presented at the National Seminar on "Partnership for Development: Holistic Approach to the North East" sponsored by the Indian Council for Social Science Research (ICSSR), New Delhi and organised by the North Eastern Regional Centre, ICSSR, Shillong from 8-9 May 2002 at Gangtok.

10. Ministry of External Affairs, Government of India, *Annual Report, 1992-93* (New Delhi, 1993), p. 18.

11. J.N. Dixit, *My South-Block Years: Memoirs of a Foreign Secretary* (New Delhi, 1997 reprint of 1996), p. 154.

12. Keynote Address given on 28 September 2001 by Arvind Dave, Governor of Arunachal Pradesh and Chancellor, Arunachal University while inaugurating the National Seminar on " Cross-Border Trade of Arunachal Pradesh Retrospect and Prospect" jointly organised by the Maulana Abul Kalam Azad Institute of Asian Studies, Kolkata and the Department of History, Arunachal University on 28-29 September 2001.Text of the address appears in S. Dutta (ed), *Cross-Border Trade of North-East India : Arunachal Perspective* (Kolkata, 2002), pp.18-25.

13. "Non-governmental "Taxes" along NH-39 Inflate Goods Prices in Manipur" ***Imphal Free Press***, 4 January 2005 wrongly entered as 4 December 2004.

14. See Indian National Congress, *Manifesto: Lok Sabha Elections – 2004, Manipur* (Imphal ?, not dated), p.7; Holkhomang Haokip, *EnSiPi Candidate ki Slogan (Slogan of the NCP candidate* (No place of publication, not dated); *Common Manifesto of the Democratic People's Alliance (DPA), 14th Lok Sabha Election, (MPP, MNC,DRPP,JD(U) &FPM,* (Imphal, not dated), not paginated; The Manifesto Committee, Bharatiya Janata Party, Manipur Pradesh, *The Election Manifesto of the Bharatiya Janata Party,* Manipur,(the 14th Lok Sabha Election, 2004), (Imphal,5th April 2004), pp. 3-4.

15. See n.5, p. 218.

16. B.G. Varghese, *Reorienting India : The New Geo-Politics of Asia* (New Delhi:Konark, 2001).p.190.

17. See *Europa Yearbook, 1999 Vol. II Far East and Australia* (London,Europa Publications,1998), p.2516 and of ***2000***

(London, 1999), pp. 762-64; C. Joshua Thomas, "Indo-Myanmar Border Trade: An Assessment on the Moreh-Tamu Sector" in Gurudas Das and R.K.Purkayastha (eds), Border Trade: North-East India and the Neighbouring Countries (New Delhi: Akansha Publishing House, 2000), pp. 151-165.

18. C. Joshua Thomas, "Indo-Myanmar Border Trade: An Assessment on the Moreh-*Tamu Sector in Gurudas Das and R.K. Purkayastha* (eds), *Border Trade : North-East India and Neighbouring Countries* (New Delhi: Akansha Publishing House, 2000), pp. 151-165.

19. n. 1

20. See for instance Mary P. Callahan, "Myanmar in 1994: New Dragon or Still Dragging" *Asian Survey* (Berkeley), vol. 35, no. 2 February 1995, p. 201-208; and see also Stephen McCarthy, "Ten Years of Chaos in Burma: Foreign Investment and Economic Liberalization under the SLORC-SPDC, 1988 to 1998" *Pacific Affairs* (Vancouver), vol. 73, no. 2 Summer 2000, pp. 233-264.

6

India's Look East Policy: Implications for Northeast India

—Prabir De

Introduction

The growth of regionalism has been one of the major developments in international relations in recent years; all countries are now members of at least one bloc and many belong to more than one.[1] In general, regionalism has shared an objective to reduce trade barriers–quantitative and qualitative. Most of the regionalism have moved away from closed model to more open model encouraging greater international commerce rather than controlling it by way of less and less tariffs and quotas. ASEAN is an example of such dynamism. In recognition of importance of faster trade, transport bottlenecks have been narrowing in regional groupings leading to "deep integration" of the economies concerned. Progress made so far in EU is a bright example of such integration in connectivity. Nonetheless, we have found equality in some regionalism, where developed countries and developing countries are equal partners. NAFTA is a case in point of such development.

There are some studies which show that rising regionalism is nothing but marching towards globalism. Okita (1989) spoke eloquently for the inter-dependence of globalism and regionalism. Regionalism has long history and has been around for hundreds of years.[2] In other words, regionalism is part of the process of globalization: a sort of sub-grouping in the broader road towards supra-national integration. Globalisation is the other name of integration–economic and otherwise. Regional integration is a long-standing concern for Asia.

Regionalism in Asia

Regionalism in Asia was never as intense as we have seen in Europe. Combined with the pull-factor of successful industrialisation at an accelerated rate for the select group of East Asian economies beyond Japan since the 1970s, plus normalization of the economic relationship with China in 1970s, and the push factor of EEC, several countries in Asia formed the Association of Southeast Asian Nations (ASEAN) and Asia-Pacific Economic Cooperation (APEC) in 1967 and 1989 respectively. While ASEAN was formed basically due to political compulsions, formation of APEC was mostly based on cohesive trading unity. Down the line, we have seen ASEAN has succeeded in opening a free trade area while APEC has little to its credit in terms of accomplishment even for the effective promotion of an intra-APEC free trade regime (Dutta, 2002). In the same direction, although much late of ASEAN and APEC, South Asian countries formed the South Asian Association for Regional Cooperation (SAARC) in 1985, only in early 2004, SAARC countries agreed to set up a free trade area with effect from 2006.[3] Regionalism in Asia got further momentum since the 1997 East Asian crisis broke out, and with its varying manifestations regionalism is on the path of rapid spread in Asia.[4] In spite of accession to WTO, countries in Asia are moving with regionalism for closer economic and trade cooperation. To promote a pan-Asian regionalism, which is quite similar to pan-European experience, there is an urge for systematic development of Asia through Asian Economic Community (AEC), which has for some time been an important consideration for policy makers of many Asian countries.[5]

In spite of having a spread of regionalism of very diverse dimensions in Asia, economic welfare remains to be attained in full. Today, Asia[6] shares 16 per cent of world surface area

(22 million sq. km.) which contains half of the world population (3.2 billion in 2001) and one third of the world poor (1.2 billion in 2001). In sharp contrast, Asia produces only 7 per cent of world output, and an Asian citizen earns on an average only 26 per cent of what a rest of world national earns. Yet, it is not easy to think of another region of the world which can surpass Asia in terms of resource endowments — natural and otherwise.[7] Notwithstanding its vast advantages of resource endowments, in terms of per capita income, Asia, on the whole, is still running far behind the developed world in terms of economic wellbeing. Economic disparity among the regions across the world is a common phenomenon but the same also prevails with varied intensity within Asia. For instance, people of South Asia earn much less than what a national from the rest of Asia earns. In terms of social development indicators, South Asia's performance happens to be poor and static; what is more, it has been hovering around the same socio-economic position for a long period of time (Srinivasan, 2002; De and Ghosh, 2003; Ghosh and De, 2004). At the same time, Asia contains world's progressive and developed countries (frontier countries) such as Japan, Singapore and Korea. Naturally, therefore, one finds regional disparity within Asia: One group of countries is attached with rising hinterland and thereby enjoying rising wealth whereas other group is endowed with relatively poor resources thereby facing burden of inertia in the era of globalisation.

Despite the rising levels general prosperity observed in some of the countries in Asia, many changes are taking place which are reshaping regional integration in Asia in many ways. The real problem that most of the Asian countries are faced with is very much economic in nature: how to ensure best trade for all the countries in the region which are willing to share the benefits of trade. Even the countries which are bound by the same land mass have utterly failed to take advantage of the wave of globalization, though it must be admitted that the Asian environment has become many times more conducive now than what it was a decade ago: China and India are coming closer; India and Pakistan are in good mood; Japan is all set to involve her in an intense way in Asian affairs than ever before; various regional cooperation groups have become very active now all on a sudden. The wave of globalisation appears to be blowing in Asia.

Another reason for focusing on Asia is also pressing if we look into the region's trade coverage. When most of the Asian economies – either through AFTA (ASEAN Free Trade Area) or through SAFTA (South Asian Free Trade Area) or combination of both[8]—are planning to promote intra-regional trade, integration of the whole region is limited by lack of an integrated and improved transport system—the life blood of the process of globalisation in tangible goods. Moreover, given the socio-cultural homogeneity and vast resources of the region, an improved and integrated regional integration process for the whole of Asia is expected to boost up the intra-regional trade when most of the economies have been growing at faster rate during the last few years. Working together for the improvement of infrastructural facilities, an essential element to promote intraregional trade, will pave the way for the region's international market access and through this to higher income.[9]

India's Association with East

India's growing association with Southeast Asia is found to be one of the major developments in international relations in recent years; her trade with East has been growing faster than her trade with West. Over time, India has not only been able to come closer to ASEAN (Association of Southeast Asian Nations) market but also to its individual members, particularly CLMV (Cambodia, Laos, Myanmar and Vietnam) countries. Apart from her bilateral initiatives in East, such as FTAs with Nepal and Thailand, and Framework Agreement for comprehensive economic cooperation with Singapore, India has already signed a Framework Agreement for comprehensive economic cooperation with ASEAN in October 2003 and Framework Agreement for opening a Free Trade Area in BIMST-EC in July 2004. Figure 6.1 portrays this network. India has

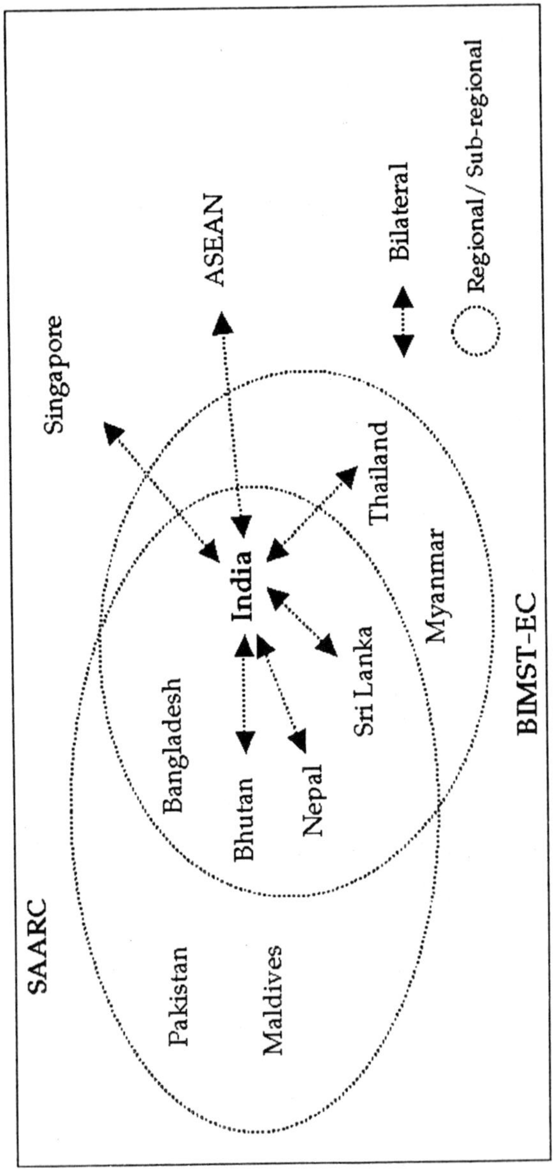

Figure 6.1.
India's Economic Engagement with East as on December 2004

also extended tariff concessions under the Bangkok Agreement to China. Proposals of bilateral free trade agreements with Bangladesh, Myanmar, among other countries, are presently being studied. Naturally therefore, India's ties with East have intensified as a part of her conscious 'Look East Policy'.

India's growing trade and investment links with East over the past few years suggest the presence of complementarities and unexploited potential. Several studies show that the integration of Indian economy with East has appeared to be mutual advantageous.[10] The pattern of development, endowments and capabilities of India open new opportunities for her Northeastern region, which is geographically located near to East. Quite naturally, this development could facilitate the exploitation of substantial complementarities and important synergies that exist between these economies and would help in expediting the process of development.

India's Association with China

The China-India economic relations and the relative spheres of activities are the most progressing issues of internal relations. China and India had a strong historical and cultural link, China and India share many similarities. They are two of the world's most populous countries sharing between them over a third of the world's population. They represent centuries old civilizations and unique history. After pursuing inward-oriented policies in the early years of their development, both China (since 1979) and India (since 1991) have increasingly deepened their economic integration with the outside world over the past two decades. While China has emerged as one of the world's fastest growing economies, Indian economy with a robust growth rate of over 8 per cent achieved in 2003-04, is also showing a healthy growth momentum. Both China and India have not only attempted to deepen their economic relations within Asia but also between themselves. Bilateral trade and investment links between the two countries have grown rapidly over the past few years suggesting the presence of complementarities and unexploited potential.

Substantial complementarities characterise the economic structures of China and India. While China has emerged as the manufacturing hub of the world, India's strengths in knowledge-based services and manufacturing are gaining recognition. The complementary strengths of the two economies can be exploited for mutual benefit. Opportunities for fruitful cooperation exist in many areas of manufacturing, services and investment. Their geographical proximity and large size of their economies would facilitate exploitation of these synergies. They can also pool resources for improving their competitiveness in third countries, particularly, Bangladesh, Bhutan, Myanmar, and Nepal. They can fruitfully share their development experiences and cooperate in several areas, especially in the critical area of energy security. India-China economic cooperation has the potential to benefit over a third of humanity. China-India cooperation could also be instrumental in building a closer border trade between them that could enable both the countries regain its place in the world economy that it had before the eighteenth century.

Economic cooperation between India and China has been deepening in the recent years. Both the countries have decided to focus on economic issues and leave unresolved political and security matters for negotiation at a later date. Both countries respect each other's success and work for common interests, particularly improving the quality of life of their citizens. Benefits of closer economic cooperation have been reflected in rising bilateral trade between the two countries. India and China officially resumed trade in 1978. Both countries singed a Trade Agreement (Most Favoured Nation Agreement) in 1984. India-China bilateral trade has grown rapidly in the last decade from US$ 338.54 million in 1992 to US$ 7.6 billion in 2003, up by 53.6 per cent over 2002. In the past few years, India-China bilateral trade exhibited a sustained pattern of growth. In view of the complementarities based on comparative and competitive advantages, the potential for further enhancement of trade is significant. The rapid growth trend continues in the current year as well. Between 1995 and 2003, the bilateral trade between China and India maintained a relatively robust annual growth rate of 26.4 per cent, which is higher than the average growth rate of the total volume of foreign trade in the same period for both China and India. In 2003, the bilateral trade volume between China and India stood at US$ 7.6 billion, of which China's export amounted to US$ 3.34 billion and India's export amounted to US$ 4.25 billion. In 2003, India became the 13th trade partner of China and the largest trade partner in South Asia. In the first quarter of 2004, bilateral trade between India and China reached a total volume of US$ 3.13 billion, representing an increase of 87.68 per cent over the corresponding period last year. It is expected to reach $10 billion by the end of 2004. Despite this rapid growth, India's share of China's imports is just 1.03 per cent (in 2003) and of China's share of India's imports is just under 5 per cent. This suggests that the potential for trade expansion is very large. Each side is now focussed to take advantage of rising opportunities for mutual gains instead of competitive challenges from each other.

In June 2003, China and India signed the Declaration on Principles for Relations and Comprehensive Cooperation and agreed to hold the ministerial meeting of the Joint Economic Group (JEG). A compact Joint Study Group (JSG) composed of government officials and economists was set up to examine the potential complementarities between two countries in enhancing trade and economic cooperation. The JSG is aimed to develop a programme for the development of China-India trade and economic cooperation for the next five years. The JSG's report together with recommendations will be submitted by the end December 2004. The recent JSG working meeting (November 29, 2004–December 3, 2004) in Beijing discussed the possibility of signing a bilateral Free Trade Agreement (FTA) as well as Comprehensive Economic Cooperation Agreement (CECA) to enhance their booming commercial ties.

Naturally, therefore, the emergence of China and India as major economic forces in world and their greater openness are the key factors for pushing closer integration between these two countries. Because of the complementarities between China and India, particularly between Northeastern India (NEI) and

Southwestern China (SWC) properly paced regional integration can help boost both the quantity and quality of economic growth, bringing benefits to all participating countries or economies. Cross-border initiatives relating to trade facilitation and investment promotion can be instrumental in generating jobs, increasing subregional gross national product (GNP), improving intra-subregional trade and deepening the economic fabric.

Southwest China (SWC), comprising five provinces, namely, Sichuan, Ghizhou, Yunnan, Tibet and Guangxi and one autonomous region, namely, Chongqing, and Eastern and Northeast India (NEI), comprising Arunachal Pradesh, Assam, Manipur, Meghalaya, Mizoram, Nagaland, Sikkim, Tripura and West Bengal, contains approximately 30 million people (out of a total of about 120 million) living below (those with incomes of less than $ 1 a day) the poverty line (Ray and De, 2004).[11] This is indeed alarming, because, in the whole of India and China, the number of people living below the poverty line (those with incomes of less than $ 1 a day) stands at about 400 million (Ray and De, 2003). The SWC and NEI are among the less developed regions of China and India respectively. However, SWC and NEI are very rich with resource endowments. The forest deposits of the States of Assam, Arunachal Pradesh and West Bengal, the hydrocarbon resources of the States of Assam, Tripura and Tibet, as well as the hydropower potential of Assam and Manipur, can supply an enormous amount of inexpensive energy — if developed and utilized in a cooperative manner. The abundance and variety of forest, livestock and mineral resources in this region are remarkable. The huge labour force in this region — with suitable training — can be mobilized to maximize the benefits from these natural resources, that would, in the process, transform the region by removing poverty, and paving the way to prosperity. For citizens of one of the less developed but potentially most prosperous areas of the world, the first decade of the 21st century begins with new challenges on environmental sustainability, economic productivity, and international competitiveness. The future quality of life and economic prosperity in these regions will depend crucially on

Table 6.1
Demographic Profile of NEI

States	*Population*		*Area*	
	2001 (million)	*Share in TIP[1] (%)*	*2001 (Sq. Km.)*	*Share in TIA[2] (%)*
Arunachal Pradesh	1.09	0.11	83743	2.83
Assam	26.64	2.59	78347	2.65
Manipur	2.39	0.23	22327	0.75
Meghalaya	2.31	0.22	22388	0.76
Mizoram	0.89	0.09	21214	0.72
Nagaland	1.99	0.19	16575	0.56
Sikkim	0.54	0.05	7096	0.24
Tripura	3.19	0.31	10497	0.35
West Bengal	80.22	7.81	88752	3.00
NEI 9	118.17	11.51	267196	9.03
India	1027.02		2959697	

States	*State GDP Share[3]*	*Per Capita Income (PCI)[4]*		*CAGR of PCI*
	2000-01 (%)	*1990-91 (Rs.)*	*2000-01 (Rs.)*	*1990-2000 (%)*
Arunachal Pradesh	0.09	5231	14587	16.26
Assam	1.58	4432	10198	11.83
Manipur	0.17	3912	12823	20.71
Meghalaya	0.19	4944	13114	15.02
Mizoram	0.08	4856	14909	18.82
Nagaland	0.16	5893	12594	10.34
Sikkim	0.05	5213	15550	18.03
Tripura	0.27	4240	14348	21.67
West Bengal	7.54	5072	16072	19.72
NEI 9	10.13	4866	13799	16.69
India		5365	16707	19.22

Notes: 1. Share in total Indian population (TIP). 2. Share in total Indian area (TIA). 3. Share of each State's net state domestic product in Indian net gross domestic product, considered in current price (new series). 4. Taken at current price (new series).

Data source: Economic Survey, 2002-03, Government of India.

how they choose to meet these challenges in a united way. Cross-border infrastructure development in this geographically integrated region is crucial to promote greater trade and investment and consequently economic prosperity (De, 2004d; Bhattacharyay and De, 2004).

Under the above backdrop, this chapter discusses India's integration with East and its implication for Northeastern region of India.

Northeastern India—Profile and Potential

While focussing on the strengths and potential business drives in individual Northeastern States, care must be taken to see the assets of these States as part of a comprehensive whole. Ninety eight per cent of this region's borders form India's international boundaries. The region shares borders with China in the North, Bangladesh in the Southwest, Bhutan in the Northwest and Myanmar in the East.

The States of India's Northeast as a whole represent 9 per cent of India's geographical area and 12 per cent of India's total population (Table 6.1). Although none of the Northeastern States has attained higher per capita income than the national average in recent years, a few of them (Manipur and Tripura) have been successful in attaining higher income growth rates compared to the national average during 1990-2000.

Northeast India has much lower population density than the rest of the country. Low population density has been reflected in low urbanization in this region. In general, urbanization is generally low here except in Assam, Mizoram and Nagaland (Table 6.1). This may be due to the fact that more than 30 per cent of the area is hilly terrain and green biosphere. While Northeastern India is potentially strong in natural endowments, due to lack of physical infrastructure networks, this region has been suffering from lack of access to the international market. In terms of availability of good quality rail and road networks, this region is still far below the national average, and so are its other physical infrastructural attributes

(Table 6.2). Nevertheless, Northeastern India has witnessed better social infrastructure characteristics.

Table 6.2
Economic Profile of NEI*

*Particulars***	*Unit*	*NEI9*	*India*
Area	Share in India (%)	9	
Population (2001)	Share in India (%)	12	
Population Density (2001)	Per Sq. Km. of Area	442	347
Literacy Rate (2001)	(%)	63	65
PCE (1998-99) (a)	Kwh	112	290
NSDP in 1970-71 (b)	Share in India (%)	10	
NSDP in 1999-2000 (b)	Share in India (%)	10	
PCI in 1970-71 (c)	US $. (at current price)	89	320
PCI in 1999-2000 (c)	US $ (at current price)	300	363
Railway Density (1998-99)	Km/'000 Sq. Km of Area	9.16	19.25
Road Density (1998-99)	Km/'000 Sq. Km of Area	583.78	862.60
Telephone Mainlines (1997-98)	Per 1000 population	1.96	3.88
Seaport Traffic (2002-2003) (d)	Million Ton	40	360
Landport Traffic (2000-2001) (e)	Million Ton	1.96	66
FDI (1991-2002) (f)	US $ billion	12	45

Notes: * Arunachal Pradesh, Assam, Manipur, Mizoram, Meghalaya, Nagaland, Sikkim, Tripura and West Bengal.

** Considers average data of nine NEs. (a) Per Capita Consumption of Electricity. (b) Net State Domestic Product (New Series). (c) Per Capita Income (New Series). (d) Overseas traffic handled by Kolkata, Haldia seaports. (e) Overseas traffic handled by Amingaon and Cossipore ICDs, and border posts like Petropole and Hili. (f) Accumulated data, considers only approved projects.

Data sources: 1. Various issues of Economic Survey, Govt. of India. 2. Various issues of Profile of States, CMIE. Preliminary Results of 2001 Census, Register of Census Operation, Govt. of India.

Northeastern India is bountifully endowed with biodiversity, hydro-potential, oil and gas, coal, limestone and forest wealth. It is ideally suited for a whole range of plantation crops, spices, fruits and vegetables, flowers and herbs, much of which could be processed and exported to neighbouring countries. There is also a huge potential for the development of a viable tourism sector. In some sense, the Northeastern States also provide a bridge to Southeast and East Asia (Verghese, 1997; NEFIT, 2004).

Industrial backwardness is one notion that is held about the region. In reality, tea industry started in 1886 and is still thriving, and the oil refinery, started in 1897, is the oldest in Asia. It is generally believed that the area is geographically isolated when in reality it could be a corridor between Southeast Asia and India.

Contrary to the notion that this region has an underdeveloped transport system associated with high transport costs, there are 12 airports, and the Brahmaputra riverway is perennial and cheapest. While it is widely believed that that power situation in the region is dismal, it has country's 38 per cent hydropower potential. Moreover, the climate for investment is most favourable owing to an almost negligible pollution, the maximum number of incentives, and a high percentage of English-speaking population. While this area has a negative image due to insurgency problems, the number of Industrial Entrepreneurs Memorandum (IEMs) filed is higher than the national average. Between 1991 and 2002, the number of IEMs filed in the Northeast region was approximately 300, with a proposed investment figure of approximately Rs. 80 billion, and an employment potential of 45,000. Between December 1999 and January 2003, the number of IEMs rose by 140 per cent compared to an increase of 17 per cent at the all-India level.[12] The region has natural gas reserves of 190 billion cubic metres, coal reserves of 909 million tonnes, hydro electric potential estimated at 49,000 MW, oil reserves of 513 million tonnes, limestone reserves of 4933 million tonnes and a forest cover which is 25 per cent of the country's forest area.

(a) Agro and Food Processing, Horticulture and Forestry

Agriculture and forestry are the bedrock on which this region has to be built (Government of India, 1997). The region's economy is primarily agrarian, but it is deficient in its food supply, importing grain, oilseeds, sugar, meat, fish and eggs, apart from other civil supplies, from distant parts of the country. The region's economy can generate a surplus, and the endeavour should be to ensure that it realises its true farm potential.

Northeastern States have vast possibilities for growing a range of fruit and vegetables, tuber crops, tapioca and spices. Mizoram, for example, is well placed to produce passion fruit. Scope for enhanced productivity exists in the cases of citrus, pineapple, banana and other varieties through tissue culture and the development of breeder seed farms. The hills can exploit niche markets and provide off-season fruit and vegetables to the plains, including Bangladesh and China. Other plantation and spice crops like ginger, turmeric, coffee, cashew, large cardamom, pepper, jackfruit, lemon grass, citronella and a host of very valuable herbs and medicinal plants, orchids and a whole range of flowers can be developed. The region is the largest producer of tea in the country, with Assam as the leading tea producer supplying 50 per cent of the country's tea output, followed by Tripura, which is the fifth largest tea producer in the country. Arunachal Pradesh also produces tea, which closely resembles the world famous Darjeeling tea of West Bengal. The lone tea unit here has been running profitably for some years now. This potential could indeed be tapped. Sikkim produces 80 per cent of India's large cardamom which enjoys high value export market in the Middle East. India is the 2nd largest producer of fruits in the world. Of the 388 million tonnes of fruit produced worldwide, 8.5 per cent are grown in Indian orchards. The paradox is that our share in the global export market is not even 0.1 per cent. The Government of India has, therefore, identified both fresh fruits and finished products as focus areas. The national target is to capture at least 1 per cent share of the global trade. Nagaland has immense potential for horticulture because of the varying soil and agro-climatic conditions. The present horticulture crops of various fruits cover an area of about 43,000 hectares with an annual production of approx. 5,00,000 tonnes. However, with proper planning and investment, the cultivated area under horticultural crops and production can easily be quadrupled.

The food products sector accounts for a bulk of industrial production in Assam. Although the contribution of this sector to the total output of the country's manufacturing sector is very minute, the importance of food products in the State's economy cannot be overlooked. In fact, there is considerable scope for the establishment of large and medium scale industries in this sector. In Nagaland, food and food products account for 11 per cent of the total output value of the State. A fruit-processing unit is proposed to be set up in Mizoram. Financial assistance of about Rs. 18 million has been extended for various projects in the Northeast and Sikkim during 2001-2002 by the Ministry of Food Processing, Government of India. According to a report prepared by the North Eastern Development Finance Corporation (NEDFI), the thrust areas identified in the agro-processing sector include canned or bottled products, packaged products, frozen products, dehydrated products, oleoresins, meat, milk, poultry, cereal based products, edible oil, fodder, jute and mesta, essential oils and fragrances and plantation crops like tea, jute, rubber and coffee.

Wood and wood based industries comprise the main industrial segment of Nagaland. It accounts for the bulk of manufacturing in Nagaland. Meghalaya is dependent on wood and wood based industries to a large extent. Most of the manufacturing units in Arunachal Pradesh are forest based, and their main raw material is wood. The quality of veneer in Arunachal Pradesh is comparable with the best in the world. Small industries of Tripura are based on forest resources like cane, and plywood. The bamboo and cane products of Tripura are exquisitely crafted, and are highly acclaimed both in India and overseas. Sikkim has a unique bio-diversity. The composition ranges from tropical Dry Deciduous Forests with Sal and its associates in the valleys of Teesta and Rangit to the

Alpine Scrub and Grasslands in high altitudes. During the last two decades, the Forest Department has laid emphasis on development of fodder and fuel wood in the agriculture fallow lands of villages, giving priority to plantations of broom grass for fodder and for economic upliftment of the villagers.

Northeast India harvests approx. 8 million tonnes of bamboo, which is about 54 per cent of the country's share. The bamboo sector is currently experiencing a big expansion in China to meet the demand of both its huge internal market and increasing exports. Average yearly household income from bamboo shoots in China, in villages specialising in the production of bamboo shoots, amounts to US$ 2,500, with some villages soaring above US$ 10,000. Given the right initiative, this region could continue effectively towards fulfilling the worldwide demand for bamboo to a considerable extent.

Sericulture is another activity which is popular in the region. Excellent quality silk of eri and muga variety are grown in Assam. In fact, the cultivation of bi-voltine variety of silk should be encouraged so that the quality of silk that is produced can compete with the best silks in the world. There are immense opportunities for setting up modern silk processing plants in this region. Manipur is set to worm its way up on the silk route. The State was once a key staging post on the ancient silk route. Traders carried silk from China's Yunnan province through Myanmar, across India and finally to Afghanistan, where they joined the main silk road. Manipur is poised to spin this tradition into business once again. Japan's Overseas Economic Cooperation Fund (OECF) has loaned Manipur $ 32.77 million in the first phase of a project to revitalize its silk industry. This project aims to increase Manipur's annual silk output to 328 tonnes from 202 tonnes by 2002-03. Sericulture accounted for 1.48 per cent of the State's real GDP. That proportion is likely to rise sharply once the industry takes hold.

(b) Energy

Energy is a crucial element for the sustained economic growth of this subregion. As this region contains high mountains and major rivers, there is a need to build power generation capacities as well as transmission grid in an optimal manner to serve the entire subregion. The development of cost-effective and environment-friendly hydro power projects is crucial for long-term development of electricity market in this region.

The region has all the resources to become the future powerhouse of India. The potential developed in the Northeastern States is only 253 MW, which is about 0.8 per cent of the total available potential. More than two-thirds of India's total hydropower potential (84,000 MW) exists in the Northeastern region.

The region houses the largest perennial water system in the country. The State of Arunachal Pradesh is known as the powerhouse of Northeast India. The untapped hydro power potential, is estimated at 49,000 MW, of which only 23.65 MW (just about 0.05 per cent of the total potential) has been harnessed. Some 15 projects with a total installed capacity of 50 MW are being set up. For ecological reasons, this State favoured power generation projects based on "run-of-the river system" and mini and micro hydel projects.

With 8000 MW of hydro-electric potential, ample opportunities exist for private sector investments in the energy sector of Sikkim. Meghalaya is one of the few States in the country with a surplus capacity of power generation. The total installed capacity of this State is 185 MW. Meghalaya has a power potential of about 3000 MW. The excess power generated in this State is presently being sold to the neighbouring States. In case of Nagaland, there are prospects for future power generation through (a) Shilloi hydroelectric project (6 MW) and (b) Tizu-Zungki basin (2000 MW). The current generation of power in Nagaland (micro-hydel) is about 2.3 MW, and the projected generation (under way) is about 30 MW.

(c) Coal

Mineral reserves in Arunachal Pradesh are reported as

follows: coal–84.23 million tonnes, dolomite–154.13 million tonnes, limestone–409.35 million tones, and semi limestone-45.82 million tonnes. In Meghalaya, the coal reserves are concentrated in the West Darrangiri area of the Garo hills possessing about 127 million tonnes.

(d) Natural Oil and Gas

Assam accounts for nearly 50 per cent onshore crude oil production in the country. It has over 1.3 billion tonnes of proven crude oil and 156 billion cubic metres of natural gas reserves. Tripura has vast reserves of natural gas in non-associate form. The gas is of high quality, with methane contents of about 97 per cent and without any presence of H_2S or Sulphur and other impurities. The Oil and Natural Gas Commission (ONGC), an Indian public sector firm has been actively engaged in exploration activities in this State since 1972. The availability of superior quality natural gas, at concessional price, offers a great opportunity to prospective investors, to set up gas-based industrial units, using natural gas as feedstock. The prospects of crude oil availability in Arunachal Pradesh have brightened after a few successful discoveries of new areas as potential reservoirs for crude oil. The oil reserves may be more than 30 million tonnes in Arunachal Pradesh.

(e) Tourism

Opening borders between Southwest China and Northeast India will enhance tourism activities. Countries could jointly develop new tourism products, marketing strategies, and invest in tourism infrastructure development.

Northeast India is a land of majestic mountains, crowned with peaks of sapphire blue, and of ambrosial water in all its brooks and pools. It is a land of lovely woods, waterfalls and trees, of clustering fruits, and of groves dense with trees and sounds of silence. While nature seems to have waved its magical wand on the region, the area has more than its share of history, pilgrimages, temples, handicrafts and wild-life.

Bordering on China and Bangladesh, this region has absorbed many waves of migrations. Here Indo-Aryan, Tibeto-Burmese, Chinese and Mon-Khmer races have mingled with the aborigines to create colourful communities and different political systems amidst the fertile Brahmaputra and Surma valleys, the resource-rich Eastern Himalayas and their foot-hills. All the eight Northeastern States offer varying attractions. Their language, customs, traditions, history, folklore, festivals and handicrafts differ as much as their people. Since 1995, the restricted areas permit requirement has been done away with for most of the States of Northeast. The Japanese were the main foreign visitors to Manipur. They came to pray at the graves of their forefathers, who perished in World War II.

Selected tourism has been permitted since the early 1980s by the Government, which recognises Northeast India's tremendous potential for adventure tourism. Sustained economic development and political stability are encouraging private investors to join the various State Tourism Corporations in creating the hotel and transport infrastructure essential for catering to growing domestic and international traffic. Twelve airports, helipads and private domestic airlines have made these States more accessible.

The whole State of Sikkim is endowed with nature's beauty. With altitudes ranging from 300 to over 5000 metres, Sikkim is covered with tropical forests, temperate forests, alpine meadows and snow-capped peaks. The tourism potential of this State is still under-exploited. An excellent opportunity exists to exploit the tourism potential in a sustainable manner without damage to the environment.

The most exciting bird habitat in Asia is found in the rainforests of the Himalayan foothills of eastern Arunachal Pradesh and the magnificent wetlands of the Brahmaputra River Valley in Assam. The extreme Northeastern part of India is one of the richest bird habitat areas on the earth. The tourism potential of the region is considerable. There is great scope for promoting adventure tourism in Arunachal Pradesh, which has quite a few fast flowing rivers and hilly terrain. River rafting and other water sports and trekking can be promoted among foreign and domestic tourists in Arunachal Pradesh. The tourism potential of Meghalaya is also considerable. Shillong, the State's capital, is already an important tourist destination. Each of the States like Sikkim, Nagaland, Manipur, Mizoram and Tripura and their rich culture, picturesque locales, rare flora and fauna, historical monuments in almost each and every district, make the region an attractive tourist destination. Although NEI is endowed with mineral resources, particularly hydro power, basic social and physical infrastructure facilities, geographical isolation has kept this region in the lower strata of economic development.

From the foregoing, it may be concluded that this region enjoys the following special advantages over other regions of India.

(i) An emerging market of 400 million people including neighbouring countries like Bangladesh, Bhutan, China, Myanmar and Nepal.

(ii) The region has the potential of developing into India's powerhouse. The area is a vibrant source of energy, rich in oil, natural gas, coal, limestone, and India's largest perennial water system in the river Brahmaputra and its tributaries, which could be tapped for energy, irrigation and transportation.

(iii) The fertile soil around the Brahmaputra valley is a veritable storehouse of horticultural products, plantation crops, vegetables, spices and rare herbs and medicinal plants.

(iv) Unlimited tourism opportunities–rare flora and fauna, natural scenic beauty, unique performing arts, varied cuisine and textiles.

(v) Locational advantages make this region attractive to foreign investment. It has unique proximity to the SAARC and ASEAN regions. Therefore this region can emerge as a strategic base for foreign/domestic investors to tap the world's largest market–SAARC and ASEAN.

(vi) Already, a border point between Myanmar and the Northeast has been opened at Moreh (Manipur) with a possibility of a second border point being opened at Champhai. Besides, Assam's internal waterway network connects it to Bangladesh, giving it access to the ports of Chittagong (Bangladesh), Kolkata and Haldia (West Bengal).

(vii) Industrial Growth Centres have already been converted into Total Tax Free Zones for next 10 years; and

(viii) Subsidies on transport, capital investment, interest on the working capital, etc. are available for industries in the region.

Northeast India is unique in terms of opportunities. It has certain peculiarities and problems, which, if tackled and leveraged in the right perspective, could yield rich dividends. While it is an industrial desert, and almost all consumables are imported from outside the region, it is the focal point of trade within a vast area. It is therefore essential to evolve a regional approach as opposed to the individual State approach. Northeast India's locational advantage and rich natural resources provide a backdrop to its development as a base for cooperation not only with China but also with neighbouring countries such as Bangladesh, Bhutan, Nepal and Myanmar. And through Myanmar, subregional cooperation can be extended to Thailand, Lao PDR, Cambodia and Viet Nam.

Trade is the easiest instrument for promotion of cooperation among countries in a region or sub-region. But the interdependence of trade and investment is apparent from the simple facts that without adequate transportation facilities, maximization of mutually beneficial trade opportunities cannot take place, that development of multimodal transportation requires large scale investments, and that economies of scale may dictate that such investments should be cross-border investments. Such investments, moreover, can benefit the poorest people in the most remote locations of Northeastern India.

Roads, railways and inland waterways are the dominant modes for trade between India and its neighbouring countries in East, roads being the most important. However, in order to minimize environmental pollution, it is advisable to lay emphasis on rail and inland water transport. Currently, trans-border rail links between India and China, and India and Myanmar do not exist. With such great rivers as the Ganga, Brahmaputra and Mekong, inland water transportation (IWT) has immense potentialities for trade ties between India's NEI and its bordering countries.

Table 6.3
Advantages of NEI

- Strategic location
- Considerable penetration of railways, roadways, and waterways
- Untapped and underutilized natural energy
- Vast reserve of natural resources
- Human resources
- Attached with a 400 million strong market
- Versatile tourism market
- Linked in India-Myanmar-Thailand Trilateral Highway, Asian Highway and Trans-Asian Railway networks

In the matter of development of hydropower potentials too, the availability of profitable commercial investment and extensive markets will depend a lot on cooperation between India and China and also neighbouring countries. Only about 3,500 MW of the hydropower potential of the Ganga and Brahmaputra basin have been or are being tapped presently, whereas the estimated total stands at 90,000 MW approximately. The Ganga basin accounts for 40 per cent of this hydropower, and the Brahmaputra basin for 57 per cent. With 37 per cent of this potential, Northeast India remains the largest reservoir of hydropower in the Eastern South Asia Subregion, whereas Bhutan commands 23 per cent, Nepal 28 per cent and north India's Ganga catchment area only 12 per cent. Much of India's unutilized hydropower potential is located in the Brahmaputra basin. To take the instance of India's Arunachal Pradesh, which has 39 per cent of India's power potential, only 2 per cent of this reserve is currently in the process of being energized. Hydropower in India's Northeast can be marketed in the Southwest provinces of China, Myanmar, and Bangladesh. It is essential to affirm that massive investments, required for the development of the hydropower resources of the Ganga-Brahmaputra basin, can be fruitful if there is ample cooperation among India and China, resulting in an integration of the power transmission and distribution networks of Bangladesh, Bhutan, China, India, Myanmar and Nepal.

Coordinated planning of hydropower investments and power transmission networks entails decision making on an exceedingly complex matter. Smaller countries usually have concern of being marginalized by big neighbours like China or India and this concern can aggravate this complexity. But there are other relatively less complex matters where a prompt exercise of administrative political will is essential for an adequate facilitation of trade and investment between India and China. Some of the requisite official decisions have to be carried out multilaterally and others bilaterally. Moreover, administrative-political will have to be directed towards an enhancement of partnership between the public and private sectors of China, India and Myanmar.

Attracting investments for mega projects in highway or hydropower development in India's Northeast may require the combined efforts of public and private agencies in concerned countries. Whereas the Asian Development Bank has launched the initiatives for such development in South and Southeast

Asia under South Asia Subregional Economic Cooperation (SASEC)[13] and Greater Mekong Region (GMS) [14] programmes respectively, much more needs to be done by India, China and Myanmar to draw investments from abroad, say, Japan, Europe and North America, for promotion of trade and investment in the region. It must be remembered that there are many other areas in the world which are also competing for investments. Therefore, public-private agencies in India, China and Myanmar must cooperate to collect/disseminate information, and adopt a strategy to secure investments from abroad. Attempts should be made to strengthen networking among chambers of commerce in the region, as also among respective government agencies, in such a way that promotional activities (e.g. in tourism) can avoid wasteful competition among various sub-regional cooperation blocs in the region and multiply mutual benefits. Such networking can ensure that investment by India in Myanmar and China and vice versa will be so designed and located as to maximize impact upon the entire area, and enhance growth by trade and employment generation.

Table 6.4
Complementarities between NEI and Southwest China and Myanmar (SCM)

NEI's Strengths	*SCM's Strengths*
Stable railways, waterways, roadways, ports and shipping networks	Stable roadways and airways network
Bordering mainland India, Bangladesh and Myanmar	Bordering mainland China and some ASEAN members
Large pool of English speaking population	English speaking population Rising
Developed IT software	Developed IT Hardware and electronic equipment
Underutilized capacity in construction	Huge potential demand for infrastructure
Presence of private capital	Scopes for private enterprises

Source: De (2004d)

As we know a major barrier to expanding India's trade with bordering countries is the lack of adequate transport network. Cross-border infrastructure development can create a sound environment in geographically proximate or integrated areas for promoting prosperity of trade and investment. In India, China and Myanmar, a majority of the poor lives in the remote and/or isolated areas, especially in the cross-border regions. These areas urgently need to set up linkage with outside world, through highway, railway, and telecommunication to take advantage of their rich resources or cheap labour. Cross-border infrastructure programmes could make use of complementarities and economies of scale in these geographically contiguous areas. The establishment of physical linkage through transportation and telecommunications would reduce the cost for factor mobility and increase trade and investment.

The development of adequate and good quality transport infrastructure such as road, air, shipping and rail networks in these regions will pave the way towards promoting international trade between the India and her immediate bordering countries and regions. Improving transport infrastructure can generate economic activities in the Northeastern States of India, i.e. increased international trade and that will, in the process, spur development, and improve the quality of life. Better transport facilities are vital in reducing inter- and intra-country inequality. To achieve substantial progress through international trade and economic cooperation, priority should be given to the development of infrastructure facilities (Das, 2000 and 2004; Ghosh and De, 2000; De and Ghosh, 2001 and 2004; De, 2002 and 2004c). Added to this, complimentary policy reforms, accompanied by improved procedural and operational efficiency in the transport sector, are essential for supporting trade liberalization. Naturally, if India, China and Myanmar cooperate with each other by sharing each other's strengths in social and economic infrastructure, the economies of both the countries, particularly regions that are relatively poor, will gain appreciably.

Improvement of transport infrastructure influences both production and household consumption. It leads to a reduction of transport costs and/or travel time. This may give rise to substantial redistribution and spillover effects among economic groups and also among regions. Trade facilitation awaits a number of bilateral and multilateral measures at various levels of complexity. These measures can increase legal trade by reducing transaction costs. What is much more important, they can remove illegal trade, which criminalizes the society, especially in border territories, and poses threats to national security by secret transfer of **areas** and narcotics.

Finally, public and private sector agencies in India, China and Myanmar shall have to pool their resources to launch a comprehensive and systematic entrepreneurship development programme, particularly in India's Northeast. New entrepreneurs, even though working on a small scale, often come up with significant innovations (as in the United States). If such entrepreneurs can hopefully provide original products in the sectors of information technology, biotechnology, or solar/wind energy, these will substantially contribute to poverty alleviation, growth, investment and trade in India, in general, and Northeastern India in particular.

Geographical contiguity can facilitate the exploitation of vast natural endowments (natural gas, coal and hydropower reserves) provided a conducive environment is created at the local level. Whatever the cross-border trade flow happening presently, there is considerable border trade potential between India and China, and India and Myanmar. These potentials can be realized by the creation of proper trade and communication facilities at the border points. Similarly, cross-border investment does not exist at present, but strengthening existing communication facilities between NEI and SCM (Southwest China and Myanmar) will generate cross-border investments. Naturally, closer cooperation among India, China and Myanmar may help in exploiting this vast and unexploited potential of cross-border cooperation for mutual benefit. The significance of such cooperation will be enormous for fostering public-private partnership in enriching the economic life of the concerned regions. This will, moreover, enable both the governments to expand the necessary infrastructure facilities and to adopt favourable policies, which will boost the competitiveness of NEI in the global market.

China, India and Myanmar are great nations that in the past created splendid civilizations in world history. Currently, these three countries are faced with high pressures of population growth, poverty and income disparity. A strong economy can be developed by learning from each other's experiences and complementarities. Some of the areas where Northeast India and Southwest China and Myanmar can cooperate include tourism, education, rail transport, ports and shipping, road transport, media and entertainment, plantation sector, and agro and food processing. Southwest China can contribute to Northeast India's development in several areas. These include infrastructure, particularly roads and airways, logistics, industrial parks, tourism, food processing, and others. Northeast India can also contribute to the development in education, IT services, telecommunication, housing and real estate, etc, in Southwest China and Myanmar. Naturally therefore, concerted and continuous cooperation between India, China and Myanmar will transform the aforesaid complementarities into the development of the concerned regions.

Concluding Remarks

A country or a region's trade volumes depend on many complex details of history, geography, income, infrastructure, administrative barriers, and the structure of demography. In this chapter we have found NEI has great potentials to become an important economic hub on the backdrop of India's growing integration with East. We have to remember that increasing integration of world goods and services are happening at rapid pace in an unprecedented way during last one decade than ever before. Countries (and regions) which have successfully integrated themselves have gone far ahead in reducing costs of transportation in particular and other infrastructure services in general over time and space. As liberalisation continues to reduce artificial barriers, the effective rate of protection provided by costs of transportation and infrastructure services is now in many cases higher than the one provided by tariffs. The lack of adequate transport infrastructure is one of the major barriers to expanding India's trade with the bordering countries. One of the key constraints for developing transport infrastructure is lack of adequate financial resources. The central and local governments and multilateral organisations have an important role to play in cross-border infrastructure development. The available sources of fund include the central government, local government, and multilateral organisations. As most transport infrastructure projects in NEI will not generate high profit in short-term, it is difficult to attract private sector or raise money from local capital markets. On the other hand, local governments in these regions do not have adequate financial resources. Hence, public-private partnerships, particularly involving local governments should be encouraged. The involvement of local governments will ensure ownership, and guarantee whereas that of private sector will provide technical expertise and efficiency as well as financing.

NOTES

1. Regional Integration Agreements (RIAs) have been around for long period of time since 1664 when a custom union of the provinces of France was proposed. As on May 2003, over 265 RIAs had been notified to the WTO, 107 dated from 1990 or after (Schiff and Winters, 2003). About 90 per cent of the RIAs are in the form of free trade arrangements (FTAs) and only 10 per cent are customs unions. WTO has allowed member countries to conclude custom unions and free-trade areas, as an exception to the fundamental principle of non-discrimination set out in the MFN Clause of GATT's Article 1.

2. For example, a customs union of the provinces of France was propose in 1664; Austria signed free trade agreements with five of its neighbours during the 18th and 19th centuries; and the colonial empires were based on preferential trade arrangements (Schiff and Winters, 2003).

3. Most of ASEAN countries have sailed through the severity of the crisis and started to ponder again about the process of their own integration within the regional and global context (Chirathivat, 2001, 2002). South Asian countries had severe geo-political differences for a long time, but they have now realised the importance of regional integration process, and finally, have signed the long-standing Free Trade Agreement at the SAARC Summit held in Islamabad in January 2004.

4. Such as BIMST-EC (Bangladesh, India, Myanmar, Sri Lanka and Thailand–Economic Cooperation), Greater Mekong Subregion (comprising Cambodia, Lao PDR, Myanmar, Vietnam, Thailand and Yunnan province of China), etc. in the last few years.

5. See, for instance, Kumar (2002, 2004), Dutta (2002), RIS (2003).

6. By Asia we mean countries in South, Southeast and East Asia only.

7. Asia produces one-third of world's commercial energy (2001), reserves half of the world's coal and limestone, and one-third of world's oil and natural gas (2001), and preserves world's one-third forest area (2000). For detailed statistical information on Asia's endowments vis-à-vis other regions, see World Resource Institute (2003), and United Nations (2000). See, also UNESCAP (2002) for a detailed survey of the natural resource endowments of Asia.

8. Such as ASEAN-China FTA signed in 2002, BIMST-EC FTA signed in 2004, etc.

9. Although the systematic development of Asia through forming an integrated economic bloc has for some time been an important consideration, there is clear lack of broader policy framework which is required for long term strategy. Moreover, there is dearth of studies to establish an appropriate causality of factors required for policy framework (De, 2004b and 2004c).

10. To name a few of such studies are Sen, Asher and Rajan (2004), Kumar (2002, 2004), De (2003, 2004a), Sarma and Mehta (2002), De and Ghosh (2004a)

11. The incidence of poverty does not count for Tibet Autonomous Region (TAR).

12. Industries already set up in the region are Godrej Sara Lee, Emami, Jyoti Laboratory, Dharampal Satyapal, Kothari

Industries, Hindustan Lever, Ozone Pharmaceutical, Ozone Ayurved Products, Guru Detergents & Chemicals, Shyam Century Ferrous, RCL Cement, Barak Vally Cement, Pancharatna Cement, S M Coke, Pepsi, Composite Jute Mill, Jericho Detergent., DSS Contact, Lafrage, etc. Some of the prominent projects under implementation in the region are H M Cement, Sai Megha Alloys, Smithkline Beecham, LG Electronics, etc.

13. There exists a subregional initiative, called, South Asia Growth Quadrangle (SAGQ) which was constituted in by the Foreign Ministers of Bangladesh, Bhutan, India and Nepal (BBIN) during the Ninth Summit of the South Asian Association for Regional Cooperation (SAARC) on May 1997 in Male. The South Asia Subregional Economic Cooperation (SASEC) of the Asian Development Bank (ADB) has as its objective to identify projects which would support development of South Asia Growth Quadrangle (SACD), endorsed by SAARC in 1997. The membership of SASEC includes Bangladesh, Bhutan, India, and Nepal.

14. Visit, for instance, http://www.adb.org/Documents/CSPs/GMS/2004/RCSP.asp

REFERENCES

Bhattacharyay, B. N. and P. De. 2004. *Promotion of Trade, Investment and Infrastructure Development between India and China: The Case of Southwest China and East and Northeast India*, CESifo Working Paper No. 1334, CESifo, Germany.

Chirathivat, S. 2001. "ASEAN's Enlargement and its Economic Implications", *Chulalongkorn Journal of Economics*, Vol. 13, pp. 229-268.

Chirathivat, S. 2002. "ASEAN-China Free Trade Area: Background, Implications and Future Development", *Journal of Asian Economics*, Vol. 13, pp. 671-686.

Das, Gurudas. 2000. "Trade between the North Eastern Region and Neighbouring Countries: Structures and Implications for Development", in Das, Gurudas and R.K. Purkayastha (ed.), *Border Trade: North East India and Neighbouring Countries*, Akansha Publishing House, New Delhi.

Das, Gurudas. 2004. "Sino-Indian Border Trade for Frontier Development: The Case of India's Northeast and China's

Southwest", in Ray, J. K and P. De (ed.), *India and China in an Era of Globalisation: Essays on Economic Cooperation*, Bookwell, New Delhi.

De, P. 2002. *Kolkata to Kunming Initiative (K2K): An Approach Paper*, Paper presented made at the International Workshop on 'Sino – India Bilateral Relations', Organised by Yunnan Development Research Centre, Kunming, November 19-21.

De, P. 2003. *Changing Profile of Regional Integration Arrangements in South Asia*, Paper presented at the International Workshop on Facilitation of Trade and Transport Cooperation between India and China, Organised by South Asia Research Society, Kolkata and Funded by Indian Council of Social Science Research, New Delhi and Moulana Abul Kalam Azad Institute of Asian Studies (MAKAIAS), Kolkata, November 27-28.

De, P. 2004a. *Transport Cooperation in BIMST-EC: Issues and Way Forward*, Discussion Paper No. 75, Research and Information System for the Non-Aligned and Other Developing Countries, New Delhi.

De, P. 2004b. *Transaction Costs as Barriers to Economic Integration in Asia: An Empirical Exploration*, Discussion Paper No. 77, Research and Information System for the Non-Aligned and Other Developing Countries, New Delhi.

De, P. 2004c. *How Do Transaction Costs Affect International Integration: Empirical Evidence from Asian Economic Community*, Paper presented at the High Level Conference on Asia's Integration at the Asian Development Bank, Manila, July 1-2. This paper also presented at the Institute of Developing Economies (IDE-JETRO), Chiba, Japan on April 30, 2004.

De, P. 2004d. *Deepening India-China Bilateral Cooperation: The Case of India's Northeast and China's Southwest*, Project report submitted to Moulana Abul Kalam Azad Institute of Asian Studies (MAKAIAS), Kolkata.

De, P. and B. Ghosh. 2001. "Transport Infrastructure and Economic Performance of Bangladesh and Indian Bordering States," *BIISS Journal*, Vol. 22, No. 4.

De, P. and B. Ghosh. 2003. *How Do Infrastructure Facilities Affect Regional Income? An Investigation with South Asian Countries*, Discussion Paper No. 66, Research and Information System for the Non-Aligned and Other Developing Countries, New Delhi.

De, P. and B. Ghosh. 2004a. "Deepening Cooperation in the BIMST-EC: A Case for Transport Integration", *BIISS Journal*, Vol. 25, No. 2.

De, P. and B. Ghosh. 2004b. "India in the BIMST-EC: Some Issues", *India Quarterly*, Vol. LIX, No. 3 & 4.

Dutta, M. 2002. "Asian Economic Community: Intra-Community Macro-and-Micro-Economic Parameters", *Journal of Asian Economics*, Vol. 13, pp. 447-491.

Ghosh, B. and P. De. 2000. "Infrastructure, Economic Growth and Trade in SAARC", *BIISS Journal*, Vol. 21, No. 2.

Ghosh, B. and P. De. 2004. "How Do Different Categories of Infrastructure Affect Development? Evidence from Indian States", *Economic and Political Weekly*, Vol. 39, No. 42.

Government of India. 1997. *High Level Commission Report to the Prime Minister: Transforming the Northeast: Tackling Backlogs in Basic Minimum Services and Infrastructural Needs*, New Delhi.

Kumar, N. 2002. *Towards an Asian Economic Community—Vision of Closer Economic Cooperation in Asia: An Overview*, Discussion Paper 32, Research and Information System for Non-Aligned and Other Developing Countries, New Delhi.

Kumar, N. 2004. *Towards an Asian Economic Community: Vision of a New Asia*, Research and Information System for Non-Aligned and Other Developing Countries, New Delhi.

North East Federation on International Trade (NEFIT). 2004. *Potential of Export from North-East to South-East Asia*, Paper presented by Mr. Sunil Kumar, General Secretary, NEFIT at the National Seminar on 'Promotion of Border Trade between India's North East and Myanmar: Problems and Prospects', Organised by ICSSR-NERC, held at Imphal, Manipur, November 8-9.

Okita, S. 1989. "Policy Approaches to the Problem", In L. Emmerji (ed.), *One World or Several?* OECD Development Centre, Paris.

Ray, J. K. and P. De. 2003. *Promotion of Trade and Investment in Eastern South Asia Subregion*, New Delhi: Bookwell.

Ray, J. K and P. De. 2004. *India and China in an Era of Globalisation: Essays on Economic Cooperation*, New Delhi: Bookwell.

Research and Information System for Non-Aligned and Other Developing Countries. 2003. *Relevance of an Asian Economic Community*, RIS Policy Briefs 1, New Delhi.

Sarma, A. and P. K. Mehta. 2002. *Exploring Indo-ASEAN Economic Partnership in Globalizing World*, New Delhi: Bookwell.

Schiff, M and L. A. Winters, 2003. *Regional Integration and Development*, New York: Oxford University Press.

Sen, Rahul, M. G. Asher and R. S. Rajan. 2004. ASEAN-India Economic Relations: Current Status and Future Prospects, Discussion Paper No. 73, Research and Information System for the Non-Aligned and Other Developing Countries, New Delhi.

Singh, B. P. 1987. *The Problem of Change: A Study of North-East India*, New Delhi: Oxford University Press.

Srinivasan, T. N. 2002. *Trade, Finance and Investment in South Asia*, New Delhi: Social Science Press.

United Nations Economic and Social Commission for Asia and Pacific. 2002. *Mineral Resources Assessment, Development and Management Series*, Vol. 8, Bangkok.

United Nations. 2000. *Industrial Commodity Statistics Yearbook*, New York.

Verghese, B. G. 1997. *India's Northeast Resurgent: Ethnicity, Insurgency, Governance, Development*, New Delhi: Konark Publishers.

World Resource Institute. 2003. *World Resources 2002-2004*, Washington.

[Views and opinions expressed in this chapter are the authors' personal, and may not necessarily be attributed to his institution. The usual disclaimers apply.]

7

Export Potential and Promotion of Trade between India's North-East and Neighbouring Countries

—Sunil Kumar

An Overview of North-East India

The North-Eastern Region of India comprising 8 states viz., Arunachal Pradesh, Assam, Manipur, Meghalaya, Mizoram, Nagaland, Sikkim and Tripura occupies an area of 2,62,264 sq.kms (accounting nearly 8 per cent of the country's total area) with a population of 3,98,35,582 (accounting for 3.88 per cent of the country's total population) as per 2001 Census. North-East has the longest international border with 5 foreign countries viz., Bhutan, Nepal, China, Myanmar and Bangladesh. The total length of the international border is more than 5000 kms. (N.E-Bangladesh 1640 km, N.E-Myanmar 1450 km, N.E-China 1000 km, N.E-Bhutan 650 km).

The North-East Region shares around 2 per cent of her border with the mainland of the country and around 98 per cent with Bhutan, China, Nepal, Myanmar and Bangladesh. Therefore the entire region can be considered as landlocked. This geographical disadvantage in terms of its proximity with the rest of the country can be turned into a boon with proper strategy and planning. It is important for the North Eastern states to come together and to avail of the geo-strategic position of the region to open up the areas as an 'entrepot' to South-East Asia. The NE states with its vast potential of mineral resources, hydro potential, agro-horticultural potential and tourism can become the golden gate of South-East Asian economy.

With the recent introduction of the first international flight between Guwahati and Bangkok, it is expected that trade between NE states and South-East Asian countries will increase tremendously in the near future. Other international Airlines like Druk Airline (Bhutan), Royal Nepal Airlines (Nepal), Biman Airlines (Bangladesh) and Union of Myanmar Airlines (Myanmar) should be allowed to operate their flights via Guwahati International Airport connecting to South-East Asian countries.

There are also proposals to open up the old Ledo-Burma Road falling under Assam and Arunachal Pradesh commonly known as Stilwell Road to facilitate trade and commerce between Myanmar, China and South-East Asian countries and the North-East.

It is high time for the NE states to take initiative to establish Free Trades Zones (FTZ), Special Economic Zones (SEZ), Export Processing Zones (EPZ), Export Oriented Units (EOUs), Export Promotion Industrial Parks (EPIP), Software Technology Parks (STP), Food Parks, Agri Export Zones (AEZ) etc., to boost export from the region and drive maximum benefits from the expanding global market.

The process of globalisation and liberalisation has opened up the economy of North-East which will lead to the expansion of trade relations with the neighbouring countries. It is being felt that border trade and opening up of the North-East may generate growth impulse in the stagnant economy of the region. North-East should take full advantage of this globalization by converting this geographical handicap into an opportunity.

Blessed with an abundance of natural, mineral and energy resources and an extremely beautiful landscape complemented by a highly literate population, the region is a fertile ground

Table: 7.1
North East at a Glance

Item	*A. P.*	*Assam*	*Manipur*	*Meghalaya*	*Mizoram*	*Nagaland*	*Tripura*	*Sikkim*
Area (Sq.km)	83743	78438	22327	22489	21087	16579	10492	7096
Total Population	1091117	26638407	2388634	2306069	891658	1988636	3191168	540493
Density of Population	13	340	107	102	42	120	304	76
Literacy rate (%)	54.74	64.28	68.87	63.31	88.49	67.11	73.66	69.68
Capital	Itanagar	Dispur	Imphal	Shillong	Aizwal	Kohima	Agartala	Gangtok
Major Crops	Rice, Maize, Millet, Wheat, Pulses, Sugarcane	Rice, Maize, Wheat, Jute, Cotton, Sugarcane	Maize, Oil Seeds, Pulse, Rice, Sugarcane, Wheat	Rice, Maize, Jute	Rice, Maze.	Rice, Sugarcane, Cotton, Jute.	Rice, Sugarcane, Cotton, Jute	Maize, Rice, Wheat, Potato
Major Plantation	Rubber, Coffee, Tea	Tea, Rubber, Coffee	Rubber, Coffee	Rubber, Coffee.	Rubber, Coffee, Tea.	Rubber, Coffee, Tea	Tea, Rubber, Coffee.	Large Cardamon of tea.
Fruits & Spices	Pineapple, Apple, Orange, Guava, Ginger, Grape	Banana, Orange, Pineapple, Onion	Potato, Pea	Banana, Pineapple, Guava, Ginger, Chilli, Uranium	Banana, Pineapple, Orange, Chilies, Ginger.	Banana, Pineapple, Ginger, Garlic	Banana, Orange, Mango, Guava, Pineapple.	Pineapple, Organe, Guava, Ginger, Banana.

(Contd...)

Item	*A.P.*	*Assam*	*Manipur*	*Meghalaya*	*Mizoram*	*Nagaland*	*Tripura*	*Sikkim*
Mineral	Coal, Limestone, Petroleum, Dolomite	Coal, Limestone, Petroleum, Gas, Granite, Iron Ore, Quarizite, Building Stone	Chzomite, Limestone, Day Nickel-Cobalt	Coal, Sillimianit, Limestone, Dolomite, Felspar, Gas, Kaolin, Iron Ore, Glass sand, Quartz	Limestone, Natural Gas, Construction Material	Coal, Limestone, Petroleum, Slate, Magnetite	Gas, Glass and Clays, Construction, Material.	Dolomite Graphite, Limestone, Silliminite, Talc
Forestry (% of Area)	82.21	30.20	77.87	69.70	86.99	85.43	54.79	36.20

Source: Data compiled from websites of NE States.

for entrepreneurs. The proposed Asian highway and Trans Asian Railway will connect the region with South-East Asian countries like Myanmar, Thailand, Laos, Cambodia, Indonesia and even Singapore. Besides the energy resources, the region is congenial for setting up export units and business houses.

The products that are currently exported from the region are as follows: tea, cotton, jute, pineapple products, medicinal herbs, broomstick, tejpatta, orchids, limestone, coal, tea processing machinery, handloom textiles, woollen carpets, cane and bamboo products.

The region has a rich agro-climatic condition which is ideally suited to produce whole range of plantation crops (including tea, rubber, coffee and cashew), spices, fruits and vegetables, flowers and herbs. The forest resources are rich, offering valuable wood, medicinal plants and roots, orchids, cut flowers, etc. It is estimated that 10.69 per cent of the forest produce requirement of the country is met from the forests of the region. The region is also well known for its traditional art and crafts, especially in the field of handloom textiles and handicraft products.

The North-East Region of India is still untapped as an export opportunity. A good market survey, excellent product pricing, packaging etc. and a will to sell globally can pay rich dividends to any enterprising businessman wishing to tap the rich natural resources and very talented and skilled manpower of the region.

India's trade with South-East Asia

Before we discuss the export potential of North Eastern region to South-East Asian countries, let us look at India's trade with these countries. Table 7.2 shows that India's trade with the South-East Asian countries is increasing over time since early 1990s. The volume of South-East Asia-India trade has increased from about US $ 4 billion in 1993-94 to US $ 12 billion in 2002–2003. India mainly exports fruits and vegetables, electronic goods, chemicals, drugs and pharmaceuticals, cotton yarn, engineering goods, vehicles, gems and jewelry, meat products and machinery and instruments.

Table 7.2
Exports/Imports From India to South-East Asia

(Value in U.S. $ Million)

Year	*Export*	*Import*	*Total Trade*	*Balance of Trade*
1993-94	1981.72	1950.00	3931.71	(+)31.71
1994-95	2326.27	3059.50	5385.76	(-)733.23
1995-96	31.77.77	3881.88	7059.65	(-)704.11
1996-97	3353.47	4492.58	7846.04	(-)1139.12
1997-98	2987.21	5177.91	8165.12	(-)2190.70
1998-99	2090.35	5865.13	7955.48	(-)3774.78
1999-00	2721.05	6281.73	9002.78	(-)3560.68
2000-01	3362.20	5210.49	8572.69	(-)1848.31
2001-02	3945.66	5767.12	9712.98	(-)1821.26
2002-03	5219.16	6565.61	11784.77	(-)1346.45

Source: Ministry of Commerce website: www.commerce.nic.in

However, there exists a huge potential for India's export to ASEAN. India's percentage share to each of the main 10 ASEAN imports is only meager (Table 7.3). This shows that there is ample scope for Indian industries to invest in these areas and enhance their export performances.

Table 7.3
India's share in ASEAN's top 10 commodities of import, 2002-3

S.No.	*Commodities*	*Value of imports**	*India's share**	*% of India's share*
1.	Machinery & electrical appliances	151,173.8	16.9	0.67
2.	Mineral Products	37,552.4	172.8	0.46
3.	Chemicals	22,246.0	487.2	2.19
4.	Base metal and metal articles	20,532.9	364.5	1.78
5.	Vehicles	17,038.6	77.7	0.46
6.	Textiles & Apparel	11,103.9	234.8	2.11
7.	Plastics	10,994.1	77.9	0.71
8.	Optical, precision & musical instruments	8.981.4	28.2	0.31
9.	Prepared foods	7,140.9	272.8	3.82
10.	Vegetable products	5,397.7	242.7	4.50

Source : Ministry of Commerce website

North-East India's Trade with the Neighbouring Countries

Of all the neighbouring countries, North-East India's Bangladesh trade is most important. Almost 50 per cent of the region's export go to Bangladesh (Table 7.4). The region enjoys favourable trade balance with Bangladesh. Much of the exports to Bangladesh consist of minerals (Table 7.5). Besides minerals, the region also exports some amount of agro-horticultural products.

Table: 7.4
North Eastern Region's Trade with neighbouring countries

Year	*Total Export*	*To B-desh*	*To Myanmar*	*To Other Countries*	*Total Import*	*From B-Desh*	*From Myanmar*
1997-98	389.69	NA	22.45	NA	49.25	NA	35.9
1998-99	406.54	NA	5.60	NA	22.10	NA	3.75
1999-2000	395.89	169.81	3.31	220.43	18.75	9.44	6.68
2000-2001	404.07	151.27	5.52	251.44	19.57	7.19	12.36
2001-2002	379.95	186.13	1.23	197.11	15.94	5.50	7.59
2002-2003	410.07	201.99	4.96	202.41	20.79	6.13	11.83
2003-2004	434.96	NA	9.41	NA	33.28	NA	13.18

Source: Custom, Shillong

Table 7.5
Major export items from north Eastern Region

Year		1999-2000	2000-2001	2001-2002	2002-2003
Item	*Mainly Exported through*	*Value (Rs. Crore)*	*Value (Rs. Crore)*	*Value (Rs. Crore)*	*Value (Rs. Crore)*
Tea	Inland Container Depot Amingoan, Guwahati	219.59	250.32	195.64	200.73
Coal	LCSs of Indo-Bangladesh border in Meghalaya, Assam	105.62	135.87	150.67	188.61
Limestone	-do-	29.20	4.34	52.44	4.46
Ginger	LCSs of Indo-Bangladesh border in Meghalaya, Assam, Tripura	2.27	0.26	2.75	26.06
Boulder stone	LCSs of Indo-Bangladesh border in Meghalaya, Assam	1.42	1.43	0.30	0.06
Crushed stone/ stone chips	-do-	2.57	2.19	1.88	1.93
Fruits (including citrus fruits, oranges, pears, pineapples, jackfruit, grapes etc.)	LCSs of Indo-Bangladesh border in Meghalaya, Assam, Tripura	0.56	0.95	1.36	1.12

(Contd...)

Year		*1999-2000*	*2000-2001*	*2001-2002*	*2002-2003*
Item	*Mainly Exported through*	*Value (Rs. Crore)*	*Value (Rs. Crore)*	*Value (Rs. Crore)*	*Value (Rs. Crore)*
Dry fish	LCSs of Indo-Bangladesh border in Tripura	0.23	0.06	0.20	0.002
Vegetables (including tomato, cauliflower etc.)	LCSs of Indo-Bangladesh border in Assam and Tripura	0.05	0	0.05	0.02
Soyabari	Moreh	2.24	4.43	0.97	1.28
Cumin Seed	-do-	0.13	0.47	0.12	1.91
Perfumery compound	LGBI	0.03	0.24	0.39	0.72
Other miscellaneous goods		**32.11**	**11.23**	**2.59**	**NA**

Source: Office of the Commissioner of Customs, Shillong. LCS= Land Custom Station

Potential Export Items of North-East India

1. *Agro-Horticulture Based Products*

NER has been ranked 6th among the top 25 bio-diversity spots in the world, a genetic treasure house of plants, animals and micro-biological resources and boast of a whopping 13,500 species of plants and 2185 varieties of vertebrates.

North-East's strength lies in agriculture, horticulture, floriculture, sericulture, etc. However, the region suffers from disadvantages like inadequate and limited public and private investment. Hence not much value addition takes place. There is utter absence of post-harvest management. Yield in agriculture has been low due to the absence of modern inputs. Ministry of Commerce and Industry, Government of India, in new Exim policy, has formulated a special policy called Vishesh Krishi Upaj Yojana in which plenty of benefits have been offered to the farmers.

We can setup following units for export from North-East.

a) **Horticulture Based Units**—like food processing, mushroom cultivation and processing.

b) **Biotechnology Based Units**—This industry is essentially knowledge-based and can function with minimum resources and limited transportation infrastructure.

c) **Tissue Culture and Orchid Units**—With orchids having a high value realization in the international markets, and Northeast accounting for 400 species of the 1300 found in India, large scale commercial exploitation in a systematic and scientific manner through tissue culture is viable. Floriculture too can be exploited in a similar way.

d) **Spices, Oleoresin and other Essential Oils Units**— A number of spices and aromatic plants grow in different parts of Northeast that can be used for the production of high value export items such as spice oils, oleoresin and other essential oils.

e) **Medicinal Plants, Tea, Rubber, Coffee & Cashew—** Medicinal plants have a good potential for development in Northeast. Commercially viable medicinal plants need to be identified and their potential assessed, based on which drugs and pharmaceuticals units would be encouraged. Northeast has good potential for cultivation of tea, coffee, cashew and rubber although their processing though large scale plantation activities has not been taken up in an organized scale.

2. *Animal Husbandry and Meat Processing Industries*

Given the large demand-supply gap of meat, Northeast needs units for hygienic and scientific processing of poultry, piggery and other meat products. The region has a high potential for development of dairy and allied products as well as for processing of animal hides and skins and for setting up leather industries.

3. *Development of Minerals based industries*

Northeast is rich in minerals like high grade limestone, coal, granite, sillimanite, industrial clay, quartz, feldspar, etc. The following mineral based industries have high potentials:

(a) **Coal-Based Industries**—Northeast produces large quantities of coal of very high calorific value with low ash content but high sulphur content. This coal can be used for production of several chemicals and other industrial products.

(b) **Limestone Based Industries**—The region has large deposits of limestone. The quality of this deposit varies from cement grade to chemical grade. The following projects are economically viable: cement plants, lime plants, calcium carbide plants, bleaching powder units, precipitated calcium carbonate units and clinker plant.

(c) Other potential mineral based industries that can come up in the region are as follows: granite mining and polishing, clay washery, sillimanite refractory and other allied industries, ceramic glazed tiles, cement based mosaic tiles, ceramic crockery and ceramic low tension insulators.

4. *Electronics and Information Technology*

The state governments may encourage setting up of electronic-based industries and complexes in the sphere of information technology in private sector and/or joint sector. Potential estimated by NASSCOM-Mckinsey study that India alone can export 81,000 crore worth IT enable services. The state governments of the region may formulate information technology (IT) policy to reap the vast potential of IT and technology related services. The state governments may expedite setting up of Software Technology Park to tap the vast English speaking population and educated unemployed youths of the region.

5. *Power Potential*

North-East has enormous recourses for producing power to the tune of 70,000 MW which can be exported to neighbouring countries as well as main land of India.

6. *Tourism Export*

The region is a land of pristine beauty. We have everything to offer which today's tourists want. We have lovely forest reserves which are foreigners delight in today's polluted world. We have water falls, majestic mountains, wild life, history, pilgrimages, temples, different language, customs, traditions, folklore, festivals etc. We can promote adventure tourism, eco tourism, cultural tourism, lake tourism, hill tourism, religious tourism, heritage tourism etc.

7. *Bamboo Based Projects*

North-East is one of the pioneer in bamboo processing and value addition. States should prepare master plan for upgradation of existing units as well as setting up of new plants in public/private/joint sector to harness the resources available in the region.

8. *Handloom and Handicraft*

North-East has long tradition in handloom and handicraft industry which can be developed on priority basis to give much needed employment opportunity as well as to earn livelihood of village population. State governments may prepare blue print to develop handloom and handicraft industry in a big way by developing rural cluster and associating Self Help Group, NGO, Village Council etc.

Table 7.6
Status of Land Custom Stations in North Eastern Region

SL. No.	*State*	*Name OF LCS and EPs.*	*Functional/ Non-Functional.*	*Counter Part L.C.S*
1.	MEGHALAYA	Dawki	Functional	Tamabil, Bangladesh
2.	MEGHALAYA	Bholaganj	Functional	Chattak, do
3.	MEGHALAYA	Borsora	Functional	Borsora, do
4.	MEGHALAYA	Shella bazaar	Functional	Chatak, do
5.	MEGHALAYA	Rynku	Non-Functional	
6.	MEGHALAYA	Baghmara	Functional	Bijoypur, do
7.	MEGHALAYA	Dalu	Functional	Nakugoan, do
8.	MEGHALAYA	Ghasuapara	Functional	Karaituli, Gobrakura,
9.	MEGHALAYA	Mahendraganj	Functional	Dhanua Kamalpur
10.	TRIPURA	Agartala	Functional	Akhaura, Bangladesh
11.	TRIPURA	Sabroom	Denotified	

(Contd...)

12.	TRIPURA	Srimantapur	Functional	Bibirbazar, Bangladesh
13.	TRIPURA	Muhurighat	Non-Functional	
14.	TRIPURA	Khowaighat	Non-Functional	
15.	TRIPURA	Dholaighat	Non-Functional	
16.	TRIPURA	Old Raghna Bazar	Functional	Juri-Batuli, Bangladesh
17.	TRIPURA	Manu	Non-Functional	
18.	ASSAM	Karimganj ferry & S.G.	Functional	Zakiganj, Bangladesh
19.	ASSAM	Sutarkandi	Functional	Sheola,Bangladesh
20.	ASSAM	Mahisasan R. STN.	Non-Functional	
21.	ASSAM	Silchar RMS Office	Non-Functional	
22.	ASSAM	Dhubri Steamer ghat	Non-Functional	
23.	ASSAM	Golakganj	Non-Functional	
24.	ASSAM	Guwahati Steamer ghat	Functional	
25.	ASSAM	Mankachar	Functional	
26.	ASSAM	Hattisar	Functional	
27.	ASSAM	Darranga	Functional	Samdrup, Jongkhar, Bhutan
28.	ASSAM	Ultapani	Non-Functional	
29.	ASSAM	ICD Amingoan	Functional	
30.	ASSAM	IGBI Airport.	Functional	
31.	ARUNACHAL PRADESH	Nampong	Non-Functional	
32.	MIZORAM	Demagiri	Non-Functional	
33.	MIZORAM	Champhai	Non-Functional	
34.	MANIPUR	Moreh	Functional	Tamu, Myanmar

Source: Office of the Commissioner of Customs, Shillong.
EP=Export Points

Measures suggested for the promotion of cross-border trade

North-East has 35 Land Custom Stations connected with Bangladesh, Myanmar and Bhutan. However, out of them only 15 are functioning properly. North-East Federation on International Trade (NEFIT) suggests the following measures to enhance border trade from the region.

1. *Development of infrastructure at Land Customs Station (LCS)*

A. *Road network*

- Improvement and construction of double lane road, RCC bridges etc, leading to all the Land Customs Stations (LCSs) of NER.
- Opening of Stillwell Road at Ledo linking central Myanmar and China on priority basis.
- Re-opening of Karimganj-Sylhet-Dhaka road for transportation.
- Extension of Amguri-Mukokchung-Twenchong Road linking Myanmar.
- Extension of Sibsagar, Sonari-Nemtola Road from Assam-Nagaland border to Lungwa in Myanmar.
- Upgradation of N.H.39 and 53 connecting Indo-Myanmar border via Dimapur and Silchar.
- Connection to Trans Asian Highways.
- Construction on priority basis 1300 km long trilateral highway connecting India, Myanmar and Thailand.

B. *Railways*

- Restore Mohisashan (Assam, India)-Shahbazpur (Bangladesh) railway traffic to facilitate export of bulk mineral (coal, limestone), food items and agro-horticulture based products from NER.

- Double tracking of the railway line from new Jalpaiguri to Tinsukia.
- Extend the Inland Container Depot, facility at Silchar, Moreh and Dimapur.
- Connection with Trans Asian Railways to North-East is must for faster movement of goods from the region.

C. *Airways*

- Creation of an air travel circuit between North-East and Bhutan, Nepal, Bangladesh, Myanmar, China, Thailand, Singapore is a must to increase export and tourism from the region.
- Provide an Air Cargo Complex at LGB Airport, Guwahati to cater to export and import of goods.
- Creation of better air connectivity between all the Northeastern states.

D. *Water-ways*

- Opening up and improvement of inland water-ways with Bangladesh and Myanmar through a number of river port existing in North-East.
- Declaration of Jogighopa, Moreh, Dawki and Karimganj as port of call.

E. *Buildings*

- Construction of integrated export complex including customs office, immigration, banking, clearing and forwarding agents buildings, truck parking bay, warehouses, cold storage facilities, post offices, telephone exchange, shopping centres, BSF complex, police outpost, electronic weigh bridges, electricity, portable drinking water facility etc at all the notified LCSs of NER.

- Development of border town and trade centre at major LCSs of NER.
- Opening of more border trading points with adequate infrastructural facilities and upgrading the infrastructure at non-functional LCS of the region.

2. *Quality Control Laboratory*

On major LCS of NER, set up organisational infrastructure like inspection house, testing facility etc. for easy issuance of phyto sanitary certificate, commodity inspection, radio-active free certificate etc. for boosting export from the region.

3. *Banking*

- Create adequate banking infrastructure for international trade and border trade in the North East, the banks functioning in the North-East should have correspondent arrangements with banks in neighbouring countries. At present this correspondent relationship are restricted to the banks functioning in Kolkata.
- Relaxation of RBI guidelines which stipulate that a bank branch need to transact a minimum of 10 crore foreign currency annually for entitlement and retention of foreign currency transaction rights. A high value currency chest may be installed at major towns near LCSs.
- Letter of Credit (LoC) arrangement between the banks of India and Myanmar need to be further regularized and institutionalised for smooth and enhanced border trade through Moreh.

- Letter of Credit advising charge may be reduced considering LOC value less then US $ 20,000. Nationalised banks may charge Rs 200/- for LoC advising instead of existing Rs.5,00/-.

Organisational Changes

- The State Level Export Promotion Committee Meeting should be held regularly by states so as to assess the status of border trade in the region and also to undertake immediate action on any problems faced thereof.
- Opening up of all the Export Promotion Council Offices relevant for North-East to facilitate export.
- It is also felt that North East Export Promotion Council should be set up to facilitate market information, to educate potential exporters and to do export promotion from the North-East.
- A local federation may be recognised by Ministry of Commerce and may be given the authority to utilize and disburse fund for various export developmental activities and to promote export from the region.
- Priority may be accorded to set up Export Promotion Industrial Park, Export Processing Zone, Special Economic Zone, Agri Export Zone, Software Technology Park, Export Oriented Units, Free Trade Zone with neighbouring countries to promote export from the region.
- Create an interactive website with all the relevant local, national and international information that would facilitate trade from the region. This website will also ensure that the interaction between the traders of NER and the traders of the neighbouring countries is productive and focused.

5. *Role of Border Management Force (BMF)*

Role of BMF in regard to export should be specifically defined and clear instructions in this regard should be circulated to BSF/Assam Riffles authorities for hassle free export movement. Otherwise, BSF/Assam Riffles authorities create a lot of problems for clearance of consignment, which is already cleared by the customs authorities. Even BSF/Assam Riffles authorities defy the timing of export on the pretext of shortage of manpower or some other excuse and they impose their own timings for export operations.

6. *Other suggestions*

a) Ministry of Commerce should take up with the Government of Bangladesh/Myanmar to give access to Chittagong Port/Mandley Port for exports from the NER to the outside world.

b) Ministry of Commerce should take up with the Ministry of External Affairs to open Counsel offices of neighbouring countries such as Nepal, Bhutan, Bangladesh, Myanmar, China, Thailand etc .in North -East which is very important to facilitate trade and commerce.

c) The Ministry of Commerce may take immediate steps to formulate North-East Exim Policy to provide incentive for export and to create required infrastructure.

d) A separate Zonal Joint Director General of Foreign Trade-cum-Development Commissioner office may be set up at Guwahati with the jurisdiction over entire Northeastern states including Sikkim.

e) North-East Council (NEC) should play a major role in the creation of infrastructure for development of export from the region and co-ordinate export promotion efforts in this region with various ministries of the Government of India.

f) Bus service along Guwahati-Imphal-Mandalay, Guwahati-Dhaka via Shillong and Guwahati-Tura-Dhaka routes may also be introduced which will facilitate easier movement of the business community. Connection with Trans Asian Highways and Railways will facilitate faster movement of goods and services from NER to South-East Asia.

g) For the development of professional manpower and creation of entrepreneurship in the field of foreign trade, government may set up a branch of Indian Institute of Foreign Trade (IIFT) in North-East.

h) Ministry of Commerce and Ministry of Foreign Affairs may request Bangladesh and Myanmar to provide transit facility and allow North-Eastern States to use Chittagong/ Mandalay port for export/ import goods to and from foreign countries.

i) The regulation of CITES certification for border trade of this flora and fauna could be reformulated taking into account the area specific situations.

j) Agricultural products at present could only pass through Karimganj, Agartala and Guwahati international Airport. It is therefore suggested that other major LCSs in the region should also be provided with systematic quarantine checking systems and set up plant-quarantine office at major LCS of the NER.

7. *To reduce informal trade the following measures may be considered*

a) A special package of incentives like Duty Entitlement Pass Book Scheme (DEPB) at enhanced rate of additional 1 per cent may be considered for export affected from L.C.S of North Eastern region in order to compensate the geographical or locational disadvantage of the region.

b) In order to bring the huge informal trade into formal trade and to encourage trade with the neighbouring countries, a special scheme in the line of duty free REP licensing scheme @ 5 per cent of F.O.B value of exports may be introduced from this region to allow the import of products from neighbouring country for payment of custom duty through this mechanism.

(c) Road transport subsidy and air freight subsidy @ 90 per cent should be considered for all the items of export through L.C.S/airport or nearest port of call located in the region since the exporters of the region have to pay double freight charge, as there is no or little import through various L.C.S of the North Eastern Region.

(d) Government of India, Bangladesh and Myanmar may take steps to declare the entire North-East Region including Sikkim as Free Trade Zone with Bangladesh and Myanmar.

(e) To check informal trade Government of India should expand the list of tradable goods and commodities under barter mechanism to the neighbouring countries of NER.

8

Trade and Development: Interrelations and Interdependence

—Ajitava Raychaudhuri

Introduction

Trade and Development are topics discussed separately as well as together for years now. The important thing is the change in the orientation of the discussion of the interrelation and interdependence of trade and development in the last few years. Broadly speaking, the earlier debate centred around the efficiency of export led growth versus import led industrialisation. The success stories in the former strategy are the Newly Industrialised Countries in the East and South-East Asia. The not so success stories in the latter are the countries in the Latin America, India and China. The major criterion for measuring success is growth. Lately, a shift of emphasis to poverty eradication and income distribution is noticeable. However, the overriding idea till the end of the last century was that growth really is the most important variable that determines the other variables like the extent of employment and poverty. However, the UN sponsored Millennium Development Goals have put aspects like targeted reforms and income distribution to the forefront which is not automatically taken care of by economic and trade reforms.

The present chapter is divided in the following sections— the first section is an overview of the trade openness and development scenario in the last few decades. The second section discusses the old theories of trade and development. The third section takes up the new theories of trade and growth. The fourth section takes up the policy issues emanating from the discussions in the preceding sections.

I

An Overview of Trade and Development issues

The pattern of world trade has undergone tremendous change in the last two decades. To quote UNCTAD Trade and Development Report 2002, the share of developing countries in the total world trade has gone up from 1/4th to 1/3rd. Manufactures, which was a mere 20 per cent of total exports from the developing countries in the 1970s went up to 70 per cent in the 1990s. The share of agricultural exports went down from 20 per cent to 10 per cent in the same period. The share of minerals and oil exports was in the downward direction too. At the same time, the share of developed countries in world income (in current dollars) increased from less than 73 per cent in 1980 to 77 per cent in 1999, while that of the developing countries remained at a constant figure of 20 per cent. This points to a pattern that emerged during the 1980s and 1990s- namely there was concentration of exports in the hands of a few East Asian countries in the developing world and the terms of trade of manufactures might have moved against the developing countries in general (Maizels, 1998).

A similar debate centres around the topic whether globalisation has done anything good for the developing countries. This is crucial since the mid-eighties and the nineties are characterised as the phase for trade openness, economic reforms and globalisation. Dollar and Kraay (2001) have gone into this question with a large data set. They reminded at the outset that the lower trade volumes of the developing countries reflect both the tariff and non-tariff barriers. Thus if globalisation implies increased trade openness and lowering of average tariff rates then it addresses one part of the problem. The other part lies in a number of non-tariff (or non-price) barriers like quotas, local content requirements and different kind of standards like labour and environmental. The authors make three points from their dataset—first, globalisers have an increase in trade to GDP ratio from 16 per cent to 33 per cent between 1970s to 1990s, which includes countries like China, Argentina, Brazil, Thailand, Malaysia etc. The second point is that globalisers experienced faster growth in the decades of 1980s and 1990s compared to non-globalisers and other rich OPEC countries. Among the spectacular cases are growth between 1980-84 and 1995-97 of Argentina (8.4 percentage points), China (3.9 percentage points), Mexico (6.5 percentage points) and the Philippines (6.2 percentage points). The third important finding is that globalisation and income inequality have mixed results where countries like China has experienced worsening of income distribution but other countries like India, Malaysia and Thailand have experienced better income equality. The point is how far is this trend results from the increased trade openness of the countries? It is always difficult to isolate impact of one event from a host of others when things move simultaneously.

The other major observation as highlighted by the previously mentioned UNCTAD Trade and Development Report 2003 is that although the developing countries are exporting a larger percentage of their products, their share in the skill intensive products is still low. Only some countries could make inroads in these products, although these are the fastest growing products in world trade. Thus, in electronic and computer related products, only few developing countries could participate as against a large participation in readymade garments or leather exports.

Another related issue often raised is the role of foreign aid in promoting economic growth. In the traditional two gap models, the developing countries suffer from low domestic savings rates and require foreign exchange to overcome it. The following tables summarise some of the stylised facts to understand the positions of the countries in the world map of growth and prosperity.

Table 8.1
Some Relevant Indicators of Development

Country/Region	*Annual percentage change of Real GDP (Base-1987)*		*ODA as percent of GNP*		*Percentage change in Manufacturing Terms of Trade with EU (NBTT)*
	1981-90	*1991-97*	*1991*	*1996*	*1979-94*
High Income	3.1	2.1	-	-	-
Developing	3.0	3.1	1.5	0.9	-2.2
East Asian	7.7	9.9	1.0	0.6	-1.2
Latin American	1.9	3.4	0.5	0.5	-3.6
South Asia	5.7	5.7	2.3	1.1	-
Sub-Saharan	1.9	2.2	6.3	5.3	-5.7

Source: 1) Real GDP growth data from Global Economic Prospects, World Bank, 1998/99
2) ODA data from World Development Report, 1998/99
3) Manufacturing Terms of Trade (TOT) data from Maizels et al.(1998)

Note: ODA is Official Development Assistance; NBTT is Net Barter Terms of Trade

The table above shows that the East Asian countries that have high savings rates required less official assistance, but they experienced high growth. The South Asian economies had lower savings rates and had higher official assistance, but they have much lower growth compared to the East Asian countries. Thus higher domestic savings rates cannot be substituted by foreign aid. However, the adverse terms of trade exist as a common factor for the developing countries irrespective of their geographical location.

But the movement of terms of trade in the present decades has an important dimensional difference than what happened in the earlier part of the twentieth century. The phenomenon of falling terms of trade (TOT) in international trade, which

Prebisch (1950), Singer (1950) and Lewis (1969) termed as the key to unfair trade and asymmetric welfare in the world, may not be ultimately so bad as it might appear. The major point is that the current world differs from Prebisch-Singer-Lewis world in one vital dimension–South (or developing countries) also now specialises in manufacturing as opposed to primary goods in many cases. Thus falling TOT and high growth may coexist together leading to the idea that welfare in the South may be improving through trade in spite of falling TOT.

Among the other important characteristics to be highlighted one is that the countries having highest growth are seen having low foreign aid levels too. At the same time, the better performers are not the ones who devote higher GNP to domestic R & D activities. However, they are the ones who have a high proportion of their imports devoted to machinery and equipments imports from the North (or, the old developed countries like EU or USA) (Yeats, 1998). Also, the same set of high performers is the ones who have reduced the illiteracy among adult population drastically.

Empirical support to the above came initially from Easterly et al (1994) and Coe and Helpman (1995). Coe and Helpman showed that for developed countries, openness with countries having larger Research and Development (R & D) produce the maximum change of total factor productivity (TFP). Coe, Helpman and Hoffmaister (1995) extended it to developing country data and showed that they benefit from foreign (or North's) R & D as well as domestic skilled labour. Their findings did support the view that trade in intermediate products (which includes machineries and equipments), which embody the fruits of R & D, do promote growth in developing countries. One finds support of this hypothesis from data produced in Caselli and Wilson (2003), Schiff, Wang and Olarreaga (2002), Caselli and Coleman II (2001) and Keller (2001). Eaton and Kortum (2000) provided the data that R & D is mostly done in the North and is transmitted to the South through equipments trade (or intermediate input trade). Easterly (1998) sums it up aptly "Development economists should shift their emphasis from increasing human and physical capital investment to increasing technology adaptation, from improving investment to improving policies". This is echoed later by Stiglitz (2002) too.

II

The Old Theories of Trade and Development

The old theories relating trade to development issues revolve around the vent for surplus theory and the theories of immiserising growth. The vent for surplus theory, popularised by Myint (1958), gives an initial basis for trade although it is not a theory to substitute comparative advantage theory to determine the types of commodities traded (Thirlwall, 1978). The vent for surplus explains the fact that a mineral or resource rich country does not have sufficient productive activities to absorb the resources. Hence exports provide them an outlet to sell these resources and pay for valuable imports. Thus this theory could explain the reasons why some countries develop export enclaves and others do not. Although vent for surplus theory was overshadowed by comparative advantage doctrines of classical and Heckscher-Ohlin varieties, this can be said to be the origin of the export-led growth theory forwarded by a number of economists.

Nurkse (1953) was one of the first economists to talk about "trade as engine of growth" which was later modified by Kravis as "trade as a handmaiden of growth". The point Kravis was trying to raise is just trade will not promote growth unless supported by other institutional changes. The export-growth nexus was later corroborated by Chenery and Strout and Balassa (Thirlwall, 1978). Maizels contradicted the finding although he found strong time-series within the countries (Thirlwall, 1978). An excellent survey on the empirical issues relating export growth and GNP growth is provided in an UNCTAD study (Medina-Smith, 2001). The chapter mentions at the outset that most successful relation between export growth and GNP/GDP growth is found in cross-section studies. Long-run time-series studies using cointegration techniques did not yield good results. It mentions 42 empirical studies done between 1967 and 1998. The first group of empirical studies used mainly bivariate spearman rank correlation tests. Among these are such well-known studies as Emery (1967), Kravis (1970), Michaely (1977), Bhagwati (1978) and Krueger (1978). All of these confirmed strong positive relationship between exports and GNP growth.

Among the second group of researchers, one may mention such well-known works as Balassa (1978), Feder (1983), Kavoussi (1984) and Ram (1985). These studies have a theoretical underpinning in that they had production function approach with traditional factors like labour and capital and a non-traditional factor export. The rationale behind introducing exports is that it generates positive externalities and productivity gains. Again, most of them used cross-section regressions on developing countries by using OLS. One of the studies which rejected the export led growth hypothesis along with the hypothesis that liberalisation promoted more growth is authored by Greeway and Sapsford (1994).

In this context, one should mention the significant results found in the book on India's exports by Marjit and Raychaudhuri (1997). The authors mention that an export led growth is only meaningful provided exports granger-cause GDP growth. This is possible if investments respond to higher exports growth leading to standard Keynesian multiplier process. However, in case regulations or inertia prevents investments to pick up, output is first distributed for the consumers in the domestic market. In case some residuals are there in any sector, efforts are made to export them such a story fits nicely for the Indian data from 1951-1994, since GDP appears to granger-cause exports. Thus, in case domestic market is big and quality factors are weak in that market, exports play a secondary role in that they are simply residuals. Thus liberalisation could promote GDP growth provided domestic markets are small and products could withstand stringent quality control standards of the developed countries.

However, the declining Terms of Trade (TOT or the relative price of exports) for the developing countries posed serious challenges to growth of the developing countries. The data in the overview section gave a clear picture in that direction. But what exactly is the connection between TOT movement, growth and welfare of a country—especially if that country happens to be a developing nation? In order to know this let us discuss some of the old theories first and then go over to the new theories gradually.

The Terms of Trade have been defined in various ways in the trade literature. The most useful one is the Barter Terms of Trade. The barter TOT is the ratio of export price to import price of the country. Apart from that one may have Double Factorial Terms of Trade or DFTT which is Barter TOT weighted by respective productivities. However, most of the theories do discuss in terms of Barter TOT. The most important question which may be posed in this case is whether growth might lead to falling TOT causing welfare loss.

The most influential traditional theory in this regard is that of Bhagwati Johnson theories of immiserising growth (Bhagwati, Panagariya and Srinivasan,1998). The assumed scenario is somewhat like this: suppose a developing country is in general small in international trade except for some primary commodity like some agricultural staple or fruit or some mineral like oil or bauxite or iron ore. In the latter case, the developing country is taken as technically a large country since it controls a large market share. Let there be two countries in the world-- the developing country and the Rest of the World (ROW). The developing country produces under incomplete specialisation two commodities—one exportable and the other importable. Both the commodities are produced with the help of two factors of production, labour and one non-labour input (capital or land). Also, suppose the exportable good is labour intensive whereas the importable good is capital intensive. We assume no lags in production so that production is instantaneous.

Now, let there be a technical progress in the developing country which increases production only in the exportable sector. By assumption, the exportable sector is a sector where the developing country has comparative advantage so that the relative price of this good is lower in the developing country compared to the ROW. Under the circumstances, the growth which is concentrated solely in the export sector, demands more labour than what is released by the import goods sector. The obvious consequence of this is a decline in the import goods production. Now, an increase in the export goods production swamps the international market by extra supply leading to a fall in developing country's TOT. The developing country now faces a double squeeze in terms of higher import prices and a lower domestic production of importables. Thus despite an outward shift in the production possibility schedule of the developing country, instead of a higher welfare, the country may experience a lower welfare in the new equilibrium. This is Bhagwati Johnson immiserising growth situation. The same result might be there even without a falling production of importable good. This requires the foreign offer curve to have an inelastic range where the equilibrium happens to occur.

This theory provided new insights to the question of growth, trade and impoverishment. The theory is almost a natural ally to the Prebisch-Singer theory of falling Terms of Trade leading to impoverishment and dependence of the developing countries. In that theory, falling terms of trade was attributed to low income and price elasticities of developing country exports to the developed world. Apart from that, the asymmetric relation of wages and prices between the developed and developing countries was also taken to be an important factor behind the falling terms of trade movements.

Emmanuel provided a Neo-Ricardian presentation of Prebisch-Singer thesis which was nicely presented by Bacha (1977). The model is Ricardian because it assumed complete specialisation for the two countries, one called the developed Centre and the other the underdeveloped Periphery. In the Prebisch-Singer version of the model, it is assumed that capitalists in the South are profit maximisers. In case the Northern wage is given due to trade union pressure or legislation, northern profit rate is determined if the labour productivity is exogenously given. Assuming Periphery is a labour surplus economy, where the surplus labour resides in a self-sufficient subsistence sector, the wage there is also given. The Balance of Payment equilibrium, then clearly expresses peripheral employment as a function of Peripheral Terms of Trade and the labour productivities of the Centre and the South.

Now, suppose the peripheral labour productivity goes up. This has the following effects—(1) TOT for the Periphery falls as its exportable becomes cheaper (under complete specialisation, only one good is produced in the Periphery and exported) (2) Employment falls to maintain Balance of Payment equilibrium since per capita import has a tendency to go up since per capita income goes up following a rise in labour productivity and (3) A reduction in TOT will increase per capita exports and decrease per capita imports, which leads to a rise in employment to maintain the BOP equilibrium. The net effect on employment then is ambiguous. The periphery will witness impoverishment in terms of falling employment in case income elasticity of import demand exceeds combined price elasticities of import and export demands (under standard Marshall-Lerner condition).

A similar exercise for the profit rate equalisation across Centre and Periphery, which Bacha has termed as the Emmanuel's case, produces identical results. In this case, a rise in the labour productivity in the centre, the employment in the Periphery unambiguously increases through the BOP condition due to income effect provided the whole gain is appropriated by the labourers in the Centre. This is rather unlikely, the gain is usually shared by both the capitalists and the labourers. In that case employment in the Periphery will go up provided the income effect in the Centre outweighs the combined price effects. Otherwise the Periphery will witness an impoverishment through a fall in employment along although there occurs a favourable movement in the TOT.

The Structuralist school also came out with their versions of TOT movement and immiserising growth. Taylor (1983) provided the seminal version of this type of models. This is a model with three countries, one being the developed North, the second being the developing South and the third is an intermediate input supplier like OPEC. The North produces the only capital goods produced in the world. The South only produces consumer goods. The OPEC produces no other goods except the intermediate input. The North is Keynesian with excess capacity and mark-up pricing. The South is capacity constrained and adjusts its price for any demand shock. Both have fixed coefficient production functions.

The North has a savings supply curve relating profit rate to growth rate of its capital and output. There is also a demand for investment function which relates the same variables. Savings supply comes from within the North and the OPEC country. Stability demands savings supply should have a steeper slope than the investment demand. The growth in the South on the other hand depends on the supply of capital goods from the North. It does not have an independent investment function. An oil price rise would thus affect the South more adversely than the North for the following reasons—(a) The North will have a reduction in profit rate due to increase in the intermediate costs, leading to a fall in savings and lower investment and growth, (b) The South will have a double squeeze since lower capacity utilisation reduces southern profit rate due to lower availability of capital goods as well as a higher Northern price due to cost rise (they mark-up their price) reduces southern profit rate directly.

The dynamic part of the model shows that over time, in the absence of any external shocks, southern growth will be faster than the north since northern rate of profit and the relative capital stock in the south, both positively affects southern growth. However, an external shock like oil price rise, affects the southern growth more adversely than the northern growth. Thus, in case the world is out of steady state, continuous shocks like oil price hike or technical progress or trade union pressure in the north will continuously disturb the growth rates in both the North and the South. This will simply disallow the two growth rates from converging and the Southern growth rate will tend to lag behind the Northern growth rates further and further.

The neo-classical economics also produced its own share of models to explain the famous Prebisch hypothesis regarding adverse TOT movements and impoverishment of Southern countries. Let us discuss one of the most representative models of Findlay (1981). The model assumes two countries called the North or developed country and the South or the developing country. The North is Solow type. The North produces output under the assumption of Constant Returns to Scale (CRS). The goods it produces is called Manufactures (M-goods). The North always experiences continuous labour augmenting technical progress. The South produces a primary commodity with CRS technology. Labour supply is Lewisian (infinitely elastic) at a fixed real wage. It further assumes all wages are consumed and a fraction of profit is saved (Keynes-Kalecki type of assumption).

The Southern capital labour ratio is easily determined by the fixed real wage rate assumption. Under CRS the common southern growth rate of employment, capital and output is determined by proportion of profit saved. Steady state is given by equality of Northern and Southern growth rates where the Northern growth rate is given by the exogenous rate of growth of its population. The link between the North and the South is given by the Balance of Trade equilibrium condition. One important result is that the long-run equilibrium TOT is completely independent of the Southern parameters and depends on the Northern parameters, although short-run movements of TOT needed to equilibriate BOT is dependent on southern parameters as well. The model clearly shows that the labour augmenting technical progress in the North continuously widens the relative income between the Northern and Southern incomes. The model however differs from the Prebisch-Singer hypothesis in one crucial respect. It concludes that a secular decline in the Terms of Trade for the South cannot continue ad infinitum. It will finally converge to a long-run steady state value.

III

New Theories of Trade and Growth

Since the late seventies and more from the mid-eighties, there a whole new school of growth theories emerged under the broad banner of endogenous growth theories. The main difference of these growth theories from the traditional neo-classical theories is their denial of growth ceasing after a time period because of diminishing marginal productivity of capital. The major contributors to the endogenous growth theories happen to be Lucas and Romer. The first one introduced human capital in the growth scenario whereas the second one explicitly brought in the role of Research and Development in the growth process. While the first type of theory of Lucas variety worked fine under competitive market assumption, Romer variety of growth could only work under imperfect market for innovation designs. Both these theories could bring in increasing returns to scale which did play pivotal roles in non-ceasing growth process of an economy. In addition, Romer type theories stressed the fact that variety of consumer goods plays an important role in the utility function of the consumers.

The role of consumer love for variety was most fruitfully introduced in the trade theory by Krugman (1979). His model introduced an innovating North or developed country along with a non-innovating South or developing country. The idea is that the North innovates and then this is imitated after a time lag by the South. The main motivation of trade in this world comes from this lag in the introduction of new products in the South. Thus trade always shows that the North exports new products and imports old products. The South enjoys technology transfer through the imitation of the innovations done in the North earlier. Thus slowing down in the rate of innovation or acceleration of technology transfer will narrow wage differentials between the North and the South because the North, then, will lose the monopoly rent which it was earning since it is the sole producer of innovations.

The model of Krugman stresses the fact that increased variety of consumer goods give higher utility to the consumers.

A fall in the relative wage in the North reduces the relative price of the Northern goods and raises the derived demand of the Northern labour. However, technology transfer to the South increases Southern production and reduces Northern derived demand for Labour. The model shows innovations in the North helps it to maintain a constant differential of per capita income from the South.

This model for the first time shows that a rapid increase in the rate of technology transfer might actually worsen the welfare of the developed North. Thus although rapid innovation move TOT against the South, as also per capita income differential, welfare in the South increases due to consumers love for variety. However, imitation of the products do not produce a similar effect, since this does not increase variety of consumer goods for the Northern consumers although this reduces TOT for the north as also per capita income differential. Thus the standard Prebisch-Singer theory was recast differently for the first time. The South was shown to have an optimistic future as also a threat to the Northern welfare.

This theory was developed with lot more sophistication by Grossman and Helpman in a number of papers. Let us concentrate on one such important paper written in 1989. In this model, a small open economy is considered. Here, the goods are produced under constant returns to scale but the Research and Development sector produces new ideas or designs in a decreasing cost set up (or increasing returns to R and D inputs). The human capital intensive R and D competes with another human capital intensive goods. The second goods is a unskilled labour intensive goods. Since every intermediate producer produces only one input, equilibrium requires the infinite stream of oligopoly profits equals the cost of production of the intermediate input.

The small country assumption suggests the Terms of Trade are given for the economy. Suppose now in the initial equilibrium, the country imposes a tariff on the importable goods and gives a subsidy to the exportable goods. In case the importable goods is human capital intensive then rewards to human capital will go up. If domestic R and D is also human capital intensive then this becomes costlier. In other words protection of the human capital intensive sector increases the competition for resources between this sector and the R and D sector. The result is that R and D activity is discouraged which simply kills the chicken laying golden egg because this sector produces increasing returns to human capital. The whole economy benefits from this since the intermediate inputs get the benefit of the decreasing costs of the designs when the economy grows. The net result of protecting a sector competing with the R and D sector is that the whole economy will slow down. Thus the best policy would be to encourage production of the exportable goods which is unskilled labour intensive thereby encouraging R and D sector indirectly. This enhances growth of the economy.

Thus the new growth theory emphasises two different strands of thought. One is that the love for variety of the consumers shows that the South may benefit from expanding variety of consumers goods production since they are in a position to imitate original innovations faster than the growth of innovations themselves. The North stops production of the old goods which then are produced by the South only (Vernon's product cycle theory). The story says South eventually produces additional goods faster than the additional goods which the North can produce, leading to faster growth in the per capita income in the South than in the North. The second avenue through which growth can be achieved in the South is to promote R and D activities which shows increasing returns to scale. The best way to do this is to give more protection to the sector which uses the input not used intensively in the R and D sector or the exportable sector.

IV

Some Policy Issues

The above discussion throws open some important policy

issues. The very basic question which the developing countries face today is how to accelerate growth in a liberalised world. The history of Trade and Development is apparently heavily loaded against the South or the developing world. The major hypothesis around which the trade issues revolved for quite a number of years is the well known Prebisch-Singer hypothesis. This theory claims that historically the developing countries gained unequally in the global trade because the southern products have low income and price elasticities. Thus they suffered from adverse Terms of Trade movement and immiserisation.

We have discussed some old theories of Trade and Development which has established theoretically the reasons for immiserisation and impoverishment of the developing countries when they participate in the international trade. The main reason behind such impoverishment is clearly (1) low income elasticity of southern products in developed countries, (2) high concentration of resources in the export sector which experiences a falling Terms of Trade effect, and (3) high dependence of the Southern countries on the developed North for capital goods or machineries.

The new theories of growth and trade make trade and development more promising. The main avenue through which trade might accelerate growth is variety of consumer goods as well as intermediate inputs. The variety effect is shown to be influencing welfare and growth in the South through two main channels--(1) South may imitate products faster than what North can innovate, thereby increasing the per capita income and welfare faster than the North and (2) they can make R and D activities which enjoy increasing returns to scale more attractive production sector by protecting sectors which utilise the competing factors of production more.

Herein comes the important role which foreign aid or Foreign direct investment might play. One clear fact is that the developing countries in general do not have very productive R and D sectors. Second is that they are dominated by small scale manufacturing units (in many cases unorganised), who has the major problem of adapting technology even if they could be borrowed, transferred or imitated. The table in the next page shows the data. Thus, it is clear that strengthening an R and D sector either by indirect or direct policies is quite a difficult proposition. Hence, the only means by which the small firms dominated manufacturing sector of the developing countries can either increase variety of production of consumer or intermediate goods is through technology adaptation. This technology adaptation can only be done either through (a) incubation method with government support through consortium of small industries in technology park, (b) targeted foreign aid, or (3) foreign direct investment through outsourcing or subcontracting (Raychaudhuri, Forthcoming).

What is the possible role of regional cooperation or border trade in this context? It is well accepted that regional cooperation is going to thrive despite globalisation. Regional Cooperation in South Asia is a difficult proposition given the political reality there. But the rationale behind such trade should be encouragement of vertical specialisation instead of horizontal specialisation. This implies instead of competing to trade in the same commodities like garments, leather or similar agricultural products like rice or potato. Rather, the principle should be more like some of the countries specialising in the supply of inputs or parts to the end products produced in some other regional economy. Such trade hold more future for both the trading partners for future rather than continuous trade in identical products. The kind of border trade practiced in South Asian countries is not really intra-industry trade. This is a trade in identical final products produced in both the trading countries except that in one country the price is cheaper. There could be more conscious effort to plan the commodities or activities which the trade partners may specialise in, so that growth prospects may increase due to either spread of increasing returns to scale of production or encouragement in the production of different varieties of similar goods.

Table 8.2
The Global Economic Scenario

Country	*Illiteracy Rate (%)*		*Manufactures as per cent of total Exports*		*Share of Manufacturing and transport equipments in total Imports*		*NBTT (1987=100)*		*R & D (% of GNP)*		*Small Firms as (%) of Total Firms*	*Small Firms as (%) of Total Output*
(1)	(2)		(3)		(4)		(5)		(6)		(7)	(8)
	'80	'99	'80	'96	'70	'93	'80	'96	'90	'95		
Argentina	5.6	3.3	23	30	31	49	123[*]	116[+]	-	0.38	-	-
Brazil	24.5	15.1	37	54	35	33	96	97[+]	-	0.84	-	-
India	59.0	43.5	59	74	23	14	71.5	96[+]	0.8	0.73	76.2[#]	13.4[#]
B'Desh	70.8	59.2	68	81[+]	-	13	148.4	94[+]	-	0.03	-	-
China	34.5	16.5	-	84	-	42	109[*]	101[+]	0.68	0.61	58.9[®]	5.2[®]
Hong Kong	14.5	6.7	91	92	17	33	100.7	100.2	-	-	97.8¢	53.8¢

(Contd...)

(1)	(2)		(3)		(4)		(5)		(6)		(7)	(8)
Thailand	12.4	4.7	25	73	36	45	116.5	103^{+}	0.18	0.13	$97.1^{ð}$	-
Malaysia	28.6	13.0	19	76	28	54	131.9	99^{+}	-	0.24	$84.0^{ð}$	$77.5^{ð}$
Korea	7.1	2.4	90	92	30	34	84.7	89.5	1.9	2.6	98.5_	-
Indonesia	30.7	13.7	2	51	40	42	145^{*}	90^{+}	-	0.07	98.7_	28.4_
Kenya	43.7	18.5	12	18^{+}	34	25	144.3	109.6	-	-	-	-
Nigeria	67.1	33.0	0	3^{+}	37	-	167^{*}	99^{+}	$0.87^{¤}$	-	-	-

Note: + = year 1993; * = year 1985; ¤ = year 1987; # = year 1992 and manufacturing only;

® = year 1991 and manufacturing only; ¢ = year 1993; ð = year 1997 and manufacturing only; _ = year 1995; Small is defined variously to have 50 to 200 employees.

Source: 1) Columns 3 and 5 from World Development Report, 1998/99
2) Column 6 from World Development Indicators, 2001
3) Columns 7 and 8 from APEC website, http:// *www.actetsme.org*
4) Column 4 from World Development Report, 1995
5) Column 2 from World Development Indicators, 2001

REFERENCES

Bala Subrahmanya, M.H. (2003), 'Technological Innovations in Small Enterprises'. *Economic and Political Weekly*, May 24.

Balassa, B. (1978), 'Exports and Economic Growth: Further Evidence'. *Journal of Development Economics*, 5, 2.

Barro, R.J. and X. Sala-i-Martin (1995), *Economic Growth*. McGraw-Hill, International edition.

Benarroch, M. and J. Gaisford (2001), 'Foreign Aid, Innovation and Technology Transfer in a North-South Model with Learning By Doing'. *Discussion Paper No. 1999-09*, University of Calgary, Department of Economics.

Bhagwati, J. (1978), *Anatomy and Consequences of Exchange Control Regimes: Liberalisation Attempts and Consequences*, Cambridge, MA: Ballinger.

Bhagwati, J.N., A. Panagariya, and T.N. Srinivasan (1998), *Lectures on International Trade*. Cambridge: The MIT Press, Chapter 16.

Boone, P (1995), 'Politics and Effectiveness of Foreign Aid'. *CEP Discussion Paper No. 272*. London: London School of Economics.

Burnside, C. and D. Dollar (1997), 'Aid, Policies and Growth'. *World Bank Policy Research Working Paper No. 1777*.

Caselli, F. and Coleman II, W. J. (2001), 'Cross-Country Technology Diffusion: The Case of Computers'. Harvard University, Mimeo.

Caselli, F. and Wilson, D. (2003), 'Importing Technology'. Paper prepared for the *Carnegie-Rochester Conference on Public Policy*, Harvard University, Mimeo.

Chatterjee, B. and A. Raychaudhuri (1996), 'Some Aspects of Production Organization and Cost Behaviors of Garments Industry in West Bengal' in A. Raychaudhuri and D. Sarkar (eds.) *Economy of West Bengal: Problems and Prospects*. New Delhi: Allied Publishers and DSA Centre for Regional Economic Studies, Jadavpur University.

Coe, D.T. and E. Helpman (1995), 'International R & D Spillovers'. *European Economic Review*, 39,859-887.

Coe, D.T., E. Helpman, and A.W. Hoffmaister (1995), 'North-South R&D Spillovers'. *NBER Working Paper No. 5048*.

Dalgaard, C-J and H. Hansen (2001), 'On Aid, Growth and Good Policies', *Journal of Development Studies*, 37(6), 17-41.

Dalgaard, C-J, H. Hansen and F.Tarp (2002), 'On the Empirics of Foreign Aid and Growth'. CREDIT working paper, University of Nottingham.

Devarajan, S., A. S. Rajkumar, and V. Swaroop (1999), 'What does Aid to Africa Finance?' *World Bank Development Research Group Working Paper*.

Dollar, D and A. Kraay (2001), 'Trade, Growth and Poverty', World Bank, Mimeo.

Easterly, W. (1998), 'Quest for Growth'. World Bank, Summary.

Easterly, W., R. King, R, Levine, and S. Rebelo (1994), 'Policy, Technology Adoption and Growth'. *NBER Working Paper No. 4681*.

Easterly, W., R. Levine and D. Roodman (2003), 'New Data, New Doubts: A Comment on Burnside and Dollars "Aid Policies and Growth"(2000)'. Centre for Global Development Working Paper No. 26.

Eaton, J. and S. Kortum (2000), 'Trade in Capital Goods'. *NBER Working Paper No. 8070*.

Emery, R.F. (1967), 'The Relation of Exports and Economic Growth', *Kyklos*, 20, May.

ESCAP (2000), Report of the Regional Consultative Meeting on Strengthening Technology Incubation System for Creating High-technology based Enterprises, Seoul, 2000.

Feder, G. (1983), 'On Exports and Economic Growth', *Journal of Development Economics*, 12, 2.

Findlay, R (1980), 'Terms of Trade and Equilibrium Growth in the World Economy'. *The American Economic Review* 70, 291-99.

--------------(1981) 'Fundamental Determinants of the Terms of Trade'. In Grossman S. and E. Lundberg, (eds), *The World Economic Order: Past and Prospects*. London: Macmillan, 425-57.

Grossman, G. and E. Helpman (1989), 'Growth and Welfare in a Small Open Economy", *Discussion Paper #145*, Woodrow Wilson School, Princeton University Press.

Heller, P.S. and R.C.Porter (1978), 'Exports and Growth: An Empirical Reinvestigation', *Journal of Development Economics*, 5, 2.

Helpman, E. (1992), 'Innovation, Imitation and Intellectual Property Rights'. *Discussion Paper No. 1597*, Harvard Institute of Economic Research, Harvard University.

Jones, R. (1979), *International Trade: Essays in Theory*. Amsterdam: North-Holland Publishing Company, Chapter 10 and 11.

Kavoussi, R.M. (1984), 'Export Expansion and Economic Growth: Further Empirical Evidence'. *Journal of Development Economics*, 14, 1/2.

Keller, W. (1996), 'Absorptive Capacity: on the Creation and Acquisition of Technology in Development'. *Journal of Development Economics* 49, 199-227.

Keller, W. (1997), 'Trade and the Transmission of Technology'. NBER Working Paper No. 6113.

Kravis,I.B. (1970), 'Trade as a Handmaiden of Growth: Similarities between the Nineteenth and Twentieth Centuries'. *Economic Journal*, 80, 320.

Krueger, A.O. (1978), *Foreign Trade Regimes and Economic Development: Liberalisation Attempts and Consequences*. Cambridge, MA: Ballinger.

Krugman, P.R. and M. Obstfeld (2000), *International Economics*. Massachusetts: Addison-Wesley.

Krugman, P.R. (1979), 'A Model of Innovation, Technology Transfer, and the World Distribution of Income'. *Journal of Political Economy*, Vol. 87, No. 21.

Lewis, A. (1969), *Aspects of Tropical Trade, 1883-1965*. Stockholm: Almqvist and Wicksell.

Lucas, R. (1988), 'On the Mechanics of Economic Development'. *Journal of Monetary Economics* 32, 3-42.

Maizels, A., T.B. Palaskas and T. Crowe (1998), 'The Prebisch-Singer Hypothesis Revisited' in D. Sapsford and Jr. Chen (eds) *Development Economics and Policy: The Conference Volume to celebrate the 85th Birthday of Professor Sir Hans Singer*. Basingstoke and London: Macmillan, 63-85.

Marjit, S. and A. Raychaudhuri (1997), *India's Exports: An Analytical Study*. Delhi: Oxford University Press.

Mayer, J. (2003), 'The Fallacy of Composition: A Review of the Literature'. *Discussion Paper No. 166*. Geneva: UNCTAD.

Medina-Smith Emilio J. (2001), 'Is the Export-Led Growth Hypothesis Valid for Developing Countries? A Case Study of Costa Rica', *Policy Issues in International Trade and Commodities Study Series No.7*, UNCTAD, New York, Mimeo.

Michaely, M.(1977), 'Exports and Growth: An Empirical Investigation'. *Journal of Development Economics*, 4, 1.

Prebisch, R. (1950), *The Economic Development of Latin America and its Principal Problems. New York*, United Nations.

Ram, R. (1985), 'Exports and Economic Growth: Some Additional Evidence'. *Economic Development and Cultural Change*, 33, 2.

Raychaudhuri, A. and J. Bhattacharya (2004), 'Endogenous Growth in a North-South Framework with Human Capital Accumulation and Technology Transfer'. *Journal of International Trade and Economic Development*, March.

Raychaudhuri, A. (Forthcoming) Subcontracting in Indian Industries, Market Structure and Product Quality: Implications under globalisation in a volume edited by Joel Ruet and others out of a conference held in Centre de Science Humaine, New Delhi on globalisation and India, China and Russia in 2002.

Rogoff, K. (2003), 'The IMF Strikes Back'. Foreign Policy, January/ February, 39-46.

Romer, P. (1986), 'Increasing Returns and Long-run Growth'. *Journal of Political Economy* 94, 1002-37.

Romer, P. (1990), 'Endogenous Technological Change'. *Journal of Political Economy*, 98 (5, Part 2), S 71- S 102.

Sarkar, P. (1999), 'Export Diversification, Market Shares and Issues of North-South Terms of Trade'. Mimeo, Centre for Studies in Social Sciences, Calcutta.

Schiff, M., Y. Wang and M. Olarreaga (2002), 'Trade-Related Technology Diffusion and The Dynamics of North-South and South-South Integration'. *World Bank Policy Research Working Paper 2861*.

Singer, H. (1950), 'The Distribution of Gains between Investing and Borrowing Countries'. *The American Economic Review* 40, 473-85.

Stiglitz, J.S. (2002), *Globalization and Its Discontents*. N.Y: W.W.Norton & Company.

Thirlwall, A. (1978), *Growth and Development*. London: Macmillan Press Limited.

UNCTAD (1996), *Trade and Development Report*, 1996 and 2003.

Vasquez, I. (2002), 'Foreign Aid and Economic Development' in Cato *Handbook for Congress*. Washington, D.C.: Cato Institute.

Watson, R., M. Crawford and S. Farley (2003), 'Strategic Approaches to Science and Technology in Development'. *World Bank Policy Research Working Paper No. 3026*.

World Development Report, Various Years. Washington, D.C.: World Bank and N.Y.: Oxford University Press.

Yeats, A.J. (1998), 'Just How Big is Global Production Sharing', *World Bank Discussion Paper*, World Bank.

Young, A (1991), 'Learning by Doing and Dynamic Effects of International Trade'. *Quarterly Journal of Economics* 106, 369-405.

9

Rescuing North Eastern Region from Economic Gloom: A Case for Relying Upon Non-Economic Factors

—Amiya Sharma

The Millennium Development goal adopted by 189 countries is about reducing extreme poverty by half between 1990 and 2015 and removing hunger in this world. On top of that India has its own target of becoming a developed country by 2020. Within the country the North Eastern Region (NER) is not developing as fast as its neighbourhood South-East Asia, a region in the fast lane of development. In this scenario, for the NER to catch up, it has to rely on a different route, non-economic one at that. It has to be understood that economic development taking place in different countries is not just the result of economic factors. Other factors matter a lot, subsumed under "residual factors" and how the economic-political and social aspects are inter-related to bring about development. It is observed that developed and developing countries seem to exist in clusters. This is more so when the borders are more open. Therefore, opening the borders with the neighbours may help to maximise the benefit to the NER because of a host of such factors. Opening up borders is a non-economic decision and therefore needs such arguments. This chapter discusses how, taking advantage of the various economic and non-economic factors, the region can move from its present state to a higher growth path.

I

The Millennium Development goals as committed by the world community of 189 nations in the UN reflect the concern for the poor and hungry people in the world today. They mean a lot for our region since while some of us have been fortunate to have a decent lifestyle, others in our own backyard are going hungry. Out of the world's total poor (living on less than $1 a day) of 1.2 billion in 1998, South Asia, East Asia and Pacific contributed more than 66.7% (World Development Report, 2000/2001). As one of the leaders in the region it is India's duty to see to it that the Millennium Development goals are fulfilled.

It has also been already heard that India would like to eradicate poverty by 2010, whatever that may mean. But even if India were to be able to eradicate poverty before 2015, there cannot be real peace and happiness unless our neighbours are also well-off and peaceful. There are neighbours in South-East Asia who have shown excellent performance in terms of development. But some are still in the bottom of the list. There has to be concerted effort to tackle the problem since individually, some of these countries may not be able to meet the target. The goals by themselves are not something very difficult to achieve as a group. Fortunately, efforts in this direction are being made, although in a rather slow fashion.

In the world today, there seem to be two distinct trends. Under the WTO regime, almost all the countries in the vicinity of India have agreed to abide by the rules that have been already framed while other areas are being worked out. The other trend is that of formation of regional groups for increased regional development. From the increase in membership, it is noticed that the countries would like to work under a universal set of rules. In that case there is reason to believe that neighbouring countries would cooperate with each other under some additional rules added to the ones under the WTO if regional advantages were added. In fact, it has been seen that there are such regional cooperation/trading blocs in almost every area in the globe today. According to Debroy (1996), *if one throws a dart at the map of the world, the probability is almost one hundred per cent that it will land on some trading bloc or the other.*

One can say that as the World is becoming unified, within that trend there are patches of different hues being formed from the dots that existed. Even if it is to only eradicate poverty from the region, India should try to form such a patch — free trade area to begin with — with its Eastern neighbours, being already a part and parcel of the WTO and hence showing willingness to cooperate. According to Dutta (1999), progress of regional blocs have been in the direction of including more contiguous economies to common fold. Expansion of European Union is an example. Dutta (1999) mentions:

> *One can indeed define the regional grouping of economies of the world in the earlier period as 'strategic', not economic. The compactness of an economic space in terms of geographic contiguity has been the prime focus of economists studying location theory. Rational economic regionalization will have to be defined by a common economic space mapped on a common geographic space.*

As far as India is concerned, according to the *NSSO* survey (55th Round of Household expenditure survey) India's poverty population was 26.1%. In terms of the poverty line $ 1 per day the figure should be higher (It was 44.2% in 1997 according to the International poverty line, according to *World Development Report*, 2002). The rate of growth of GDP is expected to be over 7% reflecting a trend for higher growth. Even at this rate the Millennium goal of removing the hunger and poverty may not be easy for the country, a concern shown by the NGOs and few intellectuals. On top of that there is a vision that India would like to be a developed country by 2020. Keeping this vision in mind the country has been taking many positive steps the fruits of which are being witnessed by everyone.

While India as a country is developing very fast, there are

areas within the country like the NER that are falling behind, relatively, if not absolutely. Because of relative backwardness there is internal strife that result in fall in growth even in absolute terms. It is true that there are other regions within India that are equally if not more backward. But in the present location like a cul-de-sac the relative backwardness problem in the region has taken a different turn. Thus, there has to be special efforts whereby such regional imbalances may be taken care of. Instead of the cul-de-sac picturisation, NER's location in the vicinity of the promising S-E Asia needs to be harnessed to the fullest extent. In any dead-end, the development process stops before that. But in case there is continuum or possibility of having a continuum, the process is carried out till the border. It is common knowledge that in the case of the NER, many important projects have been located outside or away from the border because of such thinking.

II

Going back to 1951, the state of Assam which included the present states of Nagaland, Mizoram and Meghalaya had a per capita income which was more than the national average and ranked fifth highest in the country (NEDFi study). One finds that today's Assam with a per capita income of Rs. 10,951 in 2001-02 stands almost at the bottom of the list with its PCY slightly more than half (61%) of the Indian average of Rs. 17,947. To get a better perspective, China has a per capita income (UNDP Human Development Report figures for 2001) of $ 911 while Thailand has $1874 in comparison to India's $ 462. Interestingly Bangladesh has per capita income of $ 350 (76% of India's PCY) which means that it is far above than that of Assam. Looking at all these data, one feels that under the British rule the region as a whole was in a relatively better position. One wonders if Digboi oil refinery that came up in 1901 would have at all seen the light had the present political boundaries were in existence.

It may also be pointed out that during that period the link between the region and the SE Asia was better. Does this imply that establishing better link would give the region a better advantage? Although there might have been other factors at work as to why the region could have performed relatively better during the pre-independence period, one could at least try to minimise the doubt by bringing back the old links. The following paragraphs argue that there are positive advantages of opening up borders for the region.

Verghese (2004) noted:

> *Partition severed the North-East's traditional arteries of communication with the country's heartland virtually reducing it to a landlocked region. Against an international boundary of almost 5000 kilometres, marching with Bangladesh, Myanmar, Tibet or China, Bhutan and Nepal, the tiny 22-km wide Siliguri corridor is all the connectivity that survived between the North-East and the rest of the country. Bhutan and even Nepal were yet to open up to the world and, with Tibet, Myanmar and East Pakistan becoming difficult and uncertain neighbours at different times, the North-East was geo-politically isolated. Customary border relations were disrupted or even temporarily extinguished causing both hardship and heartburn.*

In a study by *Rajiv Gandhi Institute for Contemporary Studies (RGICS) & Indicus Analytics* it has been shown that in terms of composite index which is a weighted average of general achievement, investment climate, infrastructure penetration, finance, workforce quality, social affluence, mass media penetration, consumer finance, high value agriculture, agriculture and law and order, the states in the NER perform very poorly. Among the major 20 states, Assam gets a rating of 1.0 and is placed fourth from the bottom, above Bihar, Jharkhand and Orissa.

All the other NE states including Sikkim occupy the bottom seven positions amongst the 15 small states and Union Territories. Overall the NER is placed in a precarious position. Given the location in the remotest corner, there can hardly be any "feel good" factor that helps in resurgence of the economy.

III

Clustering in the World: It is observed that countries at similar stages of development seem to belong to similar cluster. Western Europe is one cluster of developed countries. Similarly Latin American countries form middle-income group. South Asian countries, Sub-Saharan countries are other clusters. In these clusters 'other factors' seem to matter a lot in terms of development. If Mexico is not as developed as the US, there are host of non-economic factors that can be used to explain the difference. South Korea and North Korea provide another example. According to Olson (2001):

> *At the highest level there are only two possible types of explanation of the great differences in per capita income across countries that can be taken seriously. The first possibility is that as the aggregate production function methodology and the foregoing theories suggest, national borders mark differences in the scarcity of productive resources per capita; the poor countries are poor because they are short of resources... The second possibility is that national boundaries mark the borders of public policies and institutions that are not only different but in some cases better and in other cases worse. Those countries with the best policies and institutions achieve most of their potential, while other countries achieve only a tiny fraction of their potential.*

He then comes to a conclusion that 'the most important explanation of the differences in income across countries is the difference in the economic policies and institutions.'

NER does have this advantage of being near to an area that has began to show high rates of growth. Since it is very unlikely that the productive resources became abundant overnight in the SE Asian countries for such growth to take place, the factors suggested by Mancur Olson must be given the primary role.

Since there are both good policies and bad ones on both sides of the border, it is important for NER to take maximum advantage of the good effects flowing from the other side. This suggests that mere opening up of the border would not alone be sufficient for development to spill over. The society has to keep a careful watch over the unseen flows. Newspaper reports sometimes seem to stress more on the negative flows like drug trafficking, arms trafficking than positive flows like wide variety of goods and services, cultural exchanges, access to new tourist spots on each side of the border etc.

A decade and half ago interaction amongst academics, bureaucrats, economists, politicians across borders for advocating sub-regional cooperation or open border policies would not have been so common. Emergence of European Union, break down of the iron curtain together with open border policies pursued by most countries in the world these days have made it possible to look at such a factor with hope. While the world is being unified under the WTO, regional groups are being formed almost every now and then. India is adopting newer growth oriented strategies in keeping with the developments outside. At the same time one of its main objectives is also to encourage regional cooperation. Given the situation in the western border and the rapid growth in the SE Asian countries, there is a need to put more emphasis on "Look East".

The NE states have to show extra zeal towards formation of such cooperation as they have a lot to gain. One agrees with the *India Today* (August 16, 2004) which suggests opening up her border around the NER as one of only two options that the region has to increase its rate of development. One only argues further that it is non-economic/institutional factors that would matter most in improving the lot of the partners. As in the case of relationship with the West and increasing use of English language, there is a need to establish training centres for SE Asian language and even etiquettes, some of which are quite similar to our own. As of now, knowledge of each other's language on both sides of the border is not adequate for smooth business transaction. Just like the smooth exchange of Indian rupee and Nepalese rupee without any hitch, so will have to be the process of exchange between Burmese currency and the Indian currency.

For any step that involves some response from another party, a bit of marketing policies have to be worked out. Both *external* as well as *internal factors* involve in working out a cooperative relationship. As far as internal factors are concerned, in order to be able to reap the full benefits from regional cooperation, the NER states have to do some homework themselves. The states in the region must work in unison since their economic interests are interdependent to a large extent. Common tax laws, common tourism policy, agriculture, industrial policies are some of the areas that need to be worked out. It is difficult to foresee smooth cooperation between the NER and let us say Myanmar, if Assam, Nagaland, Manipur have different policies in case of some items in the state subjects like tourism or taxes. The states have to sit together and work out the possible areas where common laws, policies could be framed to boost up cross-border cooperation. As for the external factors, consistent and focussed steps must be made to involve the Indian government and the governments of the neighbouring countries. Since these are not in the hands of the people of the NER, one cannot be sure of the outcome. Internal efforts help in making the external factors yield to the pulls and pushes. According to Manmohan Singh, (Keynote address in "Destination North-East," Guwahati, on 10th Oct., 1997),

> *The Central Government has a major responsibility to assist in the expansion and modernization of infrastructure sectors in the North-East region. Infrastructure development also lends itself to fruitful regional cooperation.*

IV

Trade and beyond: Normally, when one talks about benefits of regional cooperation, one refers to trading relations. It is more or less true, as former Prime Minister A B Vajpayee pointed out that one witnesses a borderless world for illegal/ anti-social activities but not for 'social' activities. Prof. Imtiaz Ahmed of Dhaka University recently talked about the subaltern regional cooperation that has positive aspects as in NGOs' close cooperation across borders and also negative aspects as in smugglers, money launderers etc. Regional cooperation between neighbours is more than mere trading, although it starts with free trade arrangements.

Verghese (2004) observed:

> *Restoring good neighbourly cross-border ties entails more than country to country relations howsoever expansive these may be. Peripheral areas tend to be neglected, particularly if remote and marked by difficult terrain. Historically these areas have often served as buffer zones between power centers. A conscious border policy is therefore required to develop them and invest these sequestered lands with centrality and significance, covering barriers into bridges.*

Opening up of borders also involves economic, cultural and social benefits. Countries in different stages of development and with different comparative advantages would gain from such trading relationship. But even countries in similar stages and competitive advantages can gain because of the increase in productivity, innovations and choice, resulting from exchange of ideas. According to Michael E Porter, microeconomic competitiveness, not just macro policies alone, hold the key to solving problems of unemployment, trade deficit etc. This has been shown by United Kingdom recently, which improved markedly while Argentina could not keep up because of improper micro fundamentals. Based on Porter's identification of four determinants of competitive forces that the countries face one can visualise what the days ahead would bring to the NE region. He lists them as — factor conditions such as availability of factor inputs, skilled labour or infrastructure; demand conditions for that product; presence of related and supporting services and the nature of corporate structures and competition, organisational and managerial cultures. Porter, then goes on to say that differing nature of competitive advantage between nations often leads to clustering, either in industries or geographically within a region.

Given the location of the NE region and the availability of raw materials one would like to see it as a cluster of development. For such development, it would need better infrastructure and organisational as well as managerial culture. Infrastructure can be built; but the culture part has to be imbibed. After more than half century, it is commonly believed that such management and business culture has not been imbibed by the people of the region. An open border policy enhancing movement between people of similar racial stock may be able to break that inhibition. North Korea and South Korea show different pattern of development and also management culture not only because of the openness to the Western countries but also to more developed countries of the East Asia like Japan.

In Asia today, there are countries, which are still trying to maximise their comparative advantage. These are countries at the lower end of development. There are also countries, which are at the stage in which they think in terms of competitive advantage and innovations. India is one country, which is trying to move from the first stage to the second. Only through innovations and competitive advantage its manufacturing processes and service sector would be able to compete. For such competition, there is a need for an experimental market which the SE Asia would provide, being in the middle rung of the development ladder. When Japan developed its market was assured because of the cheapness of the products, not the quality. Similarly China is doing the same. Only after some market penetration can it be economical to invest more in product improvement, entailing higher cost. The feed back from the market helps to improve only those goods where the potential is huge. India would benefit from such a strategy. SE Asia is a good market for that. NER has the advantage of being the bridge-head.

In spite of the overt commitment to globalisation, developed nations do put obstacles in the path of development for countries like India. As an economy progresses the constraints to its continued advancement change the status and form requiring the whole economy to respond. This requires micro economic response, not just macro business environment.

Regional cooperation with Asian countries would help India to withstand the barriers.

Through cooperation, newer markets can be created offering more choice to the consumers. Competition will ensure efficiency of the producers. New management styles, new ideas and innovations for faster growth at a later stage can be introduced more quickly amongst the member countries. If labour movement becomes freer, then competitive advantage of the region as whole can be maximised. Macro policies as advocated by the World Bank-IMF are necessary for development—but they are not sufficient. Unless micro-economic efficiencies of the companies, which could be domestic or subsidiaries of foreign companies, are also kept attuned to the macro policies production and export on the basis of comparative advantage may not be sufficient to sustain development. India's exports of engineering goods and other non-traditional items underline this fact.

V

For the NER, much is needed in the direction of micro institutional improvements than inflow of funds. Its close proximity to the SE Asia, a region that is more developed may be seen in this light. The Global Competitiveness Report, 2002-03, shows that the countries closest to the developed ones are better off. It is not only in terms of per capita income but also in terms of macro environment like inflation; technology like internet users; public institutions and micro environment like company operations; access to loans; crime and violence, hiring and firing practices, compliance with international environment regulations, organised crimes, property rights etc. One can refer to Singapore and Malaysia who provide one such pair. South Korea and Japan, North Italy and Switzerland are other examples. It seems to be almost always true that areas contiguous to developed economies are relatively more developed even when there is no official trading relationship. Cooperation with the SE Asian countries would mean a lot for the development initiative in the region. Before facing competition from the developed world, NER would benefit from competition from slightly more developed areas. It would be like training ground for its producers.

Some economists have remarked that there is not enough surplus to export from the region. Here lies the fallacy of forecasting with given parameters. As in the case of India's new exports, the parameters themselves may change to make for new items with competitive advantage to be exported from the NER. Not many people predicted that Indian companies would be able to face the competition from abroad after the economy had opened up. Trade takes place within a free trade area for various reasons. It is not difficult to see that trading between developed countries like US and Canada has benefited them both. Therefore how much of surplus is there in the region today is of hardly any relevance for talks on open border policies.

Looking at protection of producers' interest alone would relegate the interests of the consumers who have been deprived of better choice. Product quality suffers in all cases where there is not much competition. Open borders would benefit the consumers to choose from wider varieties, tourists to 'experience' similar areas developed more professionally and students to join reputed institutions near home instead of the West.

Dutta (1999) noted:

> *In the post-cold War global order, the EU is a unique paradigm of economic regionalization, providing a macroeconomic core for microeconomic optimization–consumer satisfaction for households and profit for business corporations in all member-economies and it very much warrants our attention.*

Opening the borders with neighbouring countries should mean freer movement of goods and services along land routes. Movements through air or the sea have different implication than movements on land. In the latter case people along the route too benefit, however poor they are. If along with goods and services, the institutions are also developed as a result, then the country is firmly placed on the development path. Imbibing newer techniques and institutions for development would take place rather quickly because of cultural affinity. Distance factor too would call for lower cost of location. NER would like to belong to the stage where the SE Asian countries belong. Within India, close observations show that development in Kerala and even Tamil Nadu is more akin to that of Sri Lanka in terms of Human Development Index. Kerala and Tamil Nadu are ranked first and third respectively in the ranking of states by the *Study by RGICS & Indicus Analytics*.

Unlike Kerala, the Himalayan Mountain Chain has been a big physical barrier for NER. But more than that, the governments on both sides of the border in NE India never seem to have tried to make intra-regional movements easier. The two things combined have made regional differences much more in this case. When there is so much cultural, linguistic and racial affinity, economic development in the region should have been similar in nature. It is time that the areas next to the SE Asian Tigers get the benefit of their proximity. The gain will not be one sided. India too offers good market and an access to the Western countries through the NER. The proposed East-West Highways would put the NER and the poorly developed areas on the other side in the centre of action, not in the periphery. Railways too bring similar advantages to the local population as in the case of inland waterways and roadways. Therefore, the opening up borders to make movement along land routes assume more significance for eradicating poverty and hunger of the poor people living in these parts.

In the case of a borderless world there will be some benefits whether measurable or not. This is the feeling that one experiences in terms of being able to enjoy freer movement whether the movement actually takes place or not. Prof. A K Sen and after him even the World Bank prefers to define the term poverty as one where there is lack of opportunity to the people. Thus being able to move about freely is itself a freedom that should be counted in the measure of welfare of the people. People from the region do move out—but always through airports or ports in the mainland, which is rather inconvenient and expensive. Even if it takes some more time for the flights to actually operate from the region in a regular basis, the very feeling of openness would make the people better off.

According to Tomas Bata, innovation does not apply to technology only, but should also be applied to systems and organisations as well; and second the courage to innovate can produce some startling results. In the case of open border situation too, there will be ample opportunities for innovation but the countries have to be prepared to make innovative steps to let their people make best use of the new opportunities. One believes that in an open border environment, the NER would be able to take innovative steps to give shape to a new culture which would be able to better utilise the resources and give the needed push to be able to keep pace with the SE Asian countries. In this light, the following passage from Witzel's (2003) writing on Max Boisot becomes relevant:

> *Many earlier discussions of organizational culture had tended to discuss culture as a feature or attribute of organizations. There was often an implicit assumption that all business organizations are basically the same, and that different cultures then create adaptive responses which are in turn responsible for diversity between organizations. (Max) Boisot however argues that culture is not just a superficial set of features and attributes, but rather at the core of every organization and influences how the organizations function at the most basic of levels.*

Conclusion

India is developing very fast but the goal of becoming a developed nation by 2020 may be difficult to meet. Regions like the NER are falling behind. More effort than what is being currently done would be necessary. One such measure is cooperation with the Asian neighbours, especially those surrounding the NER. Opening borders would change things in a way that conventional economics do not seem to recognise. Neighbours benefit from each other in various ways.

Development seems to be similar in clusters as reflected by the map of the world. Close cultural affinity to a more developed region like the SE Asia would make it easier for companies to locate across the border. The underlying premise is that changes in macro policies are necessary but not sufficient for solving the problems of underdevelopment and then keeping up the process of development. It may be preferable that companies in the region first learn to compete with the neighbouring, almost middle-income group of countries before competing with the developed ones. From whatever angle one is considering, in order to be poverty free, India has to take part in encouraging open border policy in the NE and the region has to do its homework to be able to realise the benefits.

REFERENCES

Debroy, Bibek, 1996, "Beyond The Uruguay Round", in *The Indian Perspecetive on GATT*, Response Books.

Debroy Bibek and Laveesh Bhandari, 2002, "How are the States doing?," RGICS & Indicus Analytics for CII.

Dutta, M, 1999, *Economic Regionalization in the Asia-Pacific*, Edward Elgar, USA.

India Today, Special Issue, August, 2004.

Olson, Mancur, 2001, "Big Bills Left on the Sidewalk: Why some Nations are Rich, and Others Poor," in Kahkonen, Satu and Mancur Olson, *A New Approach to Economic Development*, Vistar Publications, New Delhi.

Verghese, B.G, 2004, "Borders Matter More than Boundaries: From the North-East Looking Out," in Man and Society, *a Journal of NE Studies*, ICSSR, NERC, Spring.

Witzel, Morgen, 2003, *Fifty Key Figures in Management*. Routledge, NY 10001.

World Economic Forum, 2002-03, *Global Competitiveness Report*.

10

Indo-Myanmar Border Trade: Resource Base and Export Potential of North Eastern Region

—G.P. Prasain

Introduction

The North-Eastern Region of India comprises of eight 'sister states' viz., Arunachal Pradesh, Assam, Manipur, Meghalaya, Mizoram, Nagaland, Tripura and Sikkim. The entire region is spread over 2,55,089 sq. km area which is 7.8% of the total geographical area of the country. According to census of India, 2001, the total population of North-East India is 3,65,00,108 persons which is 3.5% of the total population of India. This region is surrounded by China, Myanmar, Bangladesh and Bhutan. It is connected with mainland through what is known as 'chicken neck', a very narrow strip of land with a width of 33 km only. Because of geographical location and proximity to the foreign countries, cross-border markets are likely to be more cost effective for the goods produced in this part of the country than the distant national markets. The process of globalisation and liberalisation has also opened up the economy of the region and hence there is a good scope of promoting trade with the neighbouring countries. Border trade and economic development in the border areas are interdependent, as border trade leads to economic development, which through secondary effects increases border trade manifolds.

The geo-political situation of the North-Eastern Region is very important from two standpoints. Firstly, strategic and secondly, the feeling of alienation. The North-Eastern States are not only geographically far from the mainland India, but they are also lagging far behind in economic and industrial development. The socio-economic indicators of North-Eastern Region are presented in the Table 10.1A. It shows that the region still lags far behind from the rest of the country and in all respects. The economic backwardness and consequent unemployment problem is one of the important causes for deteriorating law and order problem in this part of the country. Therefore, the NER must be developed industrially to overcome this problem.

Regional Economic Cooperation

After the success story of European Union (EU) in the western world and the Association of South-East Association Nations (ASEAN) in South-East Asia, regional economic cooperation has become a practical proposition today. The South Asian Preferential Trade Agreement (SAPTA) was formed in 1993, which has achieved the distinction of negotiating trade concession on product by product basis. Now, India is planning to switch over from SAPTA to SAFTA (South Asian Free Trade Agreement) with the prime objective of economic liberalisation and regional cooperation, which will have direct impact on the economy of India in general, and North-Eastern states in particular. India is also a partner of BIMSTEC (Bangladesh India-Myanmar-Sri Lanka-Thailand Economic Cooperation) which is promoting joint ventures in the areas of industry, trade, technology, tourism, investment, infrastructure and human resource development. As a result of geographical proximity of North-Eastern Region of India with Myanmar, there is a good scope of economic and industrial development of the region. Geographical isolation of NER from the mainland of the country, which once considered as one of the causes of economic backwardness of the area now has become an opportunity for the entire region to accelerate growth.

Resource base of North-Eastern States

Assam

Assam is the only North-Eastern state having some industrial base. Major industries of Assam are tea, plywood, crude oil and natural gas, coal, paper, petrochemicals, fertilisers, and textiles. Assam accounts for more than 50 per cent of tea produced in the country. The state produces a variety of fruits including pineapple, banana, oranges and papaya. Sericulture is a traditional industry of Assam. Eri, muga and mulberry are special types of silk produced in the state. Muga is the monopoly of the state. Forest area, which covers 22 per cent of the total land area of Assam, contributes substantially to the state's revenue. Plywood and safety match industries are the major forest based industries of Assam. Handmade paper industry and cane and bamboo industry are the other industries at small and cottage level. Besides, there are more than 300 varieties of medicinal plants and herbs grown in the forests of Assam. Assam produces approximately 5 million tonnes of crude oil in a year, out of the total annual production of 34.4 million tonnes in the country. Natural gas output of the state is 3,740 million cubic metres per annum. Assam has rich resources of coal, limestone, china clay, granite, burleys and gypsum. The Assam Industrial Development Corporation has identified potential areas for investment. These are hydroelectric power, coal-based industries, food processing, floriculture, inland fishery, granite mining, and polishing as export-oriented industries and infrastructure projects.

Manipur

The industries which have good prospects in the state of Manipur are cycle and cycle parts, cement, pulp and paper products, vanaspati oil, drugs and pharmaceuticals, steel and iron rods, spinning and weaving mills, plastic and plastic product, fruit processing, soap and toiletry products, rubber and rubber products, disposable syringes, hosiery and hosiery products, mineral based industrial products and television sets, both colour and black and white. Most units are in the small-scale sectors catering the local needs. Moreh, on the border with Myanmar is about 108 kms from Imphal.

Meghalaya

It is predominantly an agricultural economy. The main crops of the state are rice, maize, wheat, potatoes, pulses and oilseeds. Other crops like jute, mesta cotton, ginzer, arecanut, betal leaves, pineapple, oranges and guava are grown in the state. Meghalaya has rich mineral resources like coal, limestone, clay and sillimanite. Coal and limestone are being exported to Bangladesh through the border. Rich uranium deposits are also found, but await exploitation.

Mizoram

The Mizoram border touching Myanmar has the routes at Hnablan, Champhai, Vapihai, Thingsai, Vawmbuk, Lungbun, Thaipang and Sangau. The Champhai sector has been identified as the crucial point for border trade. The distance between Champhai and Aizwal is 190 km. Mizoram is predominantly an agricultural economy. The state has rich forest resources including cane and bamboo. Teak plantations have come up in the state, which will be commercially used after 5-10 years. The state government provides cotton and woollen yarn to artisans engaged in the production of handloom products. The state has mineral resources, which have yet to be exploited. Mizoram depends heavily on trade through Champhai for a number of agricultural products. Considering the high volume of imports of gem, precious and semi-precious stones into India through the border, cutting and polishing of gem and manufacture of jewellery for export could be undertaken in the state. The required skill for manufacture of gold jewellery and diamond-studded jewellery is available in Champhai and Aizwal.

Nagaland

Agriculture is the mainstay of Nagaland. Major occupation of the Nagas is paddy cultivation. The state is rich in flora and fauna. The secondary occupation in the state includes cottage and small industries, sericulture and raising aromatic plants. Existence of industrial estate at Dimapur provides encouragement to entrepreneurs for establishing units in the district. The industrial activities in the state include sugar, transport, hotels, saw mill, engineering workshop, printing press, textile/handlooms, plastic, citronella, food products/processing, stone crusher, floor tiles, handicrafts, audio/videography, mining/coal, dress making/knitting, chemicals, metals, electronics, pulp and paper.

A large number of items including engineering products, textiles, plastic items, food products, toiletries, electrical and electronics can be developed in the state.

In addition, the state has a number of sericulture farms, reeling and spinning units and cocoon preservation centres. Besides, industrial establishment for food processing can be set up utilising local production of items like guava, pineapple, bananas, oranges and tomatoes. Other items, which can be developed in Nagaland, include bricks, cement and iron bars.

Tripura

Tripura has an international border running into 839 km with Bangladesh. Its economy is agrarian with paddy as its main agricultural crop. Other agricultural crops are pulses, oilseeds and jute. Some horticultural products including oranges, pineapples, bananas, lemons and coconuts are also grown. Natural rubber has emerged as an important plantation product in the state. It also produces a substantial quality of tea annually. Forest, covering 34 per cent of the total land area of the state, contributes significantly to the economy of Tripura. Teak, agar, mahogany and sisu are grown in the forest. Medicinal plants like nuyuomica are available in the forest of

Tripura. Bamboo-based handicraft industry is one of the main economic activities of the state. Industries having potential in the state on the basis of its natural resources are fertiliser units for urea and ammonia, power generation, natural rubber products like tyres, tubes and gloves, various processed food items, handmade paper and packing materials.

Potential Areas of Exports from North-East to Myanmar

There are certain potential areas in NER, which are to be developed for getting full benefit from the Indo-Myanmar development cooperation. These areas are:

1. *Fruits and Vegetables*

Fruits and vegetables like orange, lemon, jackfruit, ginger, papaya, bananas, potato, chilly, pineapple, guava, tezpatta, cabbage, brinjal, turmeric are available in Assam, Manipur, Mizoram and Tripura. In Myanmar, the food processing industry can not meet the demand and that country heavily depends on imports. Therefore, processing, bottling and canning facilities need to be created in Assam, Tripura and Manipur for exporting food products to the Myanmar.

2. *Tea*

Tea grows in plenty in Assam. About 50 per cent of India's supply comes from Assam. In Myanmar domestic demand of tea is met by imports. Packaged tea needs to develop in Assam. Tea blending and packaging industry has a good scope in NER.

3. *Rubber*

There is heavy demand for cycle in Myanmar. Tyres and tubes of heavy-duty vehicles are included in the list of priority items permitted for imports in Myanmar. The existing cycle producing unit in Manipur should be encouraged. Cycle parts, tyres and tubes can be manufactured in Tripura and Manipur as the rubber is produced abundantly in this region.

4. *Medicinal Plants and Herbs*

Assam, Manipur, Sikkim and Tripura are rich in plants and herbs. All medicinal items are listed under essential import items in Myanmar as there is no local production. Therefore, commercial exploitation of medicinal plants has to be taken up in NER.

5. *Drugs and Pharmaceutical Products*

Medicines are not manufactured in Myanmar. They are import. Manipur State Drugs and Pharmaceuticals Ltd. should take the advantages of this opportunity by manufacturing drugs and exporting to Myanmar.

6. *Handloom Products*

Handloom and handicrafts play a big role in the economy of NER and employ a large labour force. As per the latest census, the region accounts for half the total handloom output in the country. There is heavy demand for handloom and handicraft items in Myanmar. NER should set up more manufacturing units of handloom products.

7. *Silk*

Assam and Nagaland produce large quantities of silk. Myanmar does not produce silk. The country meet the demand for silk made items by imports only. Therefore, production of tasar, eri muga and mulberry silk needs to be commercially organised in the region.

8. *Teak Processing*

Myanmar's forest area near the Indo-Myanmar border has abundant growth of teak. High transport cost to Rangoon and Mandalay prohibits the timber to be taken for processing to these centres. This disadvantage can be exploited by India by setting up processing centres at Moreh, Champhai and Lungwa.

9. *Power Generation*

Since North-Eastern states are having a large number of rivers and other water bodies, power industry has a good scope. About 38 per cent of hydropower potential of the country lies with the north-eastern region.

10. *Cutting and Polishing of Precious Stones*

As Myanmar does not posses expertise in cutting and polishing of its large deposits of precious stones, these can be undertaken on the border area of Moreh and Champhai.

11. *Stainless Steel and Aluminium Utensils*

There is substantial demand for stainless steel utensils in Myanmar. As there is no local production, demand is met by imports, especially from Thailand. Production units can be set up at Moreh and Champhai to make stainless steel and aluminium utensils for exports to Myanmar.

12. *Cutting and Polishing of Granite*

Myanmar has large quantities of raw granites, but cutting and polishing facilities are not available there due to lack of capital or expertise. These facilities can be developed on the border area with Indian technology.

13. *Polishing and Milling of Pulses and Oilseeds*

The Pulses and Beans Trading Organisation at Mandalay in Myanmar is the wholesale market dealing with exports of these items. As polishing and milling facilities are not available in Myanmar, these items are sold without much value addition. India can enter into joint venture at Mandalay for polishing and milling of pulses and oilseeds.

The Stilwell Road

Through the border towns of Arunachal Pradesh namely,

Vijaynagar, Nampong, Khomiyeng, Laju, Wokha, Pongchou, no official trade takes place presently. The 1736 km long historic Stillwell road that runs from Ledo in Assam to Mytkiana (headquarter of Shan state of Myanmar) through Phangsau pass in Tirap-Myanmar border, if opened, could facilitate Arunachal to access Myanmar. However, about 520 km road in Myanmar is not motorable while the last leg of the road culminating to China is a double lane highway. The 12 km stretch from Nampong to Pangsan Pass on the Indo-Myanmar international border is motorable, but is a restricted area.

Reopening of the Stillwell road would usher in a new vista in regional cooperation and cross-border trade. More particularly, the route will serve as a life line for the land locked North-East India.

Conclusion

Border trade is very important for the people, living in border areas. Opening up of the border trade through the ancient Stilwell road would generate huge employment opportunities in trade, transport, tourism and related services for the youths which may reduce the tendencies of militancy and other anti-social activities in the North-Eastern Region. The Government of India has also withdrawn the ban on export of bamboo. As a result, the export of bamboo from north-eastern India to Myanmar and other South Asian countries will increase manifold. North-Eastern Council has drawn a plan for bamboo plantation in order to make the entire northeast a hub of bamboo cultivation. Recently the Government of India has decided to extend the benefit of transport subsidy to the exporters of northeast region also. This is an welcome step and this will increase export from this region.

Myanmar is an underdeveloped country with poor infrastructure and technological development. Its main exports are mostly of primary products while imports are of capital goods, consumer goods and raw materials. On the other hand, existing border trade between India and Myanmar is characterised by re-exporting of consumer goods from Myanmar and importing daily necessities from India. Commodities being traded in the border areas are mostly not of North-East origin. Although the value of border trade was estimated as high as 2000 crore per year, official trade statistics do not reflect the substantial border trade that takes place between the countries.

Therefore in the existing system, the Indian Government in general and northeastern states in particular get little benefits out of the border trade. It is due to domination of illegal trade that exits in the border. Commodities worth more than ten crore of rupees were seized every year by the Custom Department at the Indo-Myanmar border. The ongoing authorised bilateral trade between the two countries are mostly routed via Kolkata port. It may also be mentioned here that a variety of products, particularly of Indian origin are reportedly entering Myanmar through Singapore and Thailand.

Therefore, direct trade between India and Myanmar through Indo-Myanmar border should benefit the northeastern states in terms of increasing income and employment. The northeastern states, particularly those bordered with Myanmar, are landlocked and totally isolated from the other parts of the country because of their geographical location. Bringing exportables from other parts of the country would escalate the cost and ultimately the price could not compete in the international market. Therefore, it is suggested that entrepreneurs should be groomed in the potential areas like medicinal plants, pharmachemical units, tea industry, handloom and handicraft products, fruit and vegetable processing, cycle industry, paints and varnished industry, power industry and rubber plantation, teak processing industry, cutting and polishing of precious stones etc.

REFERENCES

Basic Statistics of North-Eastern Region, North Eastern Council Secretariat, Shillong.

Customs Departments, Moreh, Manipur.

Das, Gurudas and Pukayastha, R.K., *Border Trade, North-East India and Neighbouring Countries*, Akansha Publishing House, New Delhi, 2000.

Deb, R.B, and Patwari, Parto, "Revival of Stilwell Road through Regional Cooperation: A Close Review", paper presented in the Conference on Regional Cooperation, Organised by Marghreta College during 18-19th January 2004 at Marghreta.

Economic Survey of Manipur, 2002-2003.

Khuraijan, Vivek, *The Prospect of Indo-Myanmar Border Trade under New EXIM Policy*, Indian Institute of Planning and Management, New Delhi.

Journal of North-Eastern Council, Shillong.

Mahanta, Ratul, "Border Trade of Assam and Tripura with Bangladesh: Opportunities for Economic Prospects", paper presented in the workshop on Role of Government in Border Trade Between Assam and Tripura with Bangladesh, organised by SEP- HRD, Guwahati on September 6-7, 2004.

APPENDIX

Table 10.1A
Socio-Economic Indicators of North-Eastern Region

Sl.No.	*Indicators*	*NER*	*India*
1.	Literacy Ratio, 2001	68.63	65.38
2.	Urban Population (in %), 2001	15.51	27.78
3.	Sex-Ratio (Females per '000 Males), 2001	937	324
4.	Population Density (Persons per sq.km.), 2001	147	324
5.	Percentage of Workers engaged in House hold to Total Workers, 2001	3.48	4.07
6.	Percentage of Gross Cultivable Area to Total Geographical Area, 2001	25	59
7.	Land-Man Ratio (hac/man), 2001	0.66	0.32
8.	Percentage utilisation of Agricultural (Land, 2001)	58.74	73.05
9.	Per hectare use of chemical fertilisers (in kg), 2001	26.59	87.12
10.	Foodgrain production (kg per hectare) 2001	1367	1630
11.	Average population per Bank (in, 000), March, 1999	19	15
12.	Credit-Deposit Ratio (in %), 2001	28.31	57.20
13.	Percentage of Electrified villages to Total villages, 1999-2000	80.87	86.30
14.	Length of Roads per 100 sq.km. (Area in kms), 1997	54.80	74.90
15.	Percentage of roads to Total Length of Roads, 1997	24.96	58.68
16.	Area Per Post Office (in sq.km.), 2001	41.91	22.33
17.	Per Capita Income (At Current Prices in Rupees), 2000-2001.	12,202	16,487

Sources: Basic Statistics of North Eastern Region, N.E.C. Secretariat, Shillong, 2002.

Table 10.2A
Year wise volume of trade between India and Myanmar

(In Rupees)

Sl.No.	*Period*	*Export*	*Import*	*Total*
1.	April, 1995-March, 1996	10,45,27,782	5,38,99,029	15,84,26,811
2.	April, 1996-March, 1997	311,70,51,137	15,17,65,094	48,88,15,231
3.	April, 1997-March, 1998	22,44,72,930	35,08,34,823	57,53,07,753
4.	April, 1998-March, 1999	5,06,09,710	3,74,39,616	8,80,49,326
5.	April, 1999-March, 2000	3,25,65,827	3,67,97,316	6,93,63,143
6.	April,2000-March, 2001	5,29,17,530	19,38,523	5,48,56,053
7.	April,2001-March, 2002	1,25,08,345	8,29,71,255	9,54,79,600
8.	April,2002-March, 2003	3,66,74,503	12,14,60,746	15,81,35,249
		83,13,27,764/-	**83,71,05,402/-**	**166,84,33,166**

Source: Department of Commerce and Industries, Govt. of Manipur, Imphal.

Table 10.3A
Northeast Myanmar border in km.

States	*Border length*
Arunachal Pradesh	520
Manipur	398
Mizoram	510
Nagaland	215
Total	**1643**

Table 10.4A
Agreed exchangeable items between India and Myanmar

i)	Mustard/Rape Seed	ii)	Pulses and Beans
iii)	Fresh Vegetables	iv)	Fruits
v)	Garlic	vi)	Onion
vii)	Chillies	viii)	Species (excluding Nut Meg, Mace, Cloves, Cassia & Cinnamon)
ix)	Bamboo	x)	Tobacco
xi)	Minor Forest Products (Excluding Teak)	xii)	Betel Nuts and Leaves
xiii)	Food items for local consumption	xiv)	Tomato
xv)	Roasted Sunflower Seeds	xvi)	Reed Broom
xvii)	Sesame	xviii)	Soya bean
xix)	Coriander Seeds	xx)	Ginger
xxi)	Katha		
xxii)	Any other commodity as may be mutually agreed upon between the two sides.		

Source: Indo-Myanmar Border Trade Agreement.

Table 10.5A
Resource Base of North-Eastern States

State	*Sector*	*Products*
Assam	Agriculture	Tea, paddy, fruit including pineapple, banana, orange, papaya and fertilisers.
	Forestry	Plywood, paper, safety matches, cane and bamboo, medicinal plants and herbs.

(Contd...)

	Mining	Crude oil, natural gas, coal, petrochemicals and minerals.
	Textiles	Eri, muga, weaving and hosiery.
Manipur	Agriculture	Processed food, vanaspati oil and fruit processing.
	Forestry	Pulp and paper products, rubber and rubber products.
	Construction Industry	Cement
	Drugs and Pharmaceutical	Medicines, medicines equipments such as disposable syringes, bandage etc.
	Metals	Steel and iron rods.
	Textiles	Handloom, weaving mills and spinning.
	Electronics	Television, inverter, battery and other electrical equipments.
Meghalaya	Agriculture	Cereal, fruit, vegetables, oilseeds, mestra, ginger and arecanut.
	Textiles	Jute, cotton.
	Mining	Coal, clay, limestone, sillimanite.
Mizoram	Agriculture	Paddy, fruit including pineapple, bananas, papaya, oranges etc.
	Forestry	Cane, bamboo, teak.
	Textile related produce	Handloom products, Handicrafts, knitting, silk and sericulture
Nagaland	Agriculture	Paddy, food products, sugar, citronella

(Contd...)

	Textile related produce	Handloom, knitting, dressmaking, handicrafts, silk and sericulture.
	Forestry	Pulp and paper, sawmill, aromatic plants.
	Construction	Stone crushers, floor tiles.
	Mining	Coal, limestone.
	Engineering goods	Engineering workshop, electronics goods, printing press, metal and metal manufactures.
Tripura	Agriculture	Paddy, pulses, oilseeds, jute, processed food items.
	Horticulture	Oranges, pineapples, bananas, lemons, Arecanuts.
	Cash crops	Rubber and tea
	Forestry	Teak, agar, mahogany, sisu, medicinal plants, bamboo, pulp and paper.
	Fertilizer	Urea, ammonia.

Source: Directorate of Economics and Statistics of various States.

11

Good Governance for Regional Cooperation

— D.K. Sharma

A welcome development has taken place in the ASEAN countries in the recent times. The ASEAN leaders agree that economic prosperity in the future will hinge on closer ties and co-operation within the region. Look East Policy of the Government of India is a bold step in that direction. China, Japan and South Korea also have echoed the themes of regional co-operation. ASEAN and China, Japan and South Korea have already entered into a cooperative grouping called the ASEAN plus three Forum. ASEAN Leaders have also signed an agreement with India aimed at achieving free trade by 2011. The Leaders were unanimous in their view that strengthening cooperation with ASEAN would lead to economic gains for all. This realisation of the political as well as business leaders augers well for regional cooperation in the South-East Asian Countries.

The ASEAN Business and Investment Summit in Bali was launched on October 4 with a design to play a strategic role in creating momentum for the process of developing an Asian Economic Community (AEC) as it was attended by about 400 business leaders from 14 Countries—the 10 ASEAN members and other four countries namely Japan, China, South Korea and India. It was a business meet and therefore it was important. In the final analysis it is business people, not governments, who trade and make business deals. The AEC seeks to lead the 10 ASEAN countries into a more streamlined and integrated economic community through the Asian Free Trade Area (AFTA), which strives to remove tariff and non-tariff barriers–to trade in goods and services and to investment–thereby making the ASEAN countries more competitive to direct foreign investors. A common market of more than 500 million consumers is expected to make ASEAN more viable for regional production networks by capitalising on local competitive advantages and economies of scale.

However, there are still many issues to be resolved to smooth AFTA as a mechanism in paving the way for the creation of AEC stated for 2020. It is essential to understand what measures the governments in ASEAN can pursue in order to create an environment conducive to free trade and investment. To cite an example, due to 1997 economic crisis which had hit several ASEAN Countries, AFTA process was severely affected. Members preoccupied with domestic political, economic and social uncertainties tended to look inward. Indonesia, for example, has shown a stronger tendency to raise import tariffs or even erect new non-tariff barriers to protect its industries. This is where the issue of good governance becomes more relevant.

Governance is the way in which society's main players take decisions that affect the public interest. In the recent years good governance has emerged as a key focus of the international development community. In the context of globalisation Governance relates to the way a country organises itself in reaction to the challenges the world throws at it.

Aspects of governance are many–education, enterprise, the institutions of democracy and the associations of civil society–all combined together allow a society to take advantage of growing urbanised population and promote economic development. Success leads to purposeful change, civic solidarity and rapid growth. Failure on the other hand is punished by unrest, dissatisfaction and economic stagnation.

Many ASEAN governments have recognised the need to more clearly define their role. Governments need to foster an enabling environment within which the market can operate. Apart from conducive rules and effective monitoring, public-private partnerships can be strong tool for regional cooperation and development. Several seminars conferences are held in an effort to bring the policy makers together to discuss the challenges facing good governance in the South-East Asian Region. The focus in these seminars and conferences was mainly on globalisation, liberalisation and sustainable human development.

In most of the developing countries in the South-East Asian Region, the rules of the game of governance need to be simplified and applied more fairly. The need for simplification is even more important in an interdependent world where different systems must interlock and the establishment of clear standards bring mutual economic gain. A clear structure of formal rules also has the advantage of bolstering the informal norms on which the society depends. Most business is done not in the courts but in the meeting rooms where trust and reputation are essential.

The environment that South-East Asian Countries' policy makers work in today is very different to their predecessors in a decade back. It is quite astonishing to find that most of the growth is occurring in the region's poorest countries. The policy makers are now required to cope not just with vast population, but with the people quite different in capacity, awareness, alertness and urgency. Economic changes have raised their heads. Foreign investments from both within and outside the region have altered the structures of domestic economies. Old models of economic growth are not feasible in to-day's more open and more closely regulated global economy.

The only rational response to the present international economic realities is to encourage the empowerment of all sections of society through a rich dense and diverse set of social structure. Empowering as many members of the society as possible in the cause of advancing the public interest, will, in all probability, instill a widespread sense of purpose. Social capital is a strong determinant of economic growth. Government, the private sector and civil society–all have a vital role to play in strengthening social capital. In steering a society forward, the role of government possessing the legitimacy of a popular, mandate is very important. Such a government can master the art of making private sector and civil society important partners of the government.

The AEC action plan highlights are:

- Standardise customs cost and procedures and harmonise technical regulations across the region by the end 2004.
- Identify and begin breaking down non-tariff trade barriers by 2005.
- A network of free trade zones must be set up within ASEAN to make manufacturing more cost competitive and to give companies greater economics of scale.
- Capital controls must be progressively removed and intellectual property rights strengthened.
- ASEAN will overhaul and add to existing dispute settlement systems with the establishment of an ASEAN Legal Unit and other bodies.
- Visa procedures will be dramatically simplified allowing ASEAN nationals to freely travel within the area without visas by 2005 and to eventually issue a single ASEAN VISA for overseas visitors.
- Standardise requirements for professional services to enable free movement of professional and skilled labour within the region.

This action plan is expected to pave the way for better and earlier regional cooperation. The two bold and major steps in this direction are single visa for the region and introduction of single currency. Other steps are more of good governance and simplification of rules of the game. It is interesting to note that even China is proposing to enhance the so-called Chiang Mai initiatives for bilateral currency swap cooperation to multilateral swaps which would lead to development of a single currency in the region in the future. Indian Prime Minister Atal Behari Vajpayee declared that his country could be a production base for industrial goods for ASEAN investors and outsiders. In particular India was a fast growing consumer market. It is worth mentioning here that ASEAN leaders have also signed an agreement with India aiming to achieve free trade by 2011. ASEAN leaders have identified five priority sectors–(1) electrical and electronic equipments, (2) cosmetics, (3) pharmaceuticals, (4) telecommunications, and (5) processed foods. Apart from these priority sectors members have planned for full-investigation of 11 pilot sectors namely (1) wood based products (2) autos and parts (3) rubber-based products (4) textiles and apparel (5) agro based products (6) fisheries (7) electronics (8) e-ASEAN (9) health care (10) air travel and (11) tourism.

A new forecast issued by the Asian Development Bank on September 30 says growth is Asia minus Japan would accelerate even further over the coming years–thus securing its place as the world's fastest growing region.

ASEAN development model, as envisaged above is in contrast to the developed country model which is termed as capitalistic development model. The rise of such an indigenous ASEAN development model can be traced to the failure of the capitalistic development model. The most developing countries are adopting such development apparatus to create sustainable growth for the developing world over the past several decades. Daniel Lian, Senior Analyst of Morgan Stanly, one of Wall Street's biggest investment banks, observes that economic interaction between the developed and developing worlds, largely by way of investment and trade, is driven by "quest for profit" by the corporate capitalist class of the developed world, represented chiefly through multinational companies.

Leaders of South-East Asian nations signed an accord in October 2003 to layout a platform for the establishment of a European style regional community that includes the creation of a single market by 2020. It is called the Bali Accord II. The platform seeks to eliminate non-tariff barriers within the region which has about 500 million people. The Bali Accord–II has three pillars 1) ASEAN Economic Community (AEC) (2) The ASEAN Security Community (ASC) (3) The ASEAN Socio-cultural Community (ASCC). The AEC is to foster regional economic integration. It will cut tariffs for all goods and services and lead to a single market and possibly a single currency. The ASC recognises the sovereign right of member countries to pursue their individual foreign policies and defence arrangements. ASEAN leaders also touched on maritime issues agreeing that maritime co-operation would contribute to the evolution of the ASC. They also suggested formation of an ASEAN Maritime forum.

The ASCC calls for all members of society including women, youth and community groups to play a part in public affairs. It also intensifies cooperation in addressing problems related to growth, education, unemployment and prevention of infectious diseases such as HIV/AIDS and SARS. The Indian Prime Minister Atal Behari Bajpayee spoke about partnership of India and ASEAN and offered his country's willingness to support economic cooperation in his keynote address at the Bali Accord–II. India signed a Free Trade Agreement with Thailand and expected a bilateral trade worth $2 billion by the year 2004.

The Thai Message

In the year 1997 Thailand passed through a severe financial crisis which lasted for a couple of years. All parties in Thai capital market made strong efforts to once again ensure a sound economic environment, region's investors' confidence and become competitive globally. The strategy adopted was implementation of Good Corporate Governance (GCG). The government of Thailand also gave top priority to this strategy and formed a National Committee on Corporate Governance which is chaired by the Prime Minister with representatives from trade groups, security regulators and the Stock Exchange of Thailand (SET). The government made plans to aggressively implement corporate governance by creating Thai Capital Market Master Plan in order to establish a national corporate governance framework. The government had even declared 2002 to be the year of good corporate governance. A strong faith was created that GCG with its accompanying fair and transparent investment climate will attract investors and lead to much needed long-term sustainable growth. SET had embraced and progressively implemented various measures to promote GCG which subsequently emerged as the key factor of economic recovery. GCG is an efficient tool for increasing operational efficiency and effectiveness. It can monitor company's operations from the perspective of stakeholders. It also can serve as useful guidelines for adjusting and improving a company's operational workflow. GCG increases shareholders' confidence to invest more. States good governance increases the confidence of its people–and the results can be miraculous. The Thai message is a case in point.

12

Border Trade with Myanmar: Problems and Prospects

—Pradip Phanjoubam

On November 22, the Prime Minister of India, Dr Manmohan Singh, flagged off the Indo-ASEAN car rally from Guwahati, an event which much of the northeast had been awaiting with great expectations. The rally is now concluded having accomplished its mission of spreading the goodwill necessary for a long standing relations between the ASEAN countries and India, business as well as social. There can be no doubt the rally has the potential to become an important watershed in the history of the regions, for it may well turnout to be the symbolic foundation stone for India's much hyped "Look East" policy. The optimism today is this foundation stone has been laid on solid and firm ground. But like all momentous events in history, it can also very well turn out to be nothing much more than a dream that turns sour in its every infancy. It is because of this that closely studied prior planning and policy framing will be vital. Even as the central government pushes forward its macro diplomatic overtures, the Manipur government in particular and the northeast in general must wake up to the realisation that they can be left out of the sphere of influence or beneficiaries of the new thrust if it is not prepared to meet the new demands and challenges. It must be careful not to drown itself in the ambrosia of ill-timed celebration over any false sense of achievement or well-being. The attitude must be, and in fact the attitude of the entire population should be that the new policy is a major and important step towards a cherished objective but never the objective itself. Let us have no doubt that this is only a beginning; that this event is a very important launching pad to a challenging future which must be taken the best advantage of, but always with the acknowledgement that there are miles to go before the government or anybody can relax and be complacent.

What must the governments of Manipur and the other northeastern states then prepare for? First, in our opinion, they must have to be an active role in shaping the orientation of the "Look East" policy itself. The state governments must influence the central government in this regard. The fundamental question is to work out a modality by which the backward northeast region is given a lift in its effort to find an economic leg and close in the development gap that exists between it and the rest of the country. In this sense, the new shift in the vision must not be just about building an economic bridgehead between India and the ASEAN, but also of providing real, tangible opportunities to the communities in the northeast. To be specific, the entire enterprise must not be allowed to culminate in a scenario in which the local communities find themselves in the unenviable position of the dogs in the Chinese proverb, with nothing to do than bark helplessly and meaninglessly at the passing caravans. Such a scenario, rather than solve, will only accentuate the present stalemate and ennui, the northeast region is caught in.

Having said this, the next step would have to be to work out strategies to steer the course of events in the desired direction. This can be done first of all by encouraging local industries and trading to prepare to avail of the new opportunities through appropriate incentive structuring mainly by the extension of imaginative and purposeful institutional credit facilities to local entrepreneurs. This will be absolutely vital as the biggest stumbling block before the local enterprises and businesses at the moment is low investment capabilities. The second strategy would be to introduce government regulations in businesses and enterprises with the objective of maximising local involvement. This could be done by making local partnerships essential in business undertakings and investments that take advantage of this new foreign policy. The degree of this regulatory mechanism can be calibrated on a time scale drawn against projected dates of success in entrepreneurial confidence local enterprises and trades would have gained. When the required level has been reached, it can perhaps be phased out. The important thing needs to be kept in mind is the beginning of the political agenda of opening up and uplifting the Northeast which must have primacy over immediate business returns. Once the political objective of instilling confidence in the Northeast region has been achieved, all the other accepted laws of business anywhere can be allowed to take over.

Manipur's Western Doors

Almost simultaneously, as the Indo-ASEAN car rally, symbolically opens up Manipur's fabled Eastern Door, its Western Doors are also opening up. A few days ahead of the flagging off of the historic rally, the foundation stone of the Jiribam-Tupul broad gauge rail line was also laid by the Prime Minister, Manmohan Singh. When this line becomes functional, hopefully by 2010, the state capital Imphal would be more or less linked to the vast Indian rail network, Tupul being on the edge of the Imphal valley. Earlier, the line was supposed to enter Manipur territory from Diphu in Assam and after cutting across the hill ranges that surround the Imphal valley, reach at another corner of the valley at Karong in the Senapati district. This plan has been dropped for the time being, but in the future, when the need arises, hopefully it would be revived in the belief that the more connectivity there is, the better it is for the economy.

The question now is, which line would have better served the purpose. The Diphu-Karong line would have been much closer to Guwahati and would have complemented an already much used and popular route. It would have been also far closer to Dimapur and in fact would have almost been a parallel communication link to the National Highway 39. The Jiribam-Karong road likewise is a parallel link to the National Highway 53, which incidentally is not the preferred Western gate so far. However, it does not seem that the choice of this route is a result of any arbitrary political decision. In fact it appears that the preference falls in the wider picture of an integrated Asian region that includes the SAARC countries, the ASEAN and ultimately the Far East. The National Highway 53 that links Manipur with the Barak Valley of Assam is not so popular at the moment because Bangladesh is closed. If this country were to open up, then not just mainland India, but also the sea would suddenly cease to be remote to landlocked northeast. Also to be kept in mind is that it was not NH-39, but NH-53 or rather its parallel, the now disused highway that everybody fondly remembers as the Tongjei Maril that connects the Cachar district of Assam with the Bishenpur district, which formed the historic trade route that is now sought to be reopened. Indeed, the erstwhile Manipur kingdom's psychological geography of access and influence ran along this line on the one side and on the other side, the portion of the NH-39 that connects Imphal with Tamu. Hence towards the West, regions such as the Cachar, Sylhet, Tripura, Assam have found references in Manipur's stories and legends, written and unwritten. Likewise Kabaw, Kege, Ava, Khagi etc., in the East occur in Manipur's folklores and historical accounts. These are so because this trade route must have been "the path of least resistance", before artificial political obstacles came up in modern time. The removal of these obstacles will re-establish the old psychological trade geography, just as by the law of physics water seeks its own level using the "paths of least resistance". Right now, it does seem a little illogical to open up Manipur's Western door into Cachar in Assam, but when the boundaries between the adjacent valleys of Barak and the Surma, soften as per the new global and regional trends of politics, this route would suddenly become important again. Who knows the desired political shifts may come about in the period that the Jiribam-Tupul rail link is fully established and by then may be there would be the need to the push the line further on to link it to Imphal and Moreh and beyond, all along the route that the present Indo-ASEAN rally traced out in its three weeks or so on the road.

Manipur's Eastern Door

The overwhelming sense of optimism in Manipur over India's new look east policy is strongly catalysed by the general sense of an epochal change that seems to be close to a prediction in the Meitei's book of prophesy, the *Puya* that things would begin to fall back in place and prosperity return to the state after the "Nongpok Thong" (Eastern Door) opens up. We would elevate the prediction from merely the status of an occultist prophesy to one of intuitive economic vision, derived out of an innate understanding of Manipur's and the Northeast's history, geography and economic predisposition. The region lies at the junction between South Asia, South-East Asia and Far-East Asia. The great science fiction writer of the past century, Jules Verne in his "Around the World in Eighty Days" saw why this is so when he made his hero Phileas Fogg travel from India to Hong Kong through the Yunnan Province in China bordering Myanmar. The entire region that we talk of belongs to one geographical belt. It is also no wonder why China has also taken such keen interest in establishing a bridge to the ASEAN using its Yunnan Province as its bridgehead. The series of "Kunming Summits" it has been holding is evidence. The Yunnan Province, of which Kunming is the capital, like the rest of this region is settled by people of the Tibeto-Burman linguistic group, quite distinct from the Han Chinese, and it is a demonstration of China's diplomatic prudence that it is seeking to take advantage of this commonality in its ASEAN push. It is interesting to note that India already has a connection with the Yunnan. The disused Stilwell Road built during the Second World War, connects Upper Assam to this Chinese province, again an indicator that even the West saw the need to treat the region as a cohesive whole.

India, like China, has the northeast to make a similar bridge to the ASEAN and Manipur is, we must say, the right choice for a point of contact. If the western Gateway of India is in

Mumbai, there is no reason why the eastern Gateway of India must not be built at Moreh. This is no age for suspicion either, and we are sure if some kind of competition develops between India and China, it would and should be for economic opportunities alone and hence healthy. For Manipur and the northeast, this can turn out to be a big opportunity. Its geopolitical and geo-economic predicaments may suddenly change, after all the northeast can become the connecting hub between three huge and fast developing markets–the ASEAN, South Asia and Far East Asia.

In history, the western and eastern doors were always very important for Manipur. Economic and military relations with neighbours have always been through them. Unfortunately, because of certain momentous shifts in the course of history in the last century, one of these doors closed, putting to an end a traditional and historical trade route that once passed through it. That door is about to be opened, and Manipur may yet become the trade thoroughfare again it once was, ushering in with it the much needed whiffs of fresh air, both psychologically and materially. Let there also be no mistake that opening the eastern door does not mean shutting the western one. Manipur and the northeast need both the doors wide open, and in fact as many doors and windows as there are. If possible, and we are sure it will become possible one day as the SAARC grows in scope and confidence, it should have a passage to the sea as well, which incidentally is not too distant from the tip of Mizoram or Tripura.

Democracy in Myanmar

At least in matters of their policy towards the military junta in Myanmar, India and China seem to agree. Or perhaps we are understating the changing profile of the relationship between the two Asian giants. Although it will be quite sometime before the two can open up their hearts totally to each other in the backdrop of the war the two countries fought in 1962, it can be without any hesitation said that the relationship between them are not the same anymore.

Noticeably, China's attitude has visibly undergone a sea change in recent years. The country's gesture in recognising Sikkim as an integral part of India two years ago and erasing the erstwhile kingdom from its own map was an important watershed. China has since extended its hand of friendship in a big way yet again by backing India in its current bid for a seat in the Security Council, the United Nation's elite club of the rich and powerful nations. Two decades ago, such a gesture would have been unthinkable.

The two countries' Myanmar policy, it would have been noticed by all, is very much like their policy towards another common Asian neighbour, Nepal. This Himalayan kingdom, it will be recalled, is in the throes of a pro-democracy as well as a Maoist movement against the ruling heredity monarchy. India as a democracy should have aligned with the pro-democracy upsurge and Communist China with the Maoists. Neither of these is true and both seem equally comfortable with the monarchy, and their policies overtly suggest status quo in the country is just fine. The same is the case in Myanmar. There is little space for morals and principles in diplomacy, and India has made this absolutely clear by reiterating its stand that it does not matter who is in power in Myanmar for India would adjust to whoever comes to power in the country. A point of caution here that such optimism in its diplomacy misfired badly in Bangladesh in an earlier occasion. It liberated the country from Pakistan, but its assumption that the gratitude it earned by the act would be able to buy unconditional friendship proved so disastrously wrong. China too has been on a similar diplomatic track. It wants a land corridor to the ASEAN through Burma, as does India, but the latter has another vital interest. It wants a Bhutan type operation against anti-India insurgents from the Indian side camping in Myanmar territory with the active cooperation of Yangon. It is no surprise hence that it welcomed the visit to New Delhi by Myanmar's military leader Than Shwe at just about the time the European Union resolved to extend its sanctions against the country for not keeping the deadline it set for freeing the pro-democracy leader of the National League for Democracy, Aung San Swu Kyi from house arrest, and the United States' sanction on the country on the same issue. India's confidence in not being swayed by international pressures, even when it comes from the most influential lobbies, is admirable, but what also needs to be kept in sight is the long-term prudence of such diplomacy. It must be remembered that this kind of policies resulted in burning its hands pretty badly not just in Bangladesh but also in Sri Lanka. Likewise the anti-India sentiment in Nepal runs unimaginably high today. The violent, week-long anti-India carnage in Kathmandu some years ago, triggered by just one inconsequential "fictitious" comment supposedly made by Bollywood film star Hritik Roshan should be enough to substantiate the point.

While the immediate concerns of stemming violent insurrection is understandable, we are of the opinion that the long-term objectives cannot be lost sight of. It is a statistically proven fact (UNDP's annual report 2002 on Human Development) that democratic nations seldom go to war with each other and that lasting peace can result only when accountable and genuine representatives of the people chart out common diplomatic routes. Towards this end, it will not help merely paying lip services to Swu Kyi's cause or democracy in Myanmar.

Pragmatic Politics

During a recent visit to Mandalay city to participate in a seminar on border trade between India and Myanmar, some remarkable aspects of life in Myanmar came to light. In this age of information, there was hardly anybody willing to part with information in Myanmar, especially if the information is political in nature. All become tightlipped if the query is about the lady most in international news, Aung San Suu Kyi.

A local man, who became a good friend said by way of a caution that the mention of the lady's name can land you in serious problem including prison. To the question whether she would come to power if free and fair election was allowed, his prompt answer was, yes. To another question before he put on his guard again, he said it is unlikely there ever would be another election in the near future. Maybe not even in Suu Kyi's lifetime.

Except for the forced amnesia about Suu Kyi, life otherwise is very pleasantly normal in Mandalay, at least outwardly. We did not stay long enough or travel wide enough to know the nuances of dissident political undercurrents in the country. Otherwise, petty crime rate is low, although official corruption we were told is notoriously high. People of both genders, young and old are out on the streets till late into the night going about their everyday businesses and living out life as they have always known it to be.

Contrary to expectation, missing throughout thc journey was the overbearing presence of the military. In fact, the presence of the olive green would be much more in the streets of Imphal or Kohima.

No armoured vehicles, no long military convoys, no foot patrols. While we were there, we literally forgot we were in a country ruled by a military dictatorship. We did see some military personnel on our way back.

The vehicle we were travelling in had the second tire puncture about 10 km from Sikhanji town towards the dusk of November 28. Our bus being the last in the convoy of three buses and a Tata Sumo vehicle, were left stranded on the road for a long time. Some us then decided to take a lift to Sikhanji and get help.

After a long wait, a crowded local mini bus came along and stopped for us. We boarded it to find civilians and military personnel travelling together. The atmosphere was informally cordial with civil and military passengers making rooms for each other, helping unload each others luggage at stops etc.

The seeming normalcy is unmistakable. One of Mandalay's striking features is the number of eating places it boasts of, most of it with a beeline of customers. The culture of eating out seems very much a part of the average Myanmarese.

At dinner time we were surprised to see the street outside our hotel in central Myanmar fill up with make-shift eating places consisting basically of a bench or two and table, with hurricane lamps augmenting available lights from the street lamps and shops along the street. A kiosk where the cooking is done either on coal lit briars or else two burner gas stoves, stand by each of these outdoor eating arrangements.

The place, at its peak hours between 8 pm and 9 pm becomes so crowded that you literally have to walk sideway so as not push over somebody. The fares offered are also basically meat of beasts and fowls, roasted or cooked, boiled rice, salads etc.

The real taste of a place is, as they say, in roadside eating places and we did sample the food on this street, and it was to say the least, sumptuous, that is if you have no scruples about what meat you palate.

The normality of life kept a question returning to mind. Is the resistance against the military regime wearing out? Is the Nobel Peace laureate, Suu Kyi, destined to fade away? She has been under house arrest for a decade now and only recently, in total disregard of international opinion, the military junta extended her detention term by another year.

According to the sections of the media which have access to the members of her party, the National League for Democracy, NLD, she is unlikely to be released ever.

The question that follows is, what is it exactly that is making the military dictatorship so cocky and contemptuous of world opinion. Is it under no pressure to play a fair game in making the people decide who should run the country?

The more pertinent question is, and disturbing for sympathisers of the pro-democracy movement in the country is, are the Myanmarese leaders set to do another China where an event as murderous as the Tiananmen Massacre was kept under wraps and those responsible actually have come to the fore of international attention both in economical as well as political terms? Would the Myanmarese leaders also succeed in keeping the dictatorship going and win back the world by a gradual but steady liberalisation policy?

Indeed, the abiding impression that first time visitors like this writer return with is that Mandalay is a city rearing to go. There is already an increasing traffic of dollar and euro spending tourists arriving in the city. Most of these we bumped into at restaurants and tourists spots were Germans. There were many British amongst them too.

Obviously prospecting a growth in First World tourism, modern 5-Star hotels are springing up. Most of these, like the "Sedona" which overlooks the magnificent moat and fortification of the "Glass Palace" and the "Mandalay Hill Resort", are investments from ASEAN countries like Singapore and Thailand. Opposite our hotel, a 3-Star standard accommodation that sells for approximately 15 dollars a room, is a massive 25-storey shopping complex under construction at hectic pace, obviously again a foreign investment in the cash strapped country.

In short, the feeling is, there is an economic churning building up in Myanmar, and fate willing, it just might rise again.

The answer to the million dollar question, what is giving the Myanmar military junta the confidence to thumb its nose to its critics around the world is, the continued business interest the world, most specifically those in the region it belongs to, the ASEAN, China, India, Japan and indeed many European countries.

It is interesting in this light that it was when leaders of the ASEAN during the two-day summit they held in the Laotian capital Vientiane late November, intimated Myanmar to improve its human rights record and begin the process of democratisation that the latter announced its decision to extend Suu Kyi's detention by another year.

It gauged the ASEAN countries' interest in its natural resources well and rightly assumed they would not abandon it for a mere ideal as democracy. As it is, most of these countries are far from being shining examples of democracy or champions of human rights themselves.

Myanmar has also been thumbing its nose to the West in like fashion. The manner the military regime recently removed Prime Minister Khin Nyunt, a known moderate with too much ear for protests from the West is just an example. He was replaced by a known hardliner with little sympathy for the pro-democracy movement, Soe Win.

It is also not, it seems, overly worried that pressures from the West, particularly the US, would mount beyond a point, having accurately read the superpower's foreign policy priorities which grade its adversaries in terms of their status as "rogue nuclear" states. Myanmar does not have a nuclear program so it feels safe from US scrutiny on this front.

Democracy in Myanmar then seems still a far cry, that is, unless the pressures and sanctions on it come from its regional neighbours first and foremost. The developments in the recent times definitely does not suggest this is about to happen. Even India has joined the frantic prospecting of the country, with its own strategic security and business interest in mind. No matter how much it is against our moral sense of propriety, the Myanmar junta may end up having the last laugh.

The Creaking Eastern Door

There are yet other bottlenecks that became apparent during the same visit. The road to Mandalay was rough, so were the vehicles that transported us. When many amongst our delegation decided to return from Tamu, the border town adjacent to Moreh in Manipur, complaining of bad tour arrangement and poor transport, I decided otherwise, as did

64 others. For one thing, I did not expect any royal treatment in Myanmar, not that the people would not be willing to welcome visitors, but they just were unlikely to be ready or have the infrastructure to give foreign tourists their worth. We were not tourists, but a delegation to participate in a seminar that was a culmination of the new bilateral understanding between India and Myanmar, but as it became increasingly clear, not many across the border understood this. For a transit town used to low budget tourists and border traders, we were just another lot of the same economy class. If we had been visa travellers, taking the air route to Mandalay via Calcutta, Bangkok, Yangon and then Mandalay, maybe the attitude would have been different. But I did not mind it at all for sometimes a lot more of a place is revealed to low budget travellers, than to 5-Star hoppers. As the passenger traffic increase, it is only to be expected that these rough edges would be polished up. Moreover, I just had to be part of the historic opening of the Eastern Door, an event which had always been a matter of extreme interest. The journey in this sense was also very much a time travel back to a period in history when Manipur was a kingdom, very much on its own.

Our buses, beautiful Nissan vehicles, with engines in the back, would have been very comfortable if not for the modifications introduced to cater to the peculiar needs on this route as well as the terrain. The chassis suspensions of the buses have been raised at least two feet so that it needed an extra effort to board them. Midway into the journey we found out the reason why. From Moreh to Kalewa the road had been newly constructed by India so good and all weather, but beyond this point, up to another township called Mongya, a nearly 200 km stretch, there is hardly any road that can be called a road. Numerous rivulets and ravines that furrow the plains are often without bridges so that the vehicles actually have to descend into the riverbeds and climb out the other side. Especially during the wet season, it is quite imaginable that only buses with the kind of modification these buses have would be able to negotiate the terrain.

The inside of the buses are also modified. The seats have been raised a good two feet. This is to make accommodation for freight. About two thirds of the buses, towards their ends are also without seats, again the space is for freight. These buses obviously couple up as passenger as well as freight carriers. It also indicates that the passenger traffic on this rout is less than heavy. On our way up, the buses were loaded with fertilisers. Outraged, we had them removed but soon found out no sooner how uncomfortable it was to perch on raised bus seats on long distance travel with your feet two feet about the floor. On our return journey, the floors below the seats were packed with detergent packets. We allowed this, the journey home was, to say the least, decidedly more comfortable.

Myanmar is in many ways at odds with itself. This awkwardness becomes evident soon. The buses, so also most other vehicles, are right hand drive just as ours, but the roads are also right hand drive, unlike our. Apart from making driving judgment less accurate, it also left us getting off into the middle of the road every time the buses stopped for a stretch of leg. This would have been inconvenient and even dangerous on a busy highway, but the road to Mandalay from Tamu is far from this. Traffic, both of passenger buses or freight trucks were conspicuous by their absence all along the route right up to Sagaing city. Beyond Sagaing, towards Mandalay some traffic become visible. One other thing which we have come to take so much for granted—high tension electric wires—ware also missing conspicuously. In certain visibly more prosperous townships there was power, but these were from small home generators.

Myanmar's currency is the Kyat. It must be one of the most unstable currencies in the world. At the moment it sells at the rate of Rs 100 to Kyat 2000. Four years ago, when I made a trip to Tamu, the rate was Rs 100 to Kyat 750. A few more years earlier it was Rs 100 to Kyat 350. This made it extremely comfortable for Indian travellers for everything becomes so cheap. Wages are also extremely poor. A senior professor gets about Kyat 20,000, the equivalent of Rs 1000. A doctor gets around Kyat 15,000 or Rs 750. In fact there are many professions with Rs 500 salary. Within the country, this is just enough to pull along. But foreign travels, even to India, by the average Myanmarese national is beset with obvious hurdles.

The plummeting of the Kyat is understandable, for the strength of the country's currency is linked to the health of the country's economy. While the Indian economy grew at the rate of 7 per cent over the past few years, Myanmar's has been more or less stagnant. The status of the Kyat also provides an interesting contrast to the Nepalese rupees or the Bhutanese Nu, two economies which are doing no better, or even worse than the Myanmar. The currencies of these two countries have been virtually de-linked from their national GDPs and instead have come to take a piggy back ride on the strengthening Indian economy. As for instance, between 2001 and now, the Nepali rupee has gained against the Indian rupee. It was Rs 100 (INC) to Rs 170 (NC) in 2001, against Rs 100 (INC) to Rs 160 (NC) now. This is despite the fact the Indian rupees gain considerably against the dollar over the same period. The benefits Bhutan and Nepal are reaping of being a surrogate of a larger economy I suppose.

The status of the Kyat also makes you reflect on some aspects of the Indian economy. Although there is justifiable criticism against it for not fostering equitable development in all its varied regions, there are visibly other mechanisms for some semblance of an equitable distribution of national wealth. Government salaries of employees in the most prosperous state in the country, say Maharashtra, would be more or less the equivalent of those of very poor deficit economies like Manipur. It is bad that the states are not taught to fish so that all can eat forever, but the consolation is, at least the states are provided the fish if they do not have it. If the real health of Manipur's economy were to be the deciding factor of the place's salary structure, government employees would not be earning more than their counterparts in the state's fledgling private sector.

13

Trade Settlement Issues and Introduction of Letter of Credit for Promotion of Indo-Myanmar Border Trade

—Rahul Bhattacharyya

Indo-Myanmar Border Trade: A Potential 'Engine of Growth'

Development of border trade with neighbouring countries has special significance to the economic growth of the border regions. Apart from fulfilling the local needs, the scope of border trade can be further extended for the benefit of the rest of the economy through establishment of necessary backward and forward linkages.

The long and porous border between India and Myanmar stretching around 1600 kms is shared by four of our North Eastern states viz., Manipur, Mizoram, Nagaland and Arunachal Pradesh. Like our North-Eastern border states, the other side of the border i.e. the North-Western part of Myanmar is also distant from the main manufacturing and trade centres of the country. As a result, there is demand for exchange of essential commodities as well as other products for carrying out economic activities in the border region.

The geographical location of Myanmar, which acts as a natural land bridge between India and the South-East Asia, is also crucial in the context of India's 'Look East' policy. The policy that seeks to develop economic and political ties with the Southeast Asian nations has created a tremendous potential for economic growth in the region through Indo-Myanmar border trade.

It is in this backdrop that the signing of Border Trade Agreement between India and Myanmar in January 1994 has opened up new vistas of development for our North-Eastern states.

Myanmar offers opportunity for export of wide range of Indian products like iron and steel products, pharmaceuticals, agro-chemicals, cotton yarn, construction materials, machinery and spare parts for agro-based industries etc. On the other hand, there is strong demand for import of wood and wood products, pulses, sugar etc from Myanmar. An analysis of the trend in bilateral trade between India and Myanmar during the past five years reveals that:

i) The volume of trade has been doubled during the period. In fact, it has increased from US$ 203.88 million in 1998-99 to US$ 411.12 million in 2002-03.

ii) All along this period, India's balance of trade with Myanmar has been negative. This is in sharp contrast to the favourable trade balance India is maintaining with the other neighbouring countries like Bangladesh, Sri Lanka, Pakistan etc. During the year 2002-03, the exports to Myanmar were only US$ 75.07 million as against the imports of US$ 336.05 million.

iii) India has become one of the largest export markets for Myanmar.

With a view to realising the potential of Indo-Myanmar border trade, various measures have been initiated. So far, the border trade with Myanmar is being carried on through two trade point's viz. Moreh in Manipur and Champai in Mizoram. A third trade point at Longwa in Nagaland is expected to be opened shortly. Necessary infrastructural facilities like road, power, telecommunication, warehouse, trade centre, postal and banking service etc are also being created to facilitate trade through the trade points.

Nevertheless, the one key area that needs a focussed attention is the creation of a satisfactory settlement system for cross-border trade transactions. Border trade is essentially a form of international trade and is associated with the inherent complexities. As such, creation of an efficient system for smooth settlement of trade is a basic pre-requisite for the success of Indo-Myanmar Border Trade. The issue has been duly recognized by the concerned authorities and several steps have been taken in this direction. While the ground level issues have been addressed and most of them now stand resolved, some macro-level issues like the recent imposition of sanction by the US Government on Myanmar and the compulsory settlement of transactions in ACU dollar are now posing serious problem to the progress in this area.

Types of trade under the Border Trade Agreement and their settlement procedures

Unlike our border trade with Bangladesh where the mode of settlement is only by way of payment against supplies, the Indo-Myanmar Border Trade Agreement (BTA) provides for normal trade against payment as well as barter trade of identified items up to certain limits and under certain conditions. The settlement procedures for the different types of trade under the BTA are discussed below:

a) *Barter Trade of items of the value not exceeding US$1000 or its equivalent*

In this category of trade, settlement is done through barter system i.e. by way of exchange of goods and not against payment for the supplies. People residing within 40 km on either side of the border are allowed to exchange locally produced goods up to the value of US$1000 or its equivalent.

The procedure is simple and does not involve export declaration in Form GR or evidence of import in the form of Bill of Entry. The Import/Export transactions, however, should be completed within a day or two. Such transactions are monitored by the customs authority and no commercial document is required to be submitted by the exporter to the bank.

Trade under this category, though free from settlement hazards, is targeted mainly for the benefit of the local people.

b) *Barter Trade of items up to the value of US$20,000 or equivalent*

Barter trade under this category envisages exchange of 22 identified commodities up to the value of US$20,000 or its equivalent. As a form of barter trade, in this case also, there is only exchange of goods and no monetary transaction is involved. However, the settlement procedure is not as simple as in the case of barter trade up to US$1000 category. The relevant RBI guidelines provide *inter alia* that:

i) The consignments of imports and exports should be invoiced in US Dollars or any convertible currency (i.e. Euro, Japanese Yen and Sterling Pound) not exceeding US$20,000 or equivalent per transaction.

ii) The exporters should get the GR forms countersigned by the designated bank before the exports. A copy of the contract for import and export with Myanmar parties should also be submitted along with the GR forms.

iii) On completion of export, the duplicate copy of GR form along with all commercial documents viz. customs certified copy of invoice etc. should be submitted to the designated bank within 21 days from the date of export.

iv) In case of imports, where the value exceeds US$5000 or equivalent, the importer should submit the documentary evidence, i.e. Bill of Entry to the designated bank.

v) The export of goods from India to Myanmar against import of goods from Myanmar to India and vice versa should be completed within a period of six months from the date of import/export.

The most important factor that sets limit to this type of trade is the limited number of exchangeable items. As of now only 22 identified items, which are mostly agricultural/forest produce are permitted to be exchanged under the system. Another limiting factor that prevailed till recently was the stipulation that import from Myanmar should precede export from India. This has, however, been dispensed with from 5th August 2004.

Despite the above restrictions, the volume of barter trade under this system through Moreh-Tamu sector is showing an upward trend. The volume of such trade (up to US$20,000 category) during the year 2003-04 was about Rs.17.45 crore. Another important revelation is that the traders have been facing difficulty in balancing their imports with exports and as a result a good part of imports remain outstanding for a long time. Since April 2003, however, there is a sign of trend reversal and exports are now picking up at a faster rate.

c) *Normal Trade against payment for the supplies*

While a trade transaction under barter system is settled by way of exchange of goods between the buyer and the seller and no monetary transaction is involved, in a normal trade, however, there is the exchange of money and goods between them. As such, unlike in barter system, the trader in a normal trade is under no obligation to balance his imports with exports or vice versa. The export/import transaction is complete once he receives/pays in the designated currency (ACU Dollar) and in an approved manner i.e. normally within six months from the date of export/import and through the banking channel.

The normal trade is governed by the trade control and exchange control regulations of the country.

Since ACU Dollar is the settlement currency for trade between India and Myanmar, an understanding of the Asian Clearing Union (ACU) is imperative particularly in the context of the recently imposed sanction by the United States Government on Myanmar which has, for the time being, created a virtual stalemate condition in the normal trade between the two countries.

3. The Settlement currency: ACU Dollar

At the very outset it may be made clear that value-wise, there is no difference between the ACU Dollar and US Dollar. In transactions denominated in ACU Dollar, the exchange rates for US Dollar are applied. Even the forward premium/discount for different periods which are quoted for US Dollar against Indian Rupee in the ongoing market are also applicable for ACU Dollar transactions.

The term ACU Dollar is specifically used to identify the use of US Dollar in relation to Asian Clearing Union (ACU) transactions. The settlement system for ACU Dollar transactions are, however, somewhat different from those denominated in US Dollar.

a) The background and purpose of formation of Asian Clearing Union

With a view to securing regional co-operation for expansion of trade and economic relations, the Asian Clearing Union (ACU) was established in the year 1974 at the initiative of United Nations Economic and Social Commission for Asia and Pacific (ESCAP). The initial participants were the Central Banks of Iran, India, Pakistan, Bangladesh, Sri Lanka and Nepal. The Central Banks of Myanmar and Bhutan joined the Union later. The headquarters of the Union i.e. the ACU Secretariat is at Tehran, Iran. At the time of its inception, the Union sought to provide a partial solution, within a regional framework, the two major payment problems experienced by Asian countries viz. shortage of foreign exchange and non-convertibility of currencies. The focus is now on promoting monetary co-operation among the participants, to provide a facility for settlement of current international transactions on a multilateral basis among the participants and thereby contributing to the expansion of trade and economic activity among the countries of the ESCAP region.

b) Settlement procedure under ACU mechanism

The ACU mechanism has undergone several structural changes since its inception in the year 1974. Till December 1995, the settlement of eligible transactions was required to be made in the currency of the importer's or exporter's country or in Asian Monetary Unit (AMU) which was equivalent in value to one Special Drawing Right (SDR) as valued from time to time by the IMF. The modified mechanism effective from 1st January 1996 was a major departure from the earlier one when there was a switch-over from multi currency to a Dollar denominated trade among the ACU countries. The salient features of the Dollar denominated trade under ACU are as under:

i) Banks are permitted to handle commercial and other eligible transactions under ACU in much the same way they handle normal foreign exchange business. The usual procedure for opening of LC, negotiation of documents etc. is applicable for trade routed through the ACU mechanism.

ii) Payments are required to be made through ACU Dollar accounts with banks (authorised dealers) in India and the banks in the participating countries without the intervention of the central banks. Payments for export from India will be received by debit to the ACU Dollar accounts of the banks of other participating countries maintained with banks in India or by credit to the ACU Dollar accounts of

Indian banks maintained with banks in the other participating countries. The reverse will be the case for settlement of imports into India from any of the ACU countries. An exception to this rule is India's trade with Nepal and Bhutan which are, under special arrangement, settled in Rupee outside the ACU mechanism.

iii) While there is no bar on any Contract, Letter of Credit, Invoice etc. being denominated in US Dollar, it should invariably stipulate that the actual payment shall be made in ACU Dollar.

iv) While individual trade transactions are settled through the ACU Dollar accounts of banks without intervention of the central banks of the participating countries, such intervention is necessary for the purpose of funding of ACU Dollar accounts or repatriation of funds from these accounts. The issue is not discussed here in detail as it concerns the banks only.

c) *Applicability of ACU mechanism in Indo-Myanmar Border Trade*

Both India and Myanmar being the members of the eight nation conglomerate 'Asian Clearing Union', all trade transactions between the two countries are required to be compulsorily settled through the ACU mechanism. However, the transactions that take place under the barter system within the provisions of 'Indo-Myanmar Border Trade Agreement' are not subject to ACU mechanism due to the simple reason that in such cases, only goods are exchanged in settlement (though invoiced in US Dollar or any convertible currency) and no monetary transaction is involved. But the settlement of normal trade requires payment for the supplies and as such they fall within the purview of ACU mechanism. Thus, all our export/import transactions with Myanmar under the normal trade require settlement either through an ACU Dollar account of a bank in Myanmar maintained with a bank in India or through a similar account of a bank in India maintained with a bank in Myanmar.

In lines with the above requirement, the ACU Dollar account of 'Myanma Economic Bank' was opened with the Moreh Branch of 'United Bank of India' in September 2000.

Complexities Associated with International Trade and Settlement Methods

Normal trade under the Indo-Myanmar border trade is akin to any other international trade and is associated with the inherent risks and complexities.

Trading in international market involves buyer and seller from two different countries. The goods move from the seller's country to the buyer's and the money flows in the opposite direction. The exchange process is not simple. This is because the buyer and seller reside in two different countries which have different currencies, different political and legal system, the trade and exchange control regulations, market practices are all different. When placed in such complex situation, both will try to adopt a settlement system which would take care of their individual problems, apprehensions and requirements.

The seller's primary concern is to receive the contracted price in time while the buyer's concern is to receive the ordered goods in time. The usual methods of settlement between the buyer and the seller in international trade are discussed below:

i) Advance payment method

In this method the seller's interest is fully protected because he receives the money in advance. But the buyer is exposed to risk and he will not agree to such method unless he has sufficient trust in seller.

ii) Documentary Collection

Under this method the seller despatch the goods and submits the documents (including the transport document) to his bank. The seller's bank in turn forwards the documents to the buyer's bank for collection. The buyer takes delivery of the documents from his bank against payment or acceptance of the bill as per the agreement. In this case, the risk of the seller is more because he relies on the buyer and ships the goods.

iii) Open Account Payment

In this system the seller ships the goods to the buyer, allows the buyer to use or sale the goods and pay for them later as per their mutual agreement. This type of settlement is possible only when the seller has more trust in buyer.

iv) Settlement under Documentary Credit

The seller in this system gets his payment once he ships the goods and submits documents to the bank strictly as per conditions stipulated. The buyer is also assured that payment has been made to the seller only against documents in compliance with the credit terms.

'Letter of Credit': An Ideal Instrument for Settlement of International Trade Payments

An analysis of the above settlement methods reveals that in the first three cases, the common factor is 'trust'. The Advance payment method is based on buyer's trust on the seller while the opposite is the situation in Documentary Collection and Open Account Payment methods. As such, they are not considered reliable settlement systems particularly in international trade where, the trust apart, other factors like Trade and Exchange Control Regulations etc. play an important role in deciding the method of settlement. Normally, the seller would like to have control over the goods till the buyer makes payment. The buyer on the other hand, likes to make payment after ensuring that the ordered goods have been shipped/ despatched by the seller. Thus we observe that even when the buyer and the seller have mutual interest in a transaction, their financial requirements are conflicting in nature. In the circumstances, the ideal way to reconcile the conflicting interest of the parties is to use an independent third party who can ensure a satisfactory exchange of money and goods between the seller and the buyer. In a Letter of Credit transaction, a bank acts as an intermediary who can ensure definite constructive delivery of goods by the seller and definite payment by the buyer. It is due to this reason only that 'Letter of Credit' is an ideal instrument for settlement of international trade payments.

The Mechanism of 'Letter of Credit'

In simple terms, a Letter of Credit (also called a Documentary Credit) is "Bank's Conditional Undertaking of Payment". In other words the bank, in a Letter of Credit, undertakes to pay to the seller subject to his complying with certain terms and conditions. Through this "Terms and Conditions" it ensures constructive delivery of goods (in the form of documents of title to goods and not in physical form) to the buyer.

Seller and buyer enter into a sale/purchase contract for the supply of goods/services in exchange of money and they agree to utilize the service of a bank. On the basis of the sale contract, the buyer (called the '**Applicant**') approaches his bank to issue a conditional undertaking for payment (called the '**Letter of Credit**') in favour of the seller.

On being satisfied that the transaction is within the provisions of trade and exchange control regulations of the country and based on the LC application and the underlying contract between the buyer and the seller, the buyer's bank (called the '**Issuing Bank**') issues the Letter of Credit (LC) in favour of the seller (called the '**Beneficiary**'). The LC is then sent by the issuing bank to its correspondent bank in the beneficiary's country (called the '**Advising Bank**'). The Advising Bank's responsibility is to verify authenticity of the LC and then deliver the same to the beneficiary without any further engagement on their part.

At times, however, the beneficiary (the seller) insists that the LC should also contain, in addition to the undertaking of the Issuing Bank, an undertaking of payment of a bank in his own country (called the '**Confirming Bank**'). The Issuing Bank in such cases, requests the Advising Bank or any other bank in the beneficiary's country to add confirmation to the LC.

Every LC indicates whether the documents drawn under it will be available by payment/ negotiation/ acceptance with a particular bank or with any bank in the beneficiary's country. Such named bank is called the **Nominated Bank**. In a freely negotiable LC, any bank is a nominated bank.

The beneficiary i.e. the exporter, upon receipt of the LC, proceeds for despatch of the goods as per LC terms. After despatch, the exporter submits the document of title to goods viz. Bill of Lading/ Air Way Bill/ Truck Receipt etc. along with the other required documents as per terms of the LC to the Nominated Bank for negotiation of the documents.

The Nominated Bank scrutinises the documents and if they are found to be as per the LC terms, makes payment to the exporter. The Nominated Bank after making payment to the exporter (beneficiary) against negotiation of credit conform documents becomes the **Negotiating Bank**.

The Negotiating Bank, after the negotiation, forward the documents to the LC Issuing Bank and claim the reimbursement. Sometimes, while the documents are forwarded to the LC Issuing Bank, the reimbursement is claimed separately from another bank (called the '**Reimbursement Bank**'). The LC Issuing Bank, once satisfied that the documents are in conformity with the LC terms, settles the reimbursement claim of the Negotiating Bank and delivers the documents to the opener (the Buyer). With the help of the documents, the Buyer takes delivery of the goods from the carrier company. Finally, the LC Issuing bank realises payment from the buyer immediately or on the due date, depending on the tenor of the bill.

The Benefits Derived by the End-users and the Precautions to be Observed

Letters of Credit are widely used across the world as an ideal instrument of international trade settlement. This is so, because LC provides certain benefits to the end users i.e. to the exporters and the importers which are not available in other settlement methods. However, the efficacy of the system lies in the awareness of those who get associated with the Letters of Credit in various capacities.

A. *To the Exporter*

i) As the beneficiary of LC, the first and the foremost advantage to the exporter is the minimization of payment risk i.e. it gives him the assurance of payment for his supplies.

ii) The exporter can get immediate payment from the negotiating bank against submission of documents after shipment/despatch of goods.

iii) Even at the pre-shipment stage, the exporter may get financial assistance from his bank for execution of the export order under the LC.

However, it must be kept in mind that the LC issuing bank's undertaking of payment is conditional and the LC system is governed by the doctrine of strict compliance. Even a slight variation/departure from the stipulated terms renders the LC void and the exporter is deprived of the benefits.

The exporter should, on receipt of the LC, get himself satisfied that the terms and conditions of the LC are in agreement with the underlying sale/purchase contract and that they are not difficult for him to comply with. Otherwise, he should take up the matter with his counterpart i.e. the buyer (importer) for arranging necessary amendment of the LC.

B. *To the Importer*

i) The Letter of Credit enables the importer to purchase goods without making any advance payment to the seller in another country. He can thus avoid the risk of loss due to non-delivery by the seller.

ii) At the instance of the Importer, the LC may call for documents like pre-shipment inspection certificate, health certificate, packing list, weight list etc. so as to satisfy him about the quality and quantity of the goods.

iii) The importer can also ensure timely delivery of the goods by stipulating the last date of shipment/despatch in the LC.

The importer, however, should keep in mind that under a LC transaction, the banks deal in documents and not in goods. The LC can ensure him constructive delivery of goods represented by documents only and he remains liable to pay on receipt of documents as per LC terms. This is irrespective of whether he receives the goods to his satisfaction.

The importer should, while applying for issuance of the LC, advise the bank to call for appropriate documents like pre-shipment inspection certificate, health certificate (in case of perishable goods, particularly for human consumption), packing list, weight list etc. as a safe guard against this risk.

Standardisation of Letter of Credit Operation Across the World

International trade transactions involve different parties from different countries where the legal systems, usage and practice of trade are different. As such, any particular incidence or situation under a Letter of Credit transaction may be interpreted differently in the Buyer's and the Seller's countries. This may give rise to disputes and make settlement process difficult. In such a scenario, a standardized rule is necessary for smooth operations of Letter of Credit (or Documentary Credit) system.

With the objective of creating a level play-field for Letter of Credit operation in different countries, the International Chamber of Commerce (ICC), a non-governmental and independent world organisation, formulated a standard set of rules known as ' Uniform Customs and Practice for Documentary Credits' (UCPDC). These rules were first codified in the year 1933 and were revised from time to time keeping with the changes in the trade practices, transportation and communication systems that took place over the years. The current set of rules was published in the ICC Brochures No UCP-500 and became effective since 1.1.1994. The UCP-500 contains 49 articles (with sub-articles) covering different areas viz. duties and responsibilities of all the parties to a Letter of Credit, different terms used in a LC and their interpretations, various documents under LC and their acceptability under different situations etc.

The UCPDC is a set of standard rules governing LC transactions and is not a law. Hence it does not bind the parties unless they subject themselves to it. Since UCPDC has worldwide acceptance and is recognized by over 165 countries including India, we issue and accept only such LCs that are subject to the provisions of UCPDC. An expression to that effect must be incorporated in the LC.

Despite the application of UCPDC (current pub- UCP 500), some survey reports indicated that a good percentage of documents are rejected by banks due to discrepancies. This diminishes the effectiveness of LC and adds unnecessary cost and complications to the importers and exporters. With a view to minimizing the incidence of rejection of documents under LC, the ICC has recently come out with yet another publication called 'International Standard Banking Practice' (ISBP). The ISBP is not an amendment to UCP-500 but a supplement to it.

In order to realise the full benefit of Letter of Credit system and to avoid unnecessary rejection of documents under LC, it is necessary that the importers, exporters and bankers handling LCs under various capacities have a clear understanding on the UCPDC provisions.

Issues Concerning Implementation of Letter of Credit for Indo-Myanmar Border Trade and the Present Position

To facilitate border trade with Myanmar, a number of trade points have been identified. But as of now, the happenings are mostly taking place in the Moreh-Tamu sector and the other trade points are yet to take-off. To provide necessary banking arrangement for border trade (both barter and normal trade) through this sector, United Bank of India (UBI), Moreh Branch and Myanma Economic Bank (MEB), Tamu Branch have been identified as the designated banks by the Indian and Myanmarese authorities.

The two banks had entered into a Memorandum of Understanding (MOU) in April 2000 and under the MOU, an ACU Dollar account of MEB was opened with UBI, Moreh Branch in September 2000. As per provisions of the MOU, transactions under documentary Letter of Credit (LC) is to commence as soon as both UBI at Moreh and MEB at Tamu are adequately equipped.

Immediate implementation of LC system was not considered feasible as the infrastructural facilities, both in terms of technical and trained man power resources, was not available in the distant Moreh–Tamu border region at that time.

Since signing of the MOU between the two banks, however, several steps have been initiated to overcome the problems for implementation of Letter of Credit transactions. The first meeting of India-Myanmar Joint Trade Committee held in Yangon in July 2003 envisaged the need for immediate operationalisation of Letter of Credit for promotion of trade between the two countries.

The opening of ACU Dollar settlement account of MEB with UBI, Moreh Branch was the first major step towards development of normal trade through the border. This account was meant for settlement of both export and import transactions under Letters of Credit as well as against bank drafts. As regard the other facilities, arrangement has been made for communication of authenticated telegraphic messages between the two banks. This was necessary due to the absence of SWIFT facility in the region. Also, since exchange of documents between the two banks through official postal medium would take a long time, an alternative arrangement has been made for quicker exchange of documents. With a view to imparting knowledge and creating general awareness on Letter of Credit transactions, both the State Government of Manipur and the Union Government have taken initiative to organize several seminars, workshops and training programmes with active participation of the officials and traders from both sides of the border. It has also been decided that if necessary, UBI will depute one suitable officer to MEB for some time to facilitate implementation of Letter of Credit system for the border trade transactions.

Despite the above developments, the recent imposition of economic sanction by the US Government on Myanmar is now posing a serious problem in the process of commencement of LC operation for the border trade.

In so far as trade between India and Myanmar is concerned, the above sanction of the United States on Myanmar has serious implications. As we have already discussed, India and Myanmar being the members of Asian Clearing Union, settlement of trade between the two countries, as per the extant exchange control guidelines, is required to be made only in US Dollar under the ACU mechanism. But the transfer of US Dollar funds, which ultimately takes place in the United States, is not being allowed in respect of any transaction involving Myanmar. The situation has created a virtual stalemate condition in the normal trade between India and Myanmar.

Under the circumstances, the Myanmarese side has expressed willingness to transact in other currencies like Euro. Such proposal has been referred by Indian authorities to the ACU Secretariat at Tehran, the conglomerate of eight member nations. A decision in this matter is awaited.

Another impediment to the growth of normal trade

including Letter of Credit transaction is the wide difference between the official administered rate and unofficial market rate of Kyat against US Dollar or Indian Rupee.

Since both the countries are keen to promote trade for their mutual interest, it is expected that the above issues would be duly addressed by the appropriate authorities to restore the normal trade and implement Letter of Credit for border trade transactions. We have already experienced the efficacy of Letter of Credit system in the promotion of border trade between India and Bangladesh and we strongly believe that the system will play the same role of a catalyst for promotion of Indo-Myanmar border trade.

14

India-China Trade through the Stilwell Road

—H. N. Das

Considerable emphasis has been given to border trade between India and Myanmar through the Moreh-Tamu route on the Manipur-Myanmar border and also through the Mizoram-Myanmar route. Much has been written about the possibility of legalising the currently clandestine smuggling going on under the nose of customs and police on these two recognised routes. But not enough has been written or spoken about the possibility of opening up the old route between India and Myanmar which then goes to China's southern city of Kunming and beyond. This road is known as the Stilwell Road. Most of the goods imported into India, legally or illegally, through the existing routes are actually manufactured in China and brought into India through Myanmar.

The object of this chapter is to give the historical background of the Stilwell Road and to point out the issues and problems connected with its reopening for trade between India, the northern areas of Myanmar and the south-western areas of China, mainly the Yunnan province.

Available information show that for centuries there was some path linking China's Yunnan province to Assam. In the Comprehensive History of Assam, edited by late H.K. Borpujari, it has been recorded as follows: "it appears that there had been an old route from south-western Yunnan to Assam. The Tais possessed knowledge of the topography through which the route passed and also of the Brahmaputra valley".[1] The Tais came to Assam in the thirteenth century crossing the Patkai range of mountains under the leadership of Sukapha who became the first Ahom king of Assam. He ruled from 1228 to 1268. He is credited with uniting the diverse ethnic communities then inhabiting the Brahmaputra Valley. The Ahoms got absorbed in the greater Assamese society and ruled for more than six hundred years till the Yandaboo treaty of February 24, 1826, when Assam was ceded to the British.

During the Sino-Japanese war, preceding the Second World War, the Nationalist Chinese troops were supplied with their requirements "overland on a dirt road carved out of the mountains in 1937-38 by 1,60,000 Chinese with virtually no equipment. This was the famous Burma Road, a 1 000 km. haul from Lashio to Kunming."[2] This road became the Chinese portion of the Stilwell Road. The existence of this road lightened the construction cost of the Stilwell Road.

During the Second World War there were two main thrusts by the Allied Army in Burma (present Myanmar). The Southern thrust towards Rangoon (present Yangoon) was led by Field Marshall Sir William Slim who was in command of the Fourteenth Army under the South-East Asia Command (SEAC). His Army completely destroyed Japan's military power in South-East Asia. Indian troops played "a highly important role" in this campaign. Slim had observed later that "India was our base, and three quarters of everything we got from there. The best thing of all we got from India was the Indian Army. Indeed, the campaign in Burma was largely an Indian Army campaign. The bulk of the fighting troops and almost the whole of those on the fines of communication were soldiers of the Indian Army, and magnificent they were. India, too, trained and sent us our reinforcements"[3]. Again, to quote the distinguished historian Percival Spear, it was the British Indian Army to whom credit must go for "the crowning triumph of the recapture of Rangoon."[4].

However, the main body of SEAC made its thrust in the north through Myanmar to China. The details of its campaign are available in Lord Louis Mountbatten's (1900-1989) Report as the Supreme Commander of SEAC (1943-45). He had submitted a detailed "Report to the Combined Chiefs of Staff' of the Allied Army at the end of the Second World War. In this extremely unreadable but valuable chronicle of those times he has left behind nuggets of information about Assam and the neighbouring countries. It is replete with maps, charts, annexures and appendices.[5]

In the present book Mountbatten has written as follows: "On the 27th January (1945), the Ledo Road was opened. 38 Chinese Division of N.C.A.C. established contact with Chinese Army Group of the Yunnan Force on the old Burma Road at Mong Yu, on the Burma side of the frontier about 20 miles south of Wanting. On the following day, the first American Chinese convoy from India, led by Brigadier-General Pick, crossed the frontier with appropriate rejoicings." The map shows Wanting, on the Chinese side, to be 483 miles from Ledo. On the Burmese side the farthest post of Namhkan was 444 miles from Ledo. The last post on the Indian side was Loglai, 51 miles from Ledo, which connected the nearest post of Tazaplug Ga on the Burmese side which was 80 miles from Ledo. The most important place on this road in Burma, Myitkyina, which was a Railway, Road and Pipeline junction and a big market and was 253 miles from Ledo.

Mountbatten had a running feud with his American Deputy, the redoubtable 'Vineager Joe', whose real name was General J. W. Stilwell. Both of them were great soldiers. But they had different ideas and points of view. Anecdotes and incidents regarding their differences of opinion cover many pages of the book. Mountbatten had personally aired his complaint against Stilwell to the US leaders. In the book Mountbatten notes with dismay that his Deputy used to communicate with Washington directly "without informing me of the fact." While Mountbatten was dignified and restrained in his language Stilwell felt that "the world was against him and he revanged himself with black bile and an excoriating tongue." Stilwell's "diary entries became more splenetic" and he described Mountbatten as "a fatuous ass," "Childish Louis, publicity crazy," "a pisspot" etc.[6]

But Mountbatten was magnanimous and broad minded enough to record in the book as follows: "The Generalissimo christened the road the "Stilwell Road," as a compliment to the man who had the courage and the skill to push through the project and who until three months previously had commanded the forces that had carried it out." Generalissimo, Chiang Kei Shek had become the supreme leader and President of China after the death of Sun Yet Sen.

Stilwell held several simultaneous appointments including that of Chief of Staff to Chiang. But as observed by historian John Keegan in.his famous book on "the Second World War" Stilwell "displayed an impatience with the Chinese that was exceeded in degree only by his rudeness towards the British with whom he was co-operating." Keegan further notes that "the vitriolic Stilwell, who had definitely fallen out in turn with the British, the Chinese and ultimately President Roosevelt" was removed by Roosevelt on October 18, 1944.[7]

The enigmatic Chiang had vehemently opposed US President Roosevelt's proposal to put Stilwell "in direct command of all Chinese troops, both Nationalist and Communists" because he felt that it would be an insult to China. What is surprising is that on that occasion Mao Zedong, the Communist leader, had supported Roosevelt and declared that by this behaviour Chiang had "forfeited his position as leader of the war of resistance against Japan". Mao probably expected that Stilwell would be able to stop Chiang's corruption if he had been appointed to the crucial post in the Chinese Army.[8] But Chiang won at the end when Roosevelt relented and removed Stilwell.

The Stilwell Road is a marvel of engineering excellence. It was built at such a huge expense because it was important for the Allied powers to win the war against Japan. By making direct supplies possible to China it assisted in the war effort in that theatre. As mentioned by Mountbatten the Americans were "thinking solely in terms of China and of Northern Burma as a supply route to China." They were "primarily interested" in the "permanent security of the Ledo Road." For that purpose they ordered the "pushing ahead with opening the land route into China as fast as possible." The Americans believed that the "main advantage" of the Stilwell Road lay "not in the actual tonnage the road would carry, but in greatly increased supplies of petrol (gasoline) which the pipe line, running parallel with the road, would bring to the China based air forces." The British and the Americans seem to have differed on their objectives in fighting for "liberating" Burma. The British wanted their empire back. So they put more emphasis on the Southern front. The Americans were clear that "U.S. forces and resources are committed to the China-Burma-India area for the purpose of assisting China." According to them "the significance of Assam and North Burma was that they provided bases from which supplies to China could be ferried by air across the mountains loosely known as "the Hump", and eventually, it was hoped, by road."[9] The hump was the 5000 mtr. high mountain range dividing India and Burma. There lay the significance of the Stilwell Road.

The map shows three pipelines. One US pipeline ran from Kolkata to Tinsukia and then on to Mogaung near Myitkyina. The second US pipeline ran from Chittagong to Dimapur and Tinsukia. These two then jointly ran from Tinsukia to Bhamo in Burma and to Chanyi and Luliang beyond Kunming in China. The British pipeline ran from Chittagong to Dimapur and then to Tamu on the Burma border. What a configuration? And the effort and the expenses?

Chiang and his wife Sung Li had convinced Stilwell to build the road so that the petrol pipelines could be layed and protected. China needed the petrol for the Allied airborne forces operating against the Japanese from airfields in Assam, Burma and Yunnan. When Sung Li died at the age of 106 at New York on the night of October 23, 2003, I happened to be in Taipei.

From talks with Chinese friends and the newspaper reports in the next couple of days I realised how important Sung Li and Chiang were for Chinese and world history. Sung Li inspired Chiang all through his chequered career. Sung Li was one of most powerful woman of all times. Born to one of the richest families of Shanghai she was a razing beauty in her youth both in China and in the USA, where she had her education. Michael Calvert notes in his memorable biography of Field Marshal William Joseph Slim that she "had great influence in the United States" and that she "hated the British."[9] After Chiang won the war against Japan he had to retreat to Taiwan in 1949 when China was taken over by the People's Liberation Army of Mao. But he and Sung Li together built up Taiwan as one of the richest countries in the world. It has a per capita income which is seven times that of India.

I got my first opportunity to travel on the Stilwell Road only after I joined at Dibrugarh as the Deputy Commissioner of the erstwhile united Lakhimpur district in late 1969. My wife and I went by jeep from Jairampur, accompanied by Government of India officials, and reached a. Burmese Army camp on a hill overlooking the Lake of No Return. We stayed overnight in the camp and enjoyed their hospitality. It was not possible to travel the entire distance by jeep. We had to walk because the road bed was broken and at places non-existent due to landslides. It is then that I realised what an engineering feat that the Allied Army accomplished in building the road. But the scenery was breathtaking. The flora was exquisite. I had never seen such beauty and variety in orchids anywhere else, not even in the North-East of Thailand where thousands of Americans go to see orchids in the hills near Chiang Mai, Chiang Rai and Nong Khai.

There is a recent move to re-open the nearly 1,800 kms. long Stilwell Road. On the Chinese side it is now a Super Expressway stretching 1,150 kms. On the Myanmarese (Burma) side out of 525 kms. the road is reported to be bad only for 160 kms, which can be repaired and rebuilt. On the Indian side, 71 kms. from Ledo in Assam to Pheng Sau in Arunachal Pradesh, are covered by a National Highway. Only a small portion from Pheng Sau to the Myanmarese border will need complete rebuilding.[10]

It is true that international trade can be fostered if the road is reopened. The city of Kunming and its hinterland in the Yunnan province and beyond are very prosperous to-day and a substantial manufacturing industry has grown up there. The transport facilities from there to the bigger Chinese cities of Shanghai, Beijing and Guangzhou are also very advanced. But it will be necessary to ensure that India will gain from such trade. I have toured extensively across China during September-October, 2002. I have seen what tremendous economic development is taking place in that country. No one can believe how China is being transformed into an economic superpower unless he has seen that country. In 1990, India and China had the same per capita income. In 2002 China's per capita income became double that of India. It is going further ahead. Can India compete with that country? Already smuggled Chinese goods abound in the markets of the North-Eastern States. These are available in plenty in some other parts of the country too. These appear to be low-priced. What can India offer against these imports? And will the backward North-Eastern Region simply become the under belly of a bridge from China to North India?

Then there is the question of insurgency. The jungles on both sides of the Stilwell Road contain excellent hideouts for the Naga, Manipuri and Assamese insurgents. A super highway will provide easier passage to the insurgents. The same will happen in the case of the drug mafia from the nearby golden triangle.

All these questions will need deeper and detailed examination before any final decision is taken.

NOTES AND REFERENCES

1. Borpujari, H. K. (ed.), *The Comprehensive History of Assam*. Volume Two, Publication Board, Assam, Guwahati, 1992.

2. Cummings, Joe, et al., *China*. Lonely Planet Publications Pty. Ltd., Singapore, 1991.

3. Majumdar, R. C., Roychoudhury, H. C. and Datta, Kalikinkar, *An Advanced History of India*, MacMillan & Company, Delhi, 1985.

4. Spear, Percival, *The Oxford History of Modern India*, Oxford University Press, Delhi, 1992.

5. *The Earl Mountbatten of Burma, Report to the Combined Chiefs of Staff by the Supreme Allied Commander, South-East Asia Command 1943-1945,* The English Book Store, New Delhi, 1960.

6. Ziegler, Philip, *Mountbatten: The Official Biography*, Collins, London, 1985.

7. Keegan, John, *The Second World War*, Viking Penguin, New York, 1990.

8. Schram, Stuart, *Mao Tse-Tung*, Penguin Books Ltd, Harmondsworth, Middlesex, England, 1966.

9. Calvert, Michael, *Slim*, Ballantine Books Inc, New York, 1973.

10. *The Economic Times*, Wednesday, 21 January, 2004, "Stilwell Road May Be New Gateway to China", Kolkata.

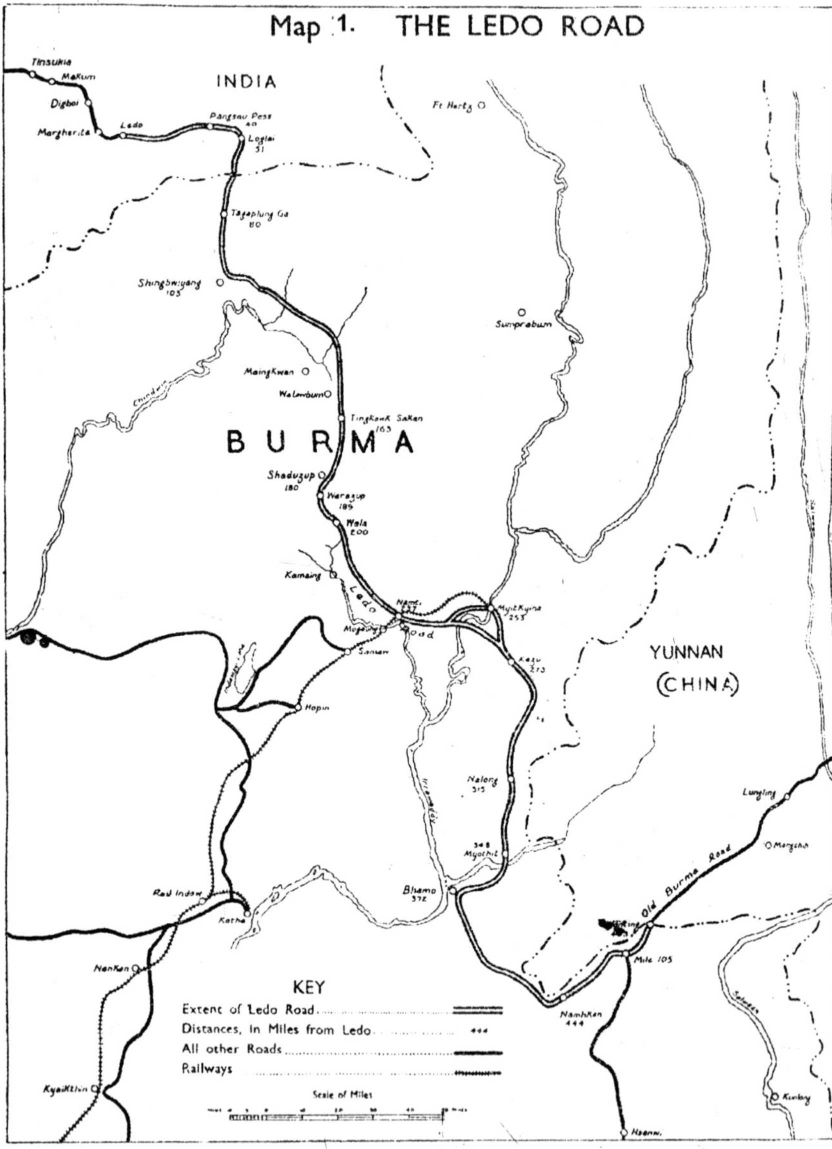
Map 1. THE LEDO ROAD
INDIA
BURMA
YUNNAN
(CHINA)
Tinsukia
Makum
Digboi
Margherita
Ledo
Pangsau Pass
40
Loglai
51
Ft Hertz
Shingbwiyang
105
Sumprabum
Maingkwan
Walawbum
Tingkawk Sakan
163
Shaduzup
180
Warazup
189
Wala
200
Kamaing
Ledo Road
Myitkyina
253
Mogaung
Sansaw
Hopin
Kazu
273
Nalong
315
348
Myothit
Bhamo
372
Lungling
Old Burma Road
Mile 105
Namhkan
444
Red Indaw
Katha
Nankan
Kyaikthin
Hsenwi
KEY
Extent of Ledo Road
Distances, in Miles from Ledo
444
All other Roads
Railways
Scale of Miles

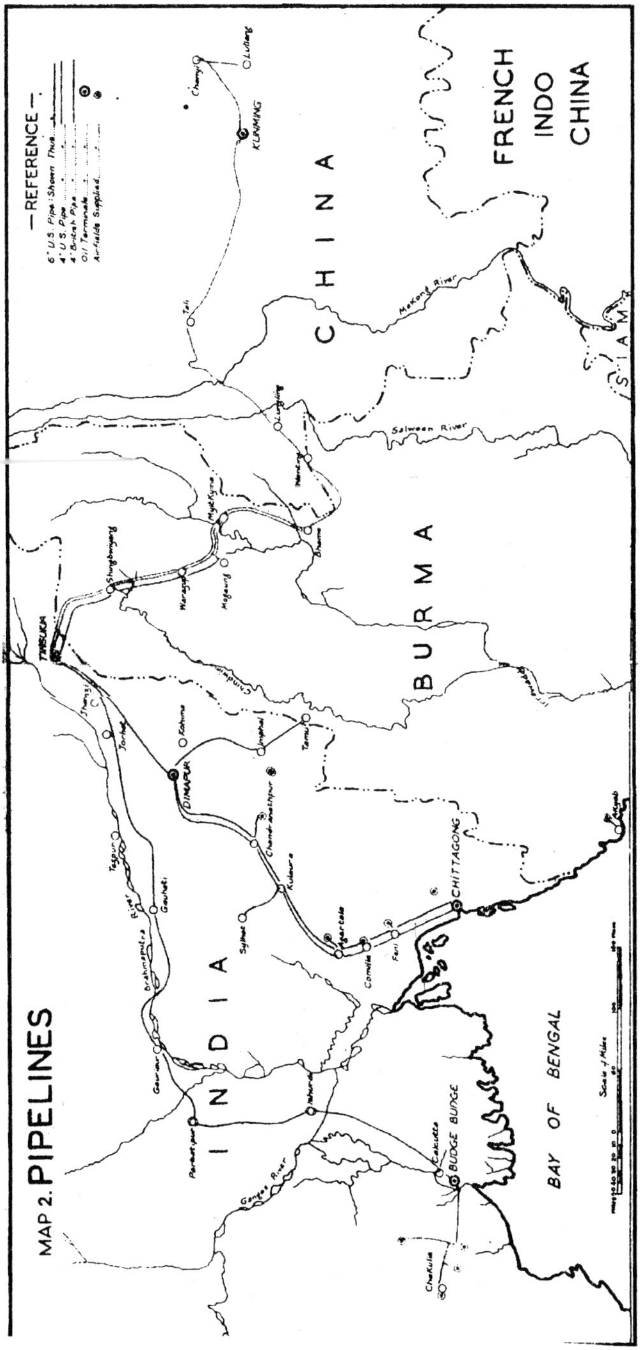

MAP 2. PIPELINES

15

Border Trade: A Note on Mizoram-Myanmar Sector

—Lallura Sailo

Salient Features of the Border Trade with Myanmar

i) Development of border trade is one of the clauses enshrined in the Mizoram Accord of 1986 signed between the MNF (which is now the party in Mizoram) and the Government of India. There has been considerable delay in implementing this invaluable clause of agreement which is the only course available to landlocked Mizoram for accelerating economic development.

ii) The sincere efforts made jointly by the Government of India and Government of Mizoram has enabled construction of Land Customs Stations (LCS) at Zokhawthar (near Champhai) on the extreme border with Myanmar. Out of the total project cost of Rs. 7.00 crores. Ministry of Commerce, Government of India has released Rs. 2.00 crores to BRO for construction of Composite Land Customs Station at Zokhawthar which will house offices of telecom, bank, postal, immigration, security and trade and commerce department. The following actions have been actively taken by the Government of Mizoram.

iii) Land measuring 18.40 bhigas (i.e., 24625.985 sq.m) was acquired at Zokhawthar at the cost of Rs. 1,44,260/- for Land Customs Stations on 7/9/2000.

iv) 147 houses within the acquired site have been evicted and rehabilitated to Phulmawitlang which is 1 km from Zokhawthar. Compensations are paid to the evicted families. The Government of Mizoram has provided electricity, water supply, school building, road to Phulmawitlang and other relief assistances to the evicted families in 2001.

v) B.R.O has set up its construction camp at Zokhawthar and it is expected to start the construction as the MOU was signed and handed over to the BRO by Government of Mizoram on 25/4/2001.

vi) Government of Mizoram is rigorously pursuing with Government of India for sanction of the balance of Rs. 5.00 crores for the development of the Indo-Myanmar border trade infrastructural facilities.

vii) A police outpost has also been set up at Zokhawthar which provides security to the construction workers as well as the traders of the international border since September 2001.

viii) The Government has also acquired 126.95 acres of land at Khawnuam (Melbuk) which is 8 km from Zokhawthar for establishment of Indo-Myanmar Border Trade township. This township has been planned systematically for accommodating staff quarters/office buildings of postal, bank, telecom, security etc. and also construction of helipad staff quarters, recreational facilities, godown etc. A detail project report for water supply for this township amounting to Rs. 3.5 crores has also been submitted to the Ministry of Commerce, Government of India. Community hall, play ground, health centre, rest house etc. have already been constructed in the border trade township from Border Area Development Fund (BADF).

ix) Secretary, North Eastern Council (NEC), Shillong accompanied by the Chief Secretary of Mizoram visited Khawnuam Indo-Myanmar border trade township and

LCS site Zokhawthar on 28.4.01. They were impressed with the developments. The 47th NEC Council Meeting also approved a sum of Rs. 9.31 crores for setting up of Special Economic Zone at Khawnuam during the 10th Plan of NEC Schemes.

x) Government of Mizoram has completed the construction of the Bailey Bridge between India & Myanmar at Zokhawthar and was inaugurated by Hon'ble Chief Minister, Mizoram.

xi) Laying of foundation stones by Minister, Trade & Commerce at Khawnuam (Melbuk) and Zokhawthar was held on 5.12.01.

xii) 2nd Border Trade Point at Zokhawthar-Rih sector was joined on 31.1.04 by Minister of Commerce, Mizoram.

Prospects of Border Trade with Myanmar

1. The people living in Mizoram and the people living in the areas of Myanmar adjacent to Mizoram will benefit from the border trade between Indo-Myanmar from Zokhawthar- Rih sector.

2. The commitment of the Government of Myanmar for the development of Rih Lake to tourist centre will enable the people of from both the countries to visit the legendary Rih Lake. This will greatly boost tourism in this sector.

3. The development of road connectivity between Rih-Zokhawthar to Falam and Kalemeo on one side and Tiddim – Kalemeo in the other will lead to more and more economic contracts between India and Myanmar and will lead to economic prosperity of the people living on both sides.

4. Development of water-ways between South Mizoram and Myanmar leading to Port of Sittwe (Akyabs) will also boost trade between the two countries and will indirectly benefit the people of Mizoram and Myanmar.

Problems of Border Trade with Myanmar

i) The construction of composite LCS at Zokhawthar by BRO could not start till date. This has affected the development of border trade with Myanmar from Zokhawthar-Rih sector.

ii) No corresponding LCS on the Myanmar side of the border

iii) Unless and until the road and water connectivity to Myanmar from Zokhawthar-Rih is developed, the trading activities from this sector cannot increase.

iv) The list of items agreed for the trade between Myanmar and India needs to be increased, as agricultural products alone does not meet the demand.

16

Moreh–Tamu: A Tale of Two Towns

—Lunminthang Haokip

Introduction

Unless halted by bundh-threat that regurlarly immobilises the line-bus services of beleaguered Manipur, Imphal's Moreh Parking at MG-Road-Kanglapark junction, every morning from 7–8.30 a.m, has scores of Moreh-bound passenger buses anxiously lined-up for profit-making departure. While drivers warm themselves up with sips of hot cups of tea, handy men, street-smart as they are, vie with one another to get more passengers through glib of the gap. In between, Tata Sumo services try to lure in some by cashing in on the impatience of the purse-prouder traveller by promising safer and faster journey ahead. Some coaches start half-empty. But they aren't bothered. Every bus registers 90 to 100 per cent occupancy before reaching Pallen, 45 km from Imphal on Moreh route where a Manipur Police Check Post compels commuters to get down to savour a plate of fresh meal in their favourite Basant (fish) hotel. Foot-loose and fancy-free, first-timers in the daily border-town trips grow curiouser as they commute closer to destination. If old-fashioned folks in the sixties hummed, "*Zindagi mein ek baar jaana Singapore....*", the consumerism-smitten domestic tourists of today's collective chant seem to be, "*Zindagi me ek bar jaana Moreh*".

Passage to Phobia–Freed Area

The 31 km up-hill drive between Pallen and Tengnoupal peak used to be every bus-driver's nightmare for more ways than one. Occurrence of more untoward incidents were reported from this dreaded stretch than from any other route in the state in the past. But such fears are passé, now. Assam Riffles patrolling and deployment of Indian Reserve Battalion (IRB) as Road Opening Party (ROP), coupled with changed mindset, no more makes the panicky commuter hide money inside his shocks or sit on the edge of his seat with a pounding heart. The secured-feeling helps the pot-belied passenger doze off after demolishing a hillock of rice at Pallen's way-side eatery only to be awakened by another round of ego-humbling security-check at Tengnoupal post High altitude Tengnoupal's Ooty-like weather chills you for a brief period of time and wish you had put on warmer clothes. Otherwise the highway is almost under control or dominated by security forces. The only terrible sight today is that of poor living conditions and pathetic undernourished children on the way.

Thai Products Better

Tachilake in Myanmar is the happening township in the Thai border from where consumer durables are transported to Namphalong or Tamu. A Chinese electric cooker may be priced at Rs, 1,600/- and a Thai one at Rs, 2,200/-. But when it comes to durability, the proportion of gain far outweigh the difference in prices. A respectable wooden sofa set costs not less than Rs. 25,000/- here at Imphal. You'll be surprised to discover that Rs. 9,000/- only can fetch you a comfortable beautifully designed Thai sofa set at Tamu. Thai-made kitchen items like cup-sets, spoon-sets, tiffin carriers, thermoflasks, plates etc. are second to none in quality although they charge a little higher. The only thing that unnerves the visiting customer is the snooty attitude of the women vendors. You see someone buying something at a price after a long bargain session. When you want the same thing at the same price, the lordly lady at the counter would turn up her nose and curtly say, "well, to come down at-that rate, we have to begin haggling all over again."

A Town of Shopkeepers

Wide streets, decent planning and a common-sense that is uncommon in Moreh makes Tamu several times a more liveable town than the former. Housing materials like cement, steel-rods, GCI-sheets used to beautify the fast-growing town of Tamu are all Indian-*phir bhi technique hai Myanmarese*. Thousands of people ferried by Japanese made Toyota utility vehicles everyday on the 3 km-long paved road between Moreh and Tamu is indicative of the volume of trade in transaction. Almost every residential house in Tamu, excepting the Church-activity centres, does some selling or buying. Truckloads of under-invoiced electronic and household goods come from Muse in China-border to Tamu. It's all a part of China's strategy to become an Asian economic super-power. The market is flooded with Chinese inverters, generators, ready-made garments, kitchen crokery. Nowhere else in Manipur can one buy a torch light at Rs, 35/- or an attractive sandal at Rs. 60/-. But the tragedy is that one is extremely lucky if the torch light can flash light for the next 35 days or the sandal bought in summer see the light after two months.

Monetary Manoeuvres

Namphalong market complex located on the fringe of Myanmarese side across the border is the venue of trade action. Small shops stuffed with durable consumer items from China and Thailand do brisk business everyday except on a monthly off-day Myanmarese observe religiously. The half-wooden and half-concrete structures are a poor replica of Bangkok's National Stadium shopping complex. In the same manner Thai shop-keepers speak heavily accented broken English like **"cannot"** with a Thai-twang, when they refuse the excessive bargain from buyers, awkwardly decked-up lady traders of Namphalong express the same sentiment by saying **"Jataleh"** in their own 'cockney' Manipuri. Shrewd as Shylock, these calculating calculator-wielding greedy hunters of the rupee will make your hackles rise before you successfully haggle a 10-rupee reduction. The feeling of gain is easily set off—balance by the bruise of your ego. However, you forget uncouth behaviours and native cunning when you get some reasonably good things at dirt-cheap rates. Tamu may be the only place where the rupee can flex its muscles against international exchange rates. The gullible traveller needs to be on his guard. There are hawks in the form of taxi handymen who will convert the benefit of doubt in exchange rates to his own profit.

Morbid Movements of Moreh

Gone are the days when the border town was synonymous with money. Once upon a time, the crime-infested town was the EI Dorads of Manipur where the rich and the wannabe rich rubbed shoulder filthied by ill-gotten lucre. Now, Moreh is a mere shadow of its flourishing past. A reticent resident commented, "Moreh is like the mother cow who everybody milks but forgets to feed". Barring the imposing recently inaugurated Yatri-Niwas near ADC's office, the partly functional shopping complex and the new 50-bedded hospital, the only small-town in Manipur's hill areas that comes under Municipal Act, is yet to get its urban act together. The wards are overcrowded with folks who can't give up rural habits in urban settlement. Unplanned growth of wooden houses in scorching tropical environs makes the entire town a potential victim of arson. For a busy tourist destination, Moreh doesn't have a single park where visitors can chill out and take a snapshot to show to home folks. All that one can see on the street are lungi-clad, chain-smoking, weather-beaten people moving to and fro to buy or sell something for a living. Business rules are changed today. Traders come and go-back pocketing a large chunk of the profit. The poor localities are left with the crumbs of loading and unloading goods when they don't sell charcoal. Seekers of manual work return home with an overload of woes. Recently, the main streets had been lit. Nights had some life ever since.

Tamu Entry Formalities

There's a natural urge for every Moreh-visitor to enter Tamu, its Myanmarese counterpart. At the border, two check-points regulate entry and exit from the twin towns. Like the twin-bed-sale ad that claimed that "one was hardly used", between the two gates of Moreh, Gate No.1 is hardly used. Whereas entry into India does not pose much of a problem, official restrictions welcome any tourist crossing the international boundary for a shopping-spree beyond Namphalong market. Uniformed immigration officials make you pay Rs,10/- per person after checking your I-Card and keeping them in their custody till you return and hand over the entry-pass they write your particulars in and issue. Those who forgot to bring their I-Cards need not worry. Any semblance of an I-Card with the stamp of any social, religious, political or administrative authority that you can conveniently get done at Moreh itself will serve the purpose. Sometimes, when the official's mood is upbeat, they allow a spouse and a bunch of kids to secure entry on the strength of the head of the family's I-Card. Of course, no visitor can stay in Myanmarese soil after 5 p.m MST which is 4 p.m IST. And if you happen to fail to deliver the I-Card you deposited earlier, while coming back, you better get a new one issued. Claiming the same in the morrow will charge you a hefty 300/- rupees.

Tamu Town

Boulevards sandwiched by painted two-storey buildings on both sides make Tamu town visually appealing to the onlooker. What the casual visitor does not know is the fact that a lot of crude and rude town planning went into the transformation of the erstwhile dusty and shabby Tamu town into a well-planned modern town that we enjoy being in today. Myanmarese military government had a way of doing things. The plot-holders on the road-frontal side were given a time-frame to build up pucca structures. The poorer ones failed to fulfil the Authority's expectations. So that the defaulters may not decrease the prestige percentage of the whole town with their ugly wooden houses, they were ordered to move out of prime plots and make do with the back-lane residential areas. This is something one can not imagine to happen in a democratic country. However, if you venture to go for a taxi-ride around the back-lanes, you will most probably come back with a back-ache. Despite neighbourly sops from big brother—India, Tamu is yet to have paved lanes outside the main-street leading to the market to join the BRTF-constructed 90 km Tamu-Kalemyo highway that is almost as smooth as fair-lady's cheeks.

Resources

The world may dub Myanmar a third-world country. But when it comes to natural resources, Myanmar has few equals. The soil itself is first-rate. It does not need repeated ploughing. Rice growers walk and stamp on the surface of the wet fields, plant rice and get bumper harvests. Manure is not required. The quality of rice they grow there is renowned world-wide. In the Kabaw valley which includes Tamu district, one comes across vast stretches of teak and Khanggra (cut as timber) growth in areas where rice is not grown. Teak used to fetch a lot of foreign exchange earlier when business with India was booming. At present, following a Supreme Court ban on transport of teak-wood via Northeastern states, the Myanmarese economy in general and that of Tamu in particular is weakened a great deal. Teakwood is not wasted altogether though. Carpenters make furniture and ready-made doors. Moreh traders buy up cut wood and finished furniture that comes in any form and shape from the neighbouring country. The endless stream of buses and lorries that do business between Imphal and Moreh further transport the wooden products to bigger markets. Burma teak is world No.1. But, due to the slump in the market, and as supply exceeds demand, like that of potatoes do in Punjab, precious teakwood, at Tamu, is being used as fencing and pig-sty materials.

Commercial Activities

A large chunk of Indian bicycles find their ultimate destination in Myanmar. Mandalay, the second town, is flooded with Hero cycles from India. Everywhere in greater Tamu, one can see womenfolk wrapping up their lungis and riding cycles meant for gents. The two-wheel 'wonder' are used for all kinds of purposes which the makers themselves could never have imagined of. Weird items like pigs, piglets, paddy, parcels of garments etc. are tied onto every visible part of the bicycle pedalled by *Tanakha* (face lotion)–smeared and lungi-clad ladies who earn the family bread in carrying goods between the twin border towns. Except for a variety of sweetened polythene-packed edibles which Indian school children can not do without, and a few other items like edibles, ready-made garments, flower-pots, fish-cans etc., Myanmar does not produce much. All that its citizens do is trade in consumer durables produced by China and Thailand.

Sticky Rice that Ticks

A crowd gathers without invitation every morning at Moreh's ward No.1 market. Another mini-mob swells up at the Meitei-dominated former Moreh parking. They are not clamouring to watch a street-show but rushing to buy and relish in the hot-favourite steamed sticky rice brought from Tamu. Every tourist visiting Moreh should make it to the morning scene. Church-folks usually go for a fast on Sundays in the morning. But the fast is broken at the sight of the irresistible palate-pleasing item that makes a mockery of Sunday-fasting. The sticky rice that sells like hot cakes comes in different colours and packages. Some like the off-white stuff and others the black one. And the exotic item that visiting guests love to take home to surprise their children with on reaching home is called '**pongden**'. The delicacy has natural flavour. Bamboo pipes are cut at a length of one foot or so, and they are filled with the right quantity of sticky rice and water. The raw bamboo pipes stuffed to the brim, are heated in fire till the contents are cooked. That is pongden served fresh for you. You taste it and will wonder how rice could smell so good. If you could not purchase the dress items your kids placed order of as "musts", you better take 'pongden' home to ensure that your kids smile from ear to ear.

Spiritual Perceptions

Buddhist stupas and monks adorn a good part of Tamu as secular delights. They do their own thing on "the middle path" without giving cause for disturbance to others. Elsewhere one comes across church buildings of different shapes and sizes with as many denominational hoardings displayed prominently at the gates. Credit must go to the tolerant military administration of Myanmar for giving so much space and liberty to Christians. Despite political upheavals and ideological clashes that made international headlines in post-independence Burma, the spirit of Adoniram Judson, the Baptist Missionary who translated the Holy Bible in Burmese, surprisingly is alive. Having had frequent fellowships together with Tamu Churches, I must admit that I had not experienced such a lively singing and worship this side of the international boundary. Tamu choirs, for sure, can teach a lesson or two to improve the low-decibel singing in Moreh Churches.

Language No Bar

The pastor of "Emmanuel Baptist Church, Tamu candidly admitted that he speaks Myanmarese more fluently than Thadou, his mother-tongue. Tamu has got its own share of linguistic divide. Tangkhul and Moyons migrated there in the previous centuries from Manipur. Second generation Nagas feel more at home in Myanmarese. Settlers from Chin state like Teddim-Chins, Paites, Falams, etc maintain their linguistic uniqueness even in spiritual grouping. Kukis are known as Thadous there. However many Churches have several linguistic minorities worshipping together in the national lingua franca. I personally believe that God allows certain languages to be spoken in common so as to undo the curse of Babel-tower.. The reluctance to learn other widely understood languages is the result of a pride-bedeviled ethno-centric bent of mind. Tamu believers have no such hang-up. This accommodating attitude singularly accounts for the tangible and palpable sense of oneness in that developing township.

17

Recommendations

A two-day national seminar on "Promotion of Border Trade Between North-East India and Myanmar: Problems and Prospects", organised by ICSSR-NERC in collaboration with Manipur University during November 8-9, 2004, at Imphal, has been attended by a cross-section of trade officials, business houses, traders, development agencies, academics and scholars from the region as well as from other parts of the country. The participants have made certain observations and unanimously adopted the following resolutions and have urged upon the concerned agencies to consider them for policy formulations and necessary action.

1. Border trade has immense importance for the development of the bordering regions of the country in general and for the northeastern region in particular. The development potential of Indo-Myanmar trade as a prelude and ultimately as a medium for full-fledged economic relationship with East and South-East Asia should be fully explored.

2. While making every effort to strengthen the weak production base of the region, the NER-Myanmar border trade promotion programmes need to focus on trade in services like tourism, health and education at least in the short-run. This has the potential for trade creation and employment generation paving the way for creation of comparative as well as competitive advantages in cross-border trade.

3. For the development of trade in services, as mentioned in 2, a regulatory framework needs to be worked out in order to facilitate the smooth and hassle-free movement of people across the Indo-Myanmar land border.

4. The growth of trade in services will strengthen people to people contacts, develop trust and bonding and hence widen networking. The formation of this social capital is thus a sine qua non for commodity trade to flow.

5. For the development of the productive base and export-oriented products, cluster approach seems to be the best options. Anciliarisation of local traditional skills and smaller production units in the region appears to hold the key for product development. This approach needs to be reflected in the state-specific industrial policies. This will lead to triadic resource-industry-trade linkages at the local level and make development sustainable.

6. It has been observed that security concerns are outweighing the trade and other developmental concerns in border management. The borders between countries should be viewed as shared borders. A framework needs to be developed where without undermining the security issues trade can flow smoothly.

7. It has been observed that border trade posts in Indian side lack in infrastructure and supportive institutional structure. A multimodal communication network and necessary institutional and infrastructural facilities need to be put in place for the efficacy of the border trade tool as a strategy for the development of the bordering regions.

8. It has been observed that in a long stretch of Indo-Myanmar land border, there are only two border trade posts that have been officially opened along Manipur-

Myanmar and Mizoram-Myamar sectors. Initiative needs to be taken to open up as many posts as possible all along Indo-Myanmar border.

9. Diplomatic activism needs to focus on opening up the Stilwell road.

10. Governments of border states should shoulder the responsibilities for product identification for exports and product development in collaboration with the stake-holders. State plans need to focus on cross-border trade dimension and accordingly this should be reflected in resource allocation.

11. Bilateral mechanism needs to be evolved to review and settle emerging issues and expand the list of goods/items to be traded across the border.

12. A bilateral advisory body needs to be formed in order to oversee the promotion of border trade. This body should include members from exporters, importers, and trade officials, local as well as central government officials, representatives of development agencies including NEC from both the parties. It will act as a lobby for the promotion of border trade and meet regularly.

13. For state governments to play effective roles, they should be empowered to negotiate business deals with agencies across the borders.

14. For a strong economic partnership to grow between NER and Myanmar, India needs to engage Myanmar in a more constructive way preferably by participating vigorously in the construction and development of Myanmar.

15. Facilitation of normal trade through banking channel in currencies other than US dollar, or in Indian Rupee, is required in view of the imposition of economic sanction by the US on Myanmar.

Appendix I

Agreement between the Government of the Republic of India and the Government of the Union of Myanmar on Border Trade between the Two Countries

The Government of the Republic of India and the Government of the Union of Myanmar, being desirous of promoting trade relations between India and Myanmar, and through friendly consultations, have agreed to the formal establishment of border trade on the basis of equality and mutual benefit and have reached the following agreement:

ARTICLE I

The border trade shall be conducted through the following designated customs posts and in accordance with the laws, regulations and procedures in force in either country:

(a) Moreh in India and Tamu in Myanmar

(b) Champai in India and Hri in Myanmar

(c) Other places that may be notified by mutual agreement between the two countries.

Adequate provisions will be made to enable buyers of either country to inspect and take delivery of goods at the customs posts in the country of the seller.

The goods to be traded on the border under this agreement shall be as permitted by both governments.

ARTICLE II

Exchange of locally produced commodities as indicated in Annexure I, by people living along both sides of the Indo-Myanmar Border will continue as per the prevailing customary practice including the barter mechanism.

ARTICLE III

Trade under this Agreement may be conducted in freely convertible currencies or in currencies mutually agreed upon by the two countries, including through counter trade arrangements.

ARTICLE IV

This Agreement shall be reviewed periodically by both sides to ensure successful implementation of its objectives and provisions. In case of difference relating to and arising out of this Agreement, the same shall be amicably settled in the spirit of mutual cooperation and friendship.

ARTICLE V

Amendment (s) and/or supplement (s) to this Agreement shall be made by Exchange of Letter between the two sides.

ARTICLE VI

This Agreement shall come into force with effect from a date mutually agreed upon by the two sides and shall remain in force for two years from that date. It shall be automatically extended for a period of two years at a time unless either side gives notice in writing of its intention to terminate this Agreement three months in advance of the date of expiry.

Done in New Delhi on the 21st day of January, 1994, in three originals, in the Hindi, Myanmar and English languages. The three texts shall be equally authentic, but in case of any divergence of interpretation, the English text shall prevail.

On behalf of the Government of the Republic of India	On behalf of the Government of the Union of Myanmar
Sd/-	Sd/-
(Tejendra Khanna) Secretary Ministry of Commerce	(Lt. Colonel Kyaw Myint) Director-General Directorate of Trade Ministry of Trade

Annexure I

The Indo-Myanmar Joint Task Force Report

Confederation of Indian Industries and Union of Myanmar Federation of Chambers of Commerce and Industries

Status

- India-Myanmar bilateral trade has grown from $203.88 million in 1998-99 to $411.12 million in 2002-03.
- India has emerged as the largest export market for Myanmar accounting nearly one fourth of Myanmar's export.
- India's major export to Myanmar are agriculture products, primary and semi finished iron and steel, pharmaceuticals, while imports consists of pulses and beans, wood and wood products.
- In 2003, India became Myanmar's fourth largest trading partner after Thailand, China and Singapore.
- Myanmar contributes one third of India's requirement of pulses and one fifth of Timber.

India-Myanmar Bilateral Trade (2000-01 to 2002-03)

(In US$ Million)

Sl. No	Year	2000-01	2001-02	2002-03
	EXPORT	52.71	60.89	75.07
1.	% of Growth	54.58	15.52	23.29
2.	India's total export	44,560.29	43,826.73	52,719.43
3.	% of Growth	21.01	-1.65	20.29
4.	% of share	0.12	0.14	0.14
5.	Import	181.69	374.43	336.04
6.	% of Growth	5.88	106.08	-10.25
7.	India' total import	50,536.46	51,413.29	61,412.13
8.	% of Growth	1.61	1.74	19.45
9.	% Of share	0.36	0.73	0.55
10.	TOTAL TRADE	234.40	435.32	411.12
11.	% of Growth	13.96	85.72	-5.56

Potential Items Identified for Exports

From India	*From Myanmar*
Dairy and related processed food products e.g. milk powder and condensed milk	Agricultural and related products, such as cardamom, poppy seeds, coconut oil, nutmeg and cinnamon, soyabean
Machinery and engineering goods including Motorcycles,	Animal hides and skins

(Contd...)

mopeds, motor parts, heavy machinery, trucks, tractors, tyres and tubes, electrical goods, cycle and parts	
Construction equipment, including metal scrap and steel	Raw material for textiles etc.– such as–silk yarn/cocoons, blankets and dress material
Cosmetics	Paraffin wax
Crockery	Stationery and toilet soaps
Textiles, especially cotton yarn	Plastic material/granules
	Wood and wood products

Suggestions for Enhancing Trade

- There is scope for export of pharmaceutical products, processed food items, medical equipment, engineering products, electrical equipment, computers, bicycle and spare parts and machinery for small industry from India.
- Myanmar offers opportunity for export of a wide range of Indian products. Besides iron and steel products and drug and pharmaceuticals, potential exists for exporting branded consumer goods, particularly kitchen items like pressure cookers, electronic ovens and steel utensils. Other products that have good export potential include agro chemicals, two wheelers, cotton garments and cotton yarn, auto components, construction materials, machinery and spare parts especially for sugar and textile industry.
- With a view to enhancing India-Myanmar economic cooperation, Indian companies could consider the investment route for increasing trading opportunities by setting up trade oriented joint ventures or wholly owned subsidiaries in Myanmar, particularly in sectors where local raw materials could be used, such as fisheries, agro and forestry based industries.
- An important pre-requisite for enhancing bilateral trade is establishment of direct shipping links between the two

countries, the opening of representative offices by Indian banks in Yangon and holding trade fairs of Indian goods at regular intervals. The proposed opening of another border trade point at Champai in Mizoram would also facilitate growth of trade between the two countries.

- Myanmar's official trade with India can be increased if direct trade links are strengthened. For example, India is presently buying more than 60 per cent of Myanmar's pulses and beans but only a portion of it enters through official and direct channels.

- Indian traders may only trade with Myanmar in US$ under the Asian Clearing Union stipulations. However, with the US sanctions on Myanmar banning the use of the US$, Letters of Credit may be issued for Myanmar through a third country only.

- India imports 800,000 MT of pulses alone from Myanmar. Traders pay an additional US$ 20 per MT to the country through which the transaction is routed, causing India a loss of 16 million US$ per year.

- Since preferential customs duties are extended to other neighbouring countries such as Afghanistan, similar concessions could be extended to Myanmar too, especially for craftsmen and artisans whose products are gaining popularity. Such a concession existed between 1976-99.

Border Trade

- Border trade between India and Myanmar has special significance and there is immense potential to enhance it due to the geographical contiguity, with India and Myanmar sharing 1,643 kms of common border.

- Trade along the Indo-Myanmar border remains relatively low in comparison with the Sino-Myanmar and Thai-Myanmar borders. India has been a late entrant but the opening of more border points will gradually increase the volume of border trade. However, lack of infrastructure on both sides of the border remains a limitation. Security is another important factor, which has been hampering border trade.

The Northeast-Myanmar border

- *In Kms*
- States — Border length
- Arunachal Pradesh — 520
- Manipur — 398
- Mizoram — 510
- Nagaland — 215
- **Total** — **1,643**

The Northeast-Myanmar border

- Bulk of Myanmar's imports consists of manufactured goods. At present, it has border trade arrangements with China, Thailand, India, and Bangladesh. India-Myanmar bilateral trade is carried out under the border trade agreement signed between India and Myanmar on 21 January 1994, which came into effect on 10 April 1995, when the India-Myanmar border was officially first declared open for trade at Moreh (Manipur, India) and Tamu (Saggine Division, Myanmar). The second official point for trading at Zowakhthar – Rhi, at Champhai in Mizoram was inaugurated on 30 January 2004.
- Under the agreement, 22 items are identified for exchange under the barter mechanism at the concessional rate of duty notified (5% ad valorem). Import of rice up to 50,000 M T is allowed per financial year. In addition, normal trade through Banking Channel for freely importable and exportable items is also allowed. Both India and Myanmar being ACU countries, the denomination of value is ACU Dollar.

Volume of Border Trade

- Formal India-Myanmar border trade through the Moreh-Tamu sector initially shot up to Rs. 59.56 crore during 1997-98. Thereafter the volume of trade registered a diminishing trend and came down to Rs. 7.45 crore only in 2000-01.
- According to the estimates of informal trade by the report of the Government of India Committee on "Informal Cross Border Trade" the value of total unofficial trade was approximately US$ 1.7 billion or Rs. 8,365 crore in the year 2000-01. This excludes under-invoicing. This estimate also excludes informal exports.
- Out of this total, a study by Indian Institute of Foreign Trade in 1995 estimated the value of informal cross border trade at the Moreh-Tamu sector at Rs. 1600 crore.

Volume of Trade between India's Northeastern States and Myanmar through the Banking Channel

- **In Rs million**

• **Year**	**Import**	**Export**
2000-01	34.0	55.3
2001-02	75.9	12.3
2002-03	118.3	49.6
2003-04	80.6	87.4

Opportunities–Resource base of the Northeast States

a) **Arunachal Pradesh:** Limited official trade is recorded across the Myanmar–Arunachal Pradesh border. The district of Chanlang borders Vijaynagar, Nampong and Khemiyong in Myanmar and the district of Tirap borders Laju, Wakka and Pongchou in Myanmar. The road communication–leading to the border points needs improvement for border trade to take place.

b) **Assam:** Assam is one of the northeast states with a reasonably good industrial base. The major industries of Assam are:

Sector	*Products*
Agriculture	Cash crops especially tea, sericulture–special types of silk e.g. eri, muga and mulberry etc. fruit including pineapple, banana, oranges and papaya, Fertilisers
Forestry/wood and related products	Plywood Paper Safety matches Cane and bamboo Medicinal plants and herbs
Mining including	Crude oil and natural gas Coal Petrochemicals Minerals
Textiles	

c) **Manipur:** The opening up of 165 kilometre Tamu-Kelemyo-Kelwa road by the Indian External Affairs Minister in February 2001 was an important initiative to link up with Myanmar. It has been further notified that banking transactions in the Moreh sector may be routed through the United Bank of India.

Existing infrastructure at Tamu point (in Manipur)

- 165 km road connecting Tamu–Kelemyo–Kelewa and along the Chindwin river

- Tamu is located at a distance of approximately 8 kilometres from Namphalong market adjacent to Gate No 1 of the border point
- Tamu is a well planned city and the Namphalong market is flooded with third country goods such as electronic goods from China, plastic products from Korea, hardware and instruments from Japan, textiles and consumer products from Thailand.

The industries operating in the state are–

Sector	*Products*
Agriculture	Processed food
	Vanaspati oil
	Fruit Processing
Forestry and forest produce	Pulp and paper products
	Rubber and rubber products
Construction industry and related products	Cement
Chemicals, drugs and pharmaceuticals	Medicines and medical equipment such as disposable syringes
	Mineral based industrial chemicals
Metals and manufactures	Steel and iron rods
Textiles	Spinning and weaving mills, hosiery
Plastics	
Cycle and cycle parts	
Soaps and toiletry	
Electrical equipment	Televisions

Existing infrastructure at Moreh (Border Township with Land Customs Station for facilitating trade with Myanmar).

At a distance of 108 km from Imphal, the capital of Manipur, the infrastructure at Moreh includes facilities such as-

- Warehousing
- Two-lane road under implementation from Imphal to Moreh
- Weighbridge under construction

Upgrading the following facilities should be considered:

- Inland container depot
- Trade centres
- Industrial growth centres
- Integrated Infrastructure Development Centre
- Export Promotion Industrial Park

Proposals are in the pipeline and/or in various stages of implementation for introduction of inland containers depot, road construction and lighting and trade centres at Imphal and Moreh.

- Moreh is also the first official trading point for cross border trading between India and Myanmar.
- The decision to construct the trilateral highway between India, Myanmar and Thailand offers exciting prospects for increasing trade between India and Myanmar as well as Thailand. The project was to be initiated from Moreh in India to Mae sot in Thailand and through Bagan in Myanmar

Meghalaya

It is predominantly an agricultural economy. The main crops of the state are

Sector	*Product*
Agricultural and related products	Cereal
	Fruit
	Vegetables
	Oilseeds
	Mesta, ginger & areca nut
Textile related produce such as —	Jute
	Cotton
Forest produce	Betel Leaves

Meghalaya also has rich mineral resources like:

- Coal
- Clay
- Limestone
- Silimanite

Coal and limestone are being exported to Bangladesh through its border. Rich uranium deposits are also found, but await exploration.

Mizoram

- **Mizoram:** The Mizoram border touching Myanmar has the following routes: Hnablan, Champhai, Vapihai/ Rarkawn, Thingsai/Ngharchhip, Vawmbuk, Lungbun, Thaipang and Sangau. The Champhai sector has been identified as the crucial point for border trade. It has been notified that banking transactions in the Champhai sector may be routed through the State Bank of India. The distance between Champhai and Aizwal is 190 km. The primary industry and resources are:

- Agriculture
- Forestry and forest produce, including
- Cane
- Bamboo
- Teak
- Minerals
- Handloom

Some sources feel that more than Rs. 2-5 crore worth of transactions occurs in the Mizoram sector. The Ministry of Commerce of the Government of India has invested in developing the infrastructure at the border town of Melbuk, a well-developed settlement, attracting immigration from nearby villages, which is expected to augment border trade in the area.

Nagaland: The following products dominate the state's produce.

Sector	*Product*
Agricultural and related products	Paddy
	Food products/ processing
	Sugar
	Citronella
Textile related produce	Handlooms
	Dressmaking/ knitting
	Handicrafts
	Silk & Sericulture
Forest produce	Aromatic plants

(Contd...)

	Veneer/saw mill
	Pulp and paper
Construction materials	Stone crushers
	Floor tiles
Mining	Coal
Engineering goods	Engineering workshop
	Electronics
	Audio / Videography
	Printing press
	Metals and Metal Manufactures
Transport	
Tourism/hotels	
Plastics & chemicals	

Border Trade Points of Nagaland

Indian Side	*Myanmar side*
Longwa (Mon district)	Yankyong
Pangsha (Tuensang district)	Pongnyo
Mimi (Tuensang district)	Robermi
Mollen (Phek district)	Sompra pasak

Progress and functioning of the centrally proposed EPIP in Nagaland needs to be monitored. On the Nagaland side, Pokhungri has been linked by an all weather road constructed by the Indian Border Roads Organisation under a project of the Northeast Council. Apart from creating other infrastructure facilities at the proposed trade centres at Pokhungri, construction of link road is required to facilitate export of minerals and mineral based products from Nagaland.

Tripura: Tripura has an international border of 839 km with Bangladesh. Its economy is agrarian, with paddy as main agricultural crop. Other agricultural crops are pulses, oilseeds and jute.

Sector	*Product*
Agricultural & related products	Paddy
	Pulses
	Oilseeds
	Jute
	Processed food items
Horticultural produce	Oranges
	Pineapples
	Bananas
	Lemons
	Arecanuts
Cash crops	Rubber and rubber products
	Tea
Forests and forestry produce	Teak
	Agar
	Mahogany
	Sisu
	Medicinal plants
	Bamboo
	Pulp and paper
Fertiliser	Urea
	Ammonia
Power	

Strategy for Promotion of Exports from Northeast States to Myanmar

- Identification of potential items for increased border trade with Myanmar has to be done with reference to the strengths and weaknesses of India's Northeastern states in terms of their location, resource-base and status of infrastructure, on the one hand, and demand for various items in Myanmar, on the other.
- Revision of the list of tradable items is of utmost importance to augment trade in high value products too, especially for Indian export.

Potential Items for Export from India for Border Trade

Sector	*Products*
Engineering goods	Electrical goods
	Machinery & spares
Vehicles, transport equipment & auto components	Heavy machinery, trucks, tractors motorcycles, mopeds, motor parts, tyres and tubes, cycle and cycle parts
Textiles	Cotton yarn, Handloom products, Readymade garments
Dairy products	Milk powder and condensed milk
Metals and metal manufactures	Industrial raw material
	Scrap

(Contd...)

Healthcare, drugs and pharmaceuticals	Allopathic & alternative traditional medicine
	Medical equipment
Agriculture and related products	Processed fruits and vegetables
	Cash crops – rubber and tea
	Agricultural implements
Forestry & forest produce	Medicinal plants & herbs
Chemicals	
Cosmetics	
Crockery	
Plastics	

Potential items for Import from Myanmar for Border Trade

Sector	*Products*
Engineering goods	Electrical goods
	Machinery & spares
Vehicles, transport equipment & auto components	Heavy machinery, trucks, tractors motorcycles, mopeds, motor parts tyres and tubes
	Cycle and cycle parts

(Contd...)

Textiles	Cotton yarn
	Handloom products
	Readymade garments
Dairy products	Milk powder and condensed milk
Metals and metal manufactures	Industrial raw material
	Scrap
Healthcare, drugs and pharmaceuticals	Allopathic and alternative traditional medicine
	Medical equipment
Agriculture and related products	Processed fruits and vegetables
	Cash crops – rubber and tea
	Agricultural implements

Suggestions

- Trade facilitation and standardisation of documents will give the requisite impetus to enhance official border trade.
- Revision of the India-Myanmar Border Trade Agreement is necessary to give a fresh impetus to border trade and revision of the list of tradable items for border trade is of utmost importance to augment trade in high value products too, especially for Indian exports.
- Myanmar continues to list a large number of items that are banned for border trade. This list is appended as Annexure-I. For increasing border trade, some of these

would have to be removed from this list. For example, "Plastic wares" and "canned food" are items, which can be exported from India but are on the list of banned items.

- The list approved for barter trade may be widened to include all freely exportable and importable items, excluding third country products, while normal custom duties may be charged for third country goods.
- The imposition of US sanction prevents the use of the US Dollar, which makes it impossible to trade through Letter of Credit under Asian Clearing Union (ACU) mechanism. Moreover, Myanmar banking officials are relatively unfamiliar with the Letter of Credit trading system. Enabling barter of most tradable items will overcome this obstacle.

Suggestions

- Trading under the Letter of Credit system should be made operational in both countries. Instead of the ACU dollar, Letter of Credit may be permitted with the Euro to conduct trade transactions.
- Unofficial trade can be converted to official trade by simplification of formalities required to register export or import of commodities across the border. Officials at trade centres should provide adequate assistance to traders filling in the details such as item name and code.
- The issue of composition of trade is as important as the trade volumes. It would be useful if India could consider adopting ASEAN Harmonised Tariff Nomenclature (AHTN). 3 version of 8 digits in India-Myanmar trade.
- Creation of adequate transport and transit infrastructure by building expressways, bridges, roads, railway linkages, containerisation, warehousing facilities, documentation services in border areas can help converting informal business to formal trade.

- Locating customs offices in the vicinity of border areas and expedited conversion of letters of credit into cash.
- Mechanisms for the expeditious disposal of required formalities at border transit points.
- Launching joint development projects to generate alternative income and increase the quantity of formal trade between the two countries.
- Reduction of tariff and non-tariff barriers.
- Concerted effort by governments of both countries to encourage interaction between business chambers and associations, greater exchange of trade delegations, tourism packages and cultural exchanges.
- Developing favourable security environment along the trade routes is essential in order to reduce the unnecessary costs and risks borne by traders.
- Enlarging the scope of ocean trade by greater and effective navigation on the Koladyn river route will clear a simple alternative route from the southern tip of Mizoram to Akyap port in Myanmar. There is a possibility for internal linkage of transit trade into the Middle East, Europe and Africa through the opening up of ocean trade.
- Development of alternative routes over the river Tiau is needed to facilitate trade movement between Zorkhathwar in India and Falam and Tiddin towns of Myanmar.
- Lack of a proper banking mechanism remains a major bottleneck for trans-border financial transactions. Myanmar has signed Account Trade Agreements with Bangladesh and Thailand but they have not been implemented mainly due to the failure to set up a proper banking system. The entire trade along the Sino-Myanmar and Sino-Thai border takes place in Yuan and Bahts.
- Establishing branches of Indian banks in the border area that we share with Myanmar could solve the Indian traders'

problem in sourcing credit and foreign exchange. The State Bank of India is considering setting up a representative office in Myanmar.

- India and Myanmar should explore various possibilities offered by the regional fora such as the BIMST-EC alliance to enhance cooperation in trade relations between India and Myanmar.
- Export Promotion Zones could be set up in the border area.
- Cold chain infrastructure and warehousing facilities need to be enhanced at existing border point. A greater number of border trading points should be opened in the states of Mizoram, Nagaland, Arunachal Pradesh and Assam.
- The list of items not permitted for export by private enterprises at cross border trade.

1. **Agricultural products**
    - Rice and rice products (rice, broken rice, vermicelli, bran of rice)
    - Sugar (white, red, brown)
    - Groundnut, groundnut oil
    - Sesame seeds, Sesame oil
    - Niger seeds, Niger oil
    - Mustard seeds, mustard oil
    - Sunflower seeds, sunflower oil
    - Oil cakes all sorts
    - Cotton and cotton products (cotton and cotton yarn etc)
2. **Mineral and metal products**
    - Petroleum
    - Gems and jewellery

- Gold
- Jade
- Pearl
- Diamond
- Lead
- Tin
- Wolfram
- Tin Scheelite
- Silver
- Copper (Bronze)
- Coal
- Other minerals and metals

Foreign Investment of Permitted Enterprises, 31 March 2003

Sl No	*Sector*	*Number*	*Approved amount*	*%*
1.	Oil & gas	56	2403.173	32.04
2.	Manufacturing	150	1604.068	21.39
3.	Hotel & tourism	43	1059.661	14.13
4.	Real estate	18	1025.140	13.67
5.	Mining	52	526.740	7.02
6.	Livestock & fisheries	23	309.758	4.13
7.	Transport & communication	14	283.272	3.78
8.	Industrial estate	3	193.113	2.57
9.	Construction	2	37.767	0.50
10.	Agriculture	4	34.351	0.46
11.	Other services	6	23.686	0.32
	Total	371	7500.729	100.00

India-Myanmar Bilateral Investments

- Investments: Indian investments in Myanmar totalled US$ 4.5 million in 2002.
- Incentives to invest in Myanmar.
- According to the Foreign Investment Law (FIL) of 1995, which regulates foreign investment, investment can be made with either "100 per cent foreign capital" or "joint venture". Chapter X of this Law lists the "exemptions" and "reliefs" which include exemption from income tax for a period of 3 years, relief from income tax on profits if they are re-invested, relief of income tax upto 50 per cent of profits if the goods are exported. Exemption of customs duty on raw materials imported for the first three years of commercial production. Chapter XI of the Law also gives the guarantee that enterprises formed under the Law will not be nationalised. Chapter XIII delineates. "Right to transfer foreign currency". According to this provision, net profits after payment of taxes can be repatriated. Most of the suggestions made by CII in its report already exist in the Foreign Investment Law of 1995.
- Despite such incentives, foreign investment in Myanmar is on the decline. Thailand is one of the few countries, which has increased its investment in Myanmar over the last five years.

As the FIL is aimed at bringing in more foreign capital into the country, it offers investment incentives and guarantees to foreign investors. An enterprise permitted by the FIL shall enjoy a tax holiday's period of three years inclusive of the year the enterprise commences its commercial operation and also up to a reasonable period upon application. In addition, the following exemptions and relief may be considered:

- Exemption or relief from income tax on reinvested profits within one year

- Accelerated depreciation rates approved by the commission
- Fifty per cent relief from income tax on profits accrued from exports
- Right to pay income tax on behalf of foreign experts and technicians employed in the business and the right to deduct such payment from the assessable income
- Right to pay income tax on the income of foreign employees at the rates applicable to Myanmar nationals
- Right to deduct R & D expenditures from the assessable income
- Right to carry forward and set off losses up to three consecutive years from the year the loss is sustained
- Exemption or relief from customs duty or other internal taxes or both on import of machinery, equipment, instruments, machinery components, spare parts and materials used in the business during the period of construction; and
- Exemption or relief on customs duty or other internal taxes or both on import raw materials for the first three years of commercial operation after completion of construction.

Analysis of Potential Sectors for Investment

Considering the nature of FDI inflows into Myanmar, analysis of the cumulative sectoral investments in Myanmar reveals that the trend of FDI flows into Myanmar has been directed to–in order of value:

- Oil & Gas
- Mining
- Manufacturing
- Hotels & Tourism

- Real Estate
- Mining
- Transport & Communication
- Livestock & fisheries
- Industrial estate
- There is a recent shift in the direction of investments, especially in terms of the emergence of business activities and trade as new sectors into which FDI is now being channelled.

Apart from the above, India has vast capacities to invest in the following sectors:

- Power
- Infrastructure
- Transport and transport equipment
- Construction
- Agriculture
- Other services
- ICT
- Healthcare and pharmaceuticals
- HRD and training
- Potential areas for investment in the border area
- Teak processing including handicrafts
- Electricity generation
- Cutting and polishing of precious and semi-precious stones
- Stainless steel utensils
- Cutting and polishing of granites
- Distillery

- Safety matches
- Polishing and milling of oilseeds
- Leather manufacturing
- Construction
- Industrial chemical gas
- Rubber products
- Exploration of coal
- Food processing

Technology transfer

Suggestions

India may offer its capacities in technology transfers in the following sectors:

- Power
- Infrastructure
- Transport and transport equipment
- Construction
- ICT
- Healthcare and pharmaceuticals
- HRD and training

Services

Observations & Suggestions

- With the initiation of a programme for computerisation and office automation in different sectors in Myanmar, scope for software exports to Myanmar will increase. Indian software companies can set up software training institutes/centres in Myanmar to train local manpower in computer systems and operations.

- In the field of banking, India can supply trained manpower to help Myanmar in its restructuring process.
- Other areas with scope for exports of services from India include engineering, marketing, insurance, auditing and accounting.
- Indian companies are well positioned to provide consultancy services in farming and food processing to Myanmar and they should invest in its agricultural, livestock and fishery sectors.
- Promotion of the tourism sector is another strategic move by which India and Myanmar may build closer cultural and social ties, apart from generating revenues out of international tourism. The reason backing up this premise is the Buddhist culture that the two countries share. There are many Buddhist pagodas and other monuments, as well as beautiful scenic locations in the region that have the potential to attract tourists.
- It is worth mentioning that Myanmar Airways has initiated a direct flight from Yangon to Delhi from 15 March 2004.
- ICT training is another area of cooperation and computerisation of Customs could be a specific area that could be offered by India.
- In healthcare, India has potential to offer health services commensurate with world standards that are also cost effective.
- In the field of education, India has the capacity to introduce new educational tools for training and skill enhancing at various levels ranging from kindergarten to vocational and professional courses.

The way forward

- Recommendations to enhance bilateral trade
- Industry-led initiatives via the investment route will

optimally engage the Myanmar market and economy with that of India and will seed rapid growth in bilateral business ties.

- Trade-oriented investments for joint ventures or wholly owned subsidiaries in Myanmar would best open up the route for enhancing India-Myanmar trade.
- Opening representative offices of Indian banks in Yangon will simplify cash and goods transactions between India and Myanmar. The procedural constraints in trading ACU Dollars and letters of credit may also be resolved in this manner.
- Holding trade fairs of Indian goods in Myanmar at regular intervals and engaging Myanmar as a manufacturing and distribution base for penetration into ASEAN markets will also promote bilateral trade to a great degree.

Recommendations to Enhance Border Trade

- There is urgent need for adequate transport and transit infrastructure by building expressways, bridges, roads, railway linkages, containerisation, warehousing facilities, documentation services etc. in border areas, which can help converting informal business to formal trade.
- This may be treated as a business opportunity by industry. Creation of infrastructural support for trade will find many takers and may be treated as a commercially viable investment.
- Joint development projects generate alternative income and increase the quantity of formal trade between the two countries.
- Interaction between business chambers and associations, greater exchange of trade delegations, tourism packages and cultural exchanges will encourage greater mingling of businesspersons and markets.

- Establishing branches of Indian banks in the border areas shared with Myanmar could solve the Indian traders problem of sourcing credit and foreign exchange.

Recommendations to enhance Bilateral Investments

- Information on bilateral investments is scarce and often inadequately updated. Information about credit lines extended by Government of India to Myanmar requires to be publicised.
- The value of Indian investment into Myanmar is far less than other countries, despite Myanmar's rich natural resources in minerals, energy and forestry etc. India should make an industry led effort to find a foot-holds in the Myanmar market.
- Myanmar can be made a lucrative tourist destination and the Indian tourism industry may engage bilaterally with Myanmar.

Recommendations to enhance Technology Transfer

- As mentioned earlier, trilateral projects, joint ventures and technology sharing, to upgrade Myanmar infrastructure, including commercial and tourism infrastructure may well be a lucrative investment.
- In the long run, technology transfer to Myanmar will upgrade the existing market in Myanmar with mutually beneficial results. India may offer its capacities in technology transfers in:
- Power
- Infrastructure
- Transport and transport equipment
- Construction
- ICT

- Healthcare and pharmaceuticals
- HRD and training

Recommendations to enhance Cooperation in Services

- The initiation of a programme for computerisation and office automation in different sectors in Myanmar increases the scope of Indian exports to Myanmar in the IT sector.
- In education and vocational training also, India has a lot to offer to Myanmar. This investment will bring long-term return in the form of an enlarged and upgraded market for either country.
- Consultancy services in farming and food processing in Myanmar and investment in its agricultural, livestock, forestry and fishery sectors–which are resources that Myanmar is rich in–can be also offered from India.
- Enhancing tourism services in the country will also encourage flow of culture, people and monies in both directions.
- Healthcare and medicine is another area where India can largely contribute Myanmar.

CII and UMFCCI are agreeable, in principle, to the following recommendations towards enhancing bilateral trade between India and Myanmar:

- India should consider adopting the ASEAN Harmonised Tariff Nomenclature (AHTN). 3 version of eight digits in India–Myanmar Trade.
- India and Myanmar should work on arriving at an agreement for cooperation in banking and financial services across borders. This will also provide support to private initiatives for setting up branches of banks across the India-Myanmar border.
- A CEOs Forum may be constituted between the Indian and Myanmar industry with the following objectives:

- To suggest ways and means to enhance bilateral trade between India and Myanmar and in particular with the North-Eastern states of India
- To constitute a study group on NTB's between India and Myanmar
- To identify opportunities for Indian investment, collaborations and joint ventures in Myanmar
- To promote tourism, particularly to Myanmar
- To frame and implement joint CII/UMFCCI work plans to be implemented each others country
- To encourage Indian companies to participate in Myanmar's economic development, especially SMEs.
- To consider and advise on participation in Multilateral fora such as ASEAN and BIMST-EC
- To identify other forms of cooperation between the two countries

CII and UMFCCI to regularly discuss pertinent areas/ implementation procedures of training that may be provided by Indian industry to Myanmar. CII and UMFCCI concur on the following possible areas of training:

a) Chamber Capacity Building
    - Chamber Management
    - Trade Facilitation and Promotion
    - Representation and Advocacy
    - Trade Fair Management

b) SMEs/SMIs Enterprise Level Industrial Skill Development
    - Technical Skill Promotion
    - Skill Standards and Certification

- Quality Controls and Standards
- Management of SMEs and SMIs

c) Business Management

- Management and Control (General)
- Efficiency and Competitiveness
- Issues in Venturing into International and Global Market

Index

❑❑❑